Cuisinart
Air Fryer Oven
Cookbook

800 Easy and Affordable Recipes for Your Whole Family

to Master Cuisinart Air Fryer Oven

Robert Beland

Disclaimer Notice:

Please note the information contained within this document is for educational and entertainment purposes only. All effort has been executed to present accurate, up to date, reliable, complete information. No warranties of any kind are declared or implied. Readers acknowledge that the author is not engaged in the rendering of legal, financial, medical or professional advice. The content within this book has been derived from various sources. Please consult a licensed professional before attempting any techniques outlined in this book.

By reading this document, the reader agrees that under no circumstances is the author responsible for any losses, direct or indirect, that are incurred as a result of the use of the information contained within this document, including, but not limited to, errors, omissions, or inaccuracies.

Table of Content

Chapter 1 Breakfasts

Tomato-Corn Frittata with Avocado Dressing

Prep time: 10 minutes | Cook time: 20 minutes | Serves 2 or 3

½ cup cherry tomatoes, halved
Kosher salt and freshly ground black pepper, to taste
6 large eggs, lightly beaten
½ cup fresh corn kernels
¼ cup milk
1 tablespoon finely chopped fresh dill
½ cup shredded Monterey Jack cheese

Avocado Dressing:

1 ripe avocado, pitted and peeled
2 tablespoons fresh lime juice
¼ cup olive oil
1 scallion, finely chopped
8 fresh basil leaves, finely chopped

1. Put the tomato halves in a colander and lightly season with salt. Set aside for 10 minutes to drain well. Pour the tomatoes into a large bowl and fold in the eggs, corn, milk, and dill. Sprinkle with salt and pepper and stir until mixed.
2. Pour the egg mixture into the baking pan.
3. Slide the baking pan into Rack Position 1, select Convection Bake, set temperature to 300ºF (150ºC) and set time to 15 minutes.
4. When done, remove the pan from the oven. Scatter the cheese on top.
5. Slide the baking pan into Rack Position 1, select Convection Bake, set temperature to 315ºF (157ºC) and set time to 5 minutes. Return the pan to the oven.
6. Meanwhile, make the avocado dressing: Mash the avocado with the lime juice in a medium bowl until smooth. Mix in the olive oil, scallion, and basil and stir until well incorporated.
7. When cooking is complete, the frittata will be puffy and set. Let the frittata cool for 5 minutes and serve alongside the avocado dressing.

Cheesy Artichoke-Mushroom Frittata

Prep time: 10 minutes | Cook time: 15 minutes | Serves 6

8 eggs
½ teaspoon kosher salt
¼ cup whole milk
¾ cup shredded Mozzarella cheese, divided
2 tablespoons unsalted butter, melted
1 cup coarsely chopped artichoke hearts
¼ cup chopped onion
½ cup mushrooms
¼ cup grated Parmesan cheese
¼ teaspoon freshly ground black pepper

1. In a medium bowl, whisk together the eggs and salt. Let rest for a minute or two, then pour in the milk and whisk again. Stir in ½ cup of the Mozzarella cheese.
2. Grease the baking pan with the butter. Stir in the artichoke hearts and onion and toss to coat with the butter.
3. Slide the baking pan into Rack Position 2, select Roast, set temperature to 375ºF (190ºC) and set time to 12 minutes.
4. After 5 minutes, remove from the oven. Spread the mushrooms over the vegetables. Pour the egg mixture on top. Stir gently just to distribute the vegetables evenly. Return the pan to the oven and continue cooking for 5 to 7 minutes, or until the edges are set. The center will still be quite liquid.
5. Select Convection Broil, set temperature to Low and set time to 3 minutes. After 1 minute, remove the pan and sprinkle the remaining ¼ cup of the Mozzarella and Parmesan cheese over the frittata. Return the pan to the oven and continue cooking for 2 minutes.
6. When cooking is complete, the cheese should be melted with the top completely set but not browned. Sprinkle the black pepper on top and serve.

Banana and Oat Bread Pudding

Prep time: 10 minutes | Cook time: 16 minutes | Serves 4

2 medium ripe bananas, mashed
½ cup low-fat milk
2 tablespoons maple syrup
2 tablespoons peanut butter
1 teaspoon vanilla extract
1 teaspoon ground cinnamon
2 slices whole-grain bread, cut into bite-sized cubes
¼ cup quick oats
Cooking spray

1. Spritz the baking pan lightly with cooking spray.
2. Mix the bananas, milk, maple syrup, peanut butter, vanilla, and cinnamon in a large mixing bowl and stir until well incorporated.
3. Add the bread cubes to the banana mixture and stir until thoroughly coated. Fold in the oats and stir to combine.
4. Transfer the mixture to the baking pan. Wrap the baking pan in aluminum foil.
5. Slide the baking pan into Rack Position 2, select Air Fry, set temperature to 350ºF (180ºC) and set time to 16 minutes.
6. After 10 minutes, remove the pan from the oven. Remove the foil. Return the pan to the oven and continue to cook for another 6 minutes.
7. When done, the pudding should be set.
8. Let the pudding cool for 5 minutes before serving.

Spicy Apple Turnovers

Prep time: 10 minutes | Cook time: 20 minutes | Serves 4

1 cup diced apple
1 tablespoon brown sugar
1 teaspoon freshly squeezed lemon juice
1 teaspoon all-purpose flour, plus more for dusting
¼ teaspoon cinnamon
⅛ teaspoon allspice
½ package frozen puff pastry, thawed
1 large egg, beaten
2 teaspoons granulated sugar

1. Whisk together the apple, brown sugar, lemon juice, flour, cinnamon and allspice in a medium bowl.
2. On a clean work surface, lightly dust with the flour and lay the puff pastry sheet. Using a rolling pin, gently roll the dough to smooth out the folds, seal any tears and form it into a square. Cut the dough into four squares.
3. Spoon a quarter of the apple mixture into the center of each puff pastry square and spread it evenly in a triangle shape over half the pastry, leaving a border of about ½ inch around the edges of the pastry. Fold the pastry diagonally over the filling to form triangles. With a fork, crimp the edges to seal them. Place the turnovers in the baking pan, spacing them evenly.
4. Cut two or three small slits in the top of each turnover. Brush with the egg. Sprinkle evenly with the granulated sugar.
5. Slide the baking pan into Rack Position 1, select Convection Bake, set temperature to 350ºF (180ºC) and set time to 20 minutes.
6. When cooking is complete, remove the pan from the oven. The turnovers should be golden brown and the filling bubbling. Let cool for about 10 minutes before serving.

Egg and Bacon Muffins

Prep time: 5 minutes | Cook time: 15 minutes | Serves 1

2 eggs
Salt and ground black pepper, to taste
1 tablespoon green pesto
3 ounces (85 g) shredded Cheddar cheese
5 ounces (142 g) cooked bacon
1 scallion, chopped

1. Preheat the air fryer oven to 350ºF (177ºC). Line a cupcake tin with parchment paper.
2. Beat the eggs with pepper, salt, and pesto in a bowl. Mix in the cheese.
3. Pour the eggs into the cupcake tin and top with the bacon and scallion.
4. Place the cupcake tin into Rack Position 1, select Convection Bake and set time to 15 minutes, or until the egg is set.
5. Serve immediately.

Maple Walnut Pancake

Prep time: 10 minutes | Cook time: 20 minutes | Serves 4

3 tablespoons melted butter, divided
1 cup flour
2 tablespoons sugar
1½ teaspoons baking powder
¼ teaspoon salt
1 egg, beaten

¾ cup milk
1 teaspoon pure vanilla extract
½ cup roughly chopped walnuts
Maple syrup or fresh sliced fruit, for serving

1. Grease the baking pan with 1 tablespoon of melted butter.
2. Mix together the flour, sugar, baking powder, and salt in a medium bowl. Add the beaten egg, milk, the remaining 2 tablespoons of melted butter, and vanilla and stir until the batter is sticky but slightly lumpy.
3. Slowly pour the batter into the greased baking pan and scatter with the walnuts.
4. Slide the baking pan into Rack Position 1, select Convection Bake, set temperature to 330ºF (166ºC) and set time to 20 minutes.
5. When cooked, the pancake should be golden brown and cooked through.
6. Let the pancake rest for 5 minutes and serve topped with the maple syrup or fresh fruit, if desired.

Asparagus and Cheese Strata

Prep time: 10 minutes | Cook time: 17 minutes | Serves 4

6 asparagus spears, cut into 2-inch pieces
1 tablespoon water
2 slices whole-wheat bread, cut into ½-inch cubes
4 eggs
3 tablespoons whole milk

2 tablespoons chopped flat-leaf parsley
½ cup grated Havarti or Swiss cheese
Pinch salt
Freshly ground black pepper, to taste
Cooking spray

1. Add the asparagus spears and 1 tablespoon of water in the baking pan.
2. Slide the baking pan into Rack Position 1, select Convection Bake, set temperature to 330ºF (166ºC) and set time to 4 minutes.

3. When cooking is complete, the asparagus spears will be crisp-tender.
4. Remove the asparagus from the pan and drain on paper towels.
5. Spritz the pan with cooking spray. Place the bread and asparagus in the pan.
6. Whisk together the eggs and milk in a medium mixing bowl until creamy. Fold in the parsley, cheese, salt, and pepper and stir to combine. Pour this mixture into the baking pan.
7. Select Bake and set time to 13 minutes. Put the pan back to the oven. When done, the eggs will be set and the top will be lightly browned.
8. Let cool for 5 minutes before slicing and serving.

Veggie Frittata

Prep time: 10 minutes | Cook time: 12 minutes | Serves 4

½ cup chopped red bell pepper
1/3 cup grated carrot
1/3 cup minced onion
1 teaspoon olive oil
1 egg

6 egg whites
1/3 cup 2% milk
1 tablespoon shredded Parmesan cheese

1. Mix together the red bell pepper, carrot, onion, and olive oil in the baking pan and stir to combine.
2. Slide the baking pan into Rack Position 1, select Convection Bake, set temperature to 350ºF (180ºC) and set time to 12 minutes.
3. After 3 minutes, remove the pan from the oven. Stir the vegetables. Return the pan to the oven and continue cooking.
4. Meantime, whisk together the egg, egg whites, and milk in a medium bowl until creamy.
5. After 3 minutes, remove the pan from the oven. Pour the egg mixture over the top and scatter with the Parmesan cheese. Return the pan to the oven and continue cooking for additional 6 minutes.
6. When cooking is complete, the eggs will be set and the top will be golden around the edges.
7. Allow the frittata to cool for 5 minutes before slicing and serving.

Fried Potatoes with Peppers and Onions

Prep time: 10 minutes | Cook time: 35 minutes | Serves 4

1 pound (454 g) red potatoes, cut into ½-inch dices
1 large red bell pepper, cut into ½-inch dices
1 large green bell pepper, cut into ½-inch dices
1 medium onion, cut into ½-inch dices
1½ tablespoons extra-virgin olive oil
1¼ teaspoons kosher salt
¾ teaspoon sweet paprika
¾ teaspoon garlic powder
Freshly ground black pepper, to taste

1. Mix together the potatoes, bell peppers, onion, oil, salt, paprika, garlic powder, and black pepper in a large mixing and toss to coat.
2. Transfer the potato mixture to the air fryer basket.
3. Put the air fryer basket on the baking pan and slide into Rack Position 2, select Air Fry, set temperature to 350ºF (180ºC) and set time to 35 minutes.
4. Stir the potato mixture three times during cooking.
5. When done, the potatoes should be nicely browned.
6. Remove from the oven to a plate and serve warm.

Carrot Banana Muffin

Prep time: 10 minutes | Cook time: 20 minutes | Serves 12

1½ cups whole-wheat flour
1 cup grated carrot
1 cup mashed banana
½ cup bran
½ cup low-fat buttermilk
2 tablespoons agave
nectar
2 teaspoons baking powder
1 teaspoon vanilla
1 teaspoon baking soda
½ teaspoon nutmeg
Pinch cloves
2 egg whites

1. Line a muffin pan with 12 paper liners.
2. In a large bowl, stir together all the ingredients. Mix well, but do not over beat.
3. Scoop the mixture into the muffin cups.

4. Place the muffin pan into Rack Position 1, select Convection Bake, set temperature to 400ºF (205ºC) and set time to 20 minutes.
5. When cooking is complete, remove from the oven and let rest for 5 minutes.
6. Serve warm or at room temperature.

Egg and Avocado Burrito

Prep time: 10 minutes | Cook time: 4 minutes | Serves 4

4 low-sodium whole-wheat flour tortillas
Filling:
1 hard-boiled egg, chopped
2 hard-boiled egg whites, chopped
1 ripe avocado, peeled, pitted, and chopped
1 red bell pepper,
chopped
1 (1.2-ounce / 34-g) slice low-sodium, low-fat American cheese, torn into pieces
3 tablespoons low-sodium salsa, plus additional for serving (optional)

Special Equipment:
4 toothpicks (optional), soaked in water for at least 30 minutes

1. Make the filling: Combine the egg, egg whites, avocado, red bell pepper, cheese, and salsa in a medium bowl and stir until blended.
2. Assemble the burritos: Arrange the tortillas on a clean work surface and place ¼ of the prepared filling in the middle of each tortilla, leaving about 1½-inch on each end unfilled. Fold in the opposite sides of each tortilla and roll up. Secure with toothpicks through the center, if needed.
3. Transfer the burritos to the air fryer basket.
4. Put the air fryer basket on the baking pan and slide into Rack Position 2, select Air Fry, set temperature to 390ºF (199ºC) and set time to 4 minutes.
5. When cooking is complete, the burritos should be crisp and golden brown.
6. Allow to cool for 5 minutes and serve with salsa, if desired.

Olives, Kale, and Pecorino Baked Eggs

Prep time: 5 minutes | Cook time: 11 minutes | Serves 2

1 cup roughly chopped kale leaves, stems and center ribs removed
¼ cup grated pecorino cheese
¼ cup olive oil
1 garlic clove, peeled
3 tablespoons whole almonds
Kosher salt and freshly ground black pepper, to taste
4 large eggs
2 tablespoons heavy cream
3 tablespoons chopped pitted mixed olives

1. Place the kale, pecorino, olive oil, garlic, almonds, salt, and pepper in a small blender and blitz until well incorporated.
2. One at a time, crack the eggs in the baking pan. Drizzle the kale pesto on top of the egg whites. Top the yolks with the cream and swirl together the yolks and the pesto.
3. Slide the baking pan into Rack Position 1, select Convection Bake, set temperature to 300ºF (150ºC) and set time to 11 minutes.
4. When cooked, the top should begin to brown and the eggs should be set.
5. Allow the eggs to cool for 5 minutes. Scatter the olives on top and serve warm.

Breakfast Blueberry Cobbler

Prep time: 5 minutes | Cook time: 15 minutes | Serves 4

¾ teaspoon baking powder
1/3 cup whole-wheat pastry flour
Dash sea salt
1/3 cup unsweetened nondairy milk
2 tablespoons maple
syrup
½ teaspoon vanilla
Cooking spray
½ cup blueberries
¼ cup granola
Nondairy yogurt, for topping (optional)

1. Spritz the baking pan with cooking spray.
2. Mix together the baking powder, flour, and salt in a medium bowl. Add the milk, maple syrup, and vanilla and whisk to combine.
3. Scrape the mixture into the prepared pan. Scatter the blueberries and granola on top.
4. Slide the baking pan into Rack Position 1, select Convection Bake, set temperature to 347ºF (175ºC) and set time to 15 minutes.
5. When done, the top should begin to brown and a knife inserted in the center should come out clean.
6. Let the cobbler cool for 5 minutes and serve with a drizzle of nondairy yogurt.

Corned Beef Hash with Eggs

Prep time: 10 minutes | Cook time: 25 minutes | Serves 4

2 medium Yukon Gold potatoes, peeled and cut into ¼-inch cubes
1 medium onion, chopped
1/3 cup diced red bell pepper
3 tablespoons vegetable oil
½ teaspoon dried
thyme
½ teaspoon kosher salt, divided
½ teaspoon freshly ground black pepper, divided
¾ pound (340 g) corned beef, cut into ¼-inch pieces
4 large eggs

1. In a large bowl, stir together the potatoes, onion, red pepper, vegetable oil, thyme, ¼ teaspoon of the salt and ¼ teaspoon of the pepper. Spread the vegetable mixture into the baking pan in an even layer.
2. Slide the baking pan into Rack Position 2, select Roast, set temperature to 375ºF (190ºC) and set time to 25 minutes.
3. After 15 minutes, remove the pan from the oven and add the corned beef. Stir the mixture to incorporate the corned beef. Return the pan to the oven and continue cooking.
4. After 5 minutes, remove the pan from the oven. Using a large spoon, create 4 circles in the hash to hold the eggs. Gently crack an egg into each circle. Season the eggs with the remaining ¼ teaspoon of the salt and ¼ teaspoon of the pepper. Return the pan to the oven. Continue cooking for 3 to 5 minutes, depending on how you like your eggs.
5. When cooking is complete, remove the pan from the oven. Serve immediately.

Whole-Wheat Blueberry Scones

Prep time: 5 minutes | Cook time: 20 minutes | Serves 14

½ cup low-fat buttermilk
¾ cup orange juice
Zest of 1 orange
2¼ cups whole-wheat pastry flour
⅓ cup agave nectar
¼ cup canola oil
1 teaspoon baking soda
1 teaspoon cream of tartar
1 cup fresh blueberries

1. In a small bowl, stir together the buttermilk, orange juice and orange zest.
2. In a large bowl, whisk together the flour, agave nectar, canola oil, baking soda and cream of tartar.
3. Add the buttermilk mixture and blueberries to the bowl with the flour mixture. Mix gently by hand until well combined.
4. Transfer the batter onto a lightly floured baking pan. Pat into a circle about ¾ inch thick and 8 inches across. Use a knife to cut the circle into 14 wedges, cutting almost all the way through.
5. Slide the baking pan into Rack Position 1, select Convection Bake, set temperature to 375ºF (190ºC) and set time to 20 minutes.
6. When cooking is complete, remove the pan and check the scones. They should be lightly browned.
7. Let rest for 5 minutes and cut completely through the wedges before serving.

French Toast Sticks

Prep time: 5 minutes | Cook time: 12 minutes | Serves 4

3 slices low-sodium whole-wheat bread, each cut into 4 strips
1 tablespoon unsalted butter, melted
1 tablespoon 2 percent milk
1 tablespoon sugar
1 egg, beaten
1 egg white
1 cup sliced fresh strawberries
1 tablespoon freshly squeezed lemon juice

1. Arrange the bread strips on a plate and drizzle with the melted butter.
2. In a bowl, whisk together the milk, sugar, egg and egg white.
3. Dredge the bread strips into the egg mixture and place on a wire rack to let the batter drip off. Arrange half the coated bread strips in the air fryer basket.
4. Put the air fryer basket on the baking pan and slide into Rack Position 2, select Air Fry, set temperature to 380ºF (193ºC) and set time to 6 minutes.
5. After 3 minutes, remove from the oven and turn the strips over. Return to the oven to continue cooking.
6. When cooking is complete, the strips should be golden brown. Repeat with the remaining strips.
7. In a small bowl, mash the strawberries with a fork and stir in the lemon juice. Serve the French toast sticks with the strawberry sauce.

Sweet Banana Bread Pudding

Prep time: 10 minutes | Cook time: 18 minutes | Serves 4

2 medium ripe bananas, mashed
½ cup low-fat milk
2 tablespoons maple syrup
2 tablespoons peanut butter
1 teaspoon vanilla
extract
1 teaspoon ground cinnamon
2 slices whole-grain bread, torn into bite-sized pieces
¼ cup quick oats
Cooking spray

1. Spritz the baking pan with cooking spray.
2. In a large bowl, combine the bananas, milk, maple syrup, peanut butter, vanilla extract and cinnamon. Use an immersion blender to mix until well combined.
3. Stir in the bread pieces to coat well. Add the oats and stir until everything is combined.
4. Transfer the mixture to the baking pan. Cover with the aluminum foil.
5. Put the baking pan into Rack Position 2, select Air Fry, set temperature to 375ºF (190ºC) and set time to 18 minutes.
6. After 10 minutes, remove the foil and continue to cook for 8 minutes.
7. Serve immediately.

Chicken Breakfast Sausages

Prep time: 15 minutes | Cook time: 10 minutes | Makes 8 patties

1 Granny Smith apple, peeled and finely chopped
2 tablespoons apple juice
2 garlic cloves, minced
1 egg white

1/3 cup minced onion
3 tablespoons ground almonds
1/8 teaspoon freshly ground black pepper
1 pound (454 g) ground chicken breast

1. Combine all the ingredients except the chicken in a medium mixing bowl and stir well.
2. Add the chicken breast to the apple mixture and mix with your hands until well incorporated.
3. Divide the mixture into 8 equal portions and shape into patties. Arrange the patties in the air fryer basket.
4. Put the air fryer basket on the baking pan and slide into Rack Position 2, select Air Fry, set temperature to 330ºF (166ºC) and set time to 10 minutes.
5. When done, a meat thermometer inserted in the center of the chicken should reach at least 165ºF (74ºC).
6. Remove from the oven to a plate. Let the chicken cool for 5 minutes and serve warm.

Mini Brown Rice Quiches

Prep time: 10 minutes | Cook time: 14 minutes | Serves 6

4 ounces (113 g) diced green chilies
3 cups cooked brown rice
1 cup shredded reduced-fat Cheddar cheese, divided
1/2 cup egg whites
1/3 cup fat-free milk

1/4 cup diced pimiento
1/2 teaspoon cumin
1 small eggplant, cubed
1 bunch fresh cilantro, finely chopped
Cooking spray

1. Spritz a 12-cup muffin pan with cooking spray.
2. In a large bowl, stir together all the ingredients, except for 1/2 cup of the cheese.

3. Scoop the mixture evenly into the muffin cups and sprinkle the remaining 1/2 cup of the cheese on top.
4. Put the muffin pan into Rack Position 1, select Convection Bake, set temperature to 400ºF (205ºC) and set time to 14 minutes.
5. When cooking is complete, remove from the oven and check the quiches. They should be set.
6. Carefully transfer the quiches to a platter and serve immediately.

All-in-One Toast

Prep time: 10 minutes | Cook time: 10 minutes | Serves 1

1 strip bacon, diced
1 slice 1-inch thick bread
1 egg
Salt and freshly

ground black pepper, to taste
1/4 cup grated Colby cheese

1. Preheat the air fryer oven to 400ºF (204ºC).
2. Put the bacon in the air fryer basket.
3. Place the air fryer basket onto the baking pan and slide into Rack Position 2, select Air Fry and set time to 3 minutes, shaking the basket once or twice while it cooks.
4. Remove the bacon to a paper towel-lined plate and set aside.
5. Use a sharp paring knife to score a large circle in the middle of the slice of bread, cutting halfway through, but not all the way through to the cutting board. Press down on the circle in the center of the bread slice to create an indentation.
6. Transfer the slice of bread, hole-side up, to the air fryer basket. Crack the egg into the center of the bread, and season with salt and pepper.
7. Reduce the temperature to 380ºF (193ºC) and air fry for 5 minutes. Sprinkle the grated cheese around the edges of the bread, leaving the center of the yolk uncovered, and top with the cooked bacon. Press the cheese and bacon into the bread lightly.
8. Air fry for 1 or 2 more minutes, just to melt the cheese and finish cooking the egg. Serve immediately.

Creamy Quesadillas with Blueberries

Prep time: 5 minutes | Cook time: 4 minutes | Serves 2

¼ cup nonfat Ricotta cheese
¼ cup plain nonfat Greek yogurt
2 tablespoons finely ground flaxseeds
1 tablespoon granulated stevia
½ teaspoon cinnamon
¼ teaspoon vanilla extract
2 (8-inch) low-carb whole-wheat tortillas
½ cup fresh blueberries, divided

1. Line the baking pan with aluminum foil.
2. In a small bowl, whisk together the Ricotta cheese, yogurt, flaxseeds, stevia, cinnamon and vanilla.
3. Place the tortillas on the prepared pan. Spread half of the yogurt mixture on each tortilla, almost to the edges. Top each tortilla with ¼ cup of blueberries. Fold the tortillas in half.
4. Slide the baking pan into Rack Position 1, select Convection Bake, set temperature to 400ºF (205ºC) and set time to 4 minutes.
5. When cooking is complete, remove the pan from the oven. Serve immediately.

Whole-Wheat Muffins with Blueberries

Prep time: 5 minutes | Cook time: 25 minutes | Makes 8 muffins

½ cup unsweetened applesauce
½ cup plant-based milk
½ cup maple syrup
1 teaspoon vanilla extract
2 cups whole-wheat flour
½ teaspoon baking soda
1 cup blueberries
Cooking spray

1. Spritz a 8-cup muffin pan with cooking spray.
2. In a large bowl, stir together the applesauce, milk, maple syrup and vanilla extract. Whisk in the flour and baking soda until no dry flour is left and the batter is smooth. Gently mix in the blueberries until they are evenly distributed throughout the batter.
3. Spoon the batter into the muffin cups, three-quarters full.

4. Put the muffin pan into Rack Position 1, select Convection Bake, set temperature to 375ºF (190ºC) and set time to 25 minutes.
5. When cooking is complete, remove from the oven and check the muffins. You can stick a knife into the center of a muffin and it should come out clean.
6. Let rest for 5 minutes before serving.

Potatoes Lyonnaise

Prep time: 10 minutes | Cook time: 31 minutes | Serves 4

1 Vidalia onion, sliced
1 teaspoon butter, melted
1 teaspoon brown sugar
2 large russet potatoes (about 1
pound / 454 g in total), sliced ½-inch thick
1 tablespoon vegetable oil
Salt and freshly ground black pepper, to taste

1. Preheat the air fryer oven to 370ºF (188ºC).
2. Toss the sliced onions, melted butter and brown sugar together in the air fryer basket.
3. Place the air fryer basket onto the baking pan and slide into Rack Position 2, select Air Fry and set time to 8 minutes, shaking the basket occasionally to help the onions cook evenly.
4. While the onions are cooking, bring a saucepan of salted water to a boil on the stovetop. Par-cook the potatoes in boiling water for 3 minutes. Drain the potatoes and pat them dry with a clean kitchen towel.
5. Add the potatoes to the onions in the air fryer basket and drizzle with vegetable oil. Toss to coat the potatoes with the oil and season with salt and freshly ground black pepper.
6. Increase the temperature to 400ºF (204ºC) and air fry for 20 minutes, tossing the vegetables a few times during the cooking time to help the potatoes brown evenly.
7. Season with salt and freshly ground black pepper and serve warm.

Blueberry Cake

Prep time: 5 minutes | Cook time: 10 minutes | Serves 8

1½ cups Bisquick
¼ cup granulated sugar
2 large eggs, beaten
¾ cup whole milk
1 teaspoon vanilla

extract
½ teaspoon lemon zest
Cooking spray
2 cups blueberries

1. Stir together the Bisquick and sugar in a medium bowl. Stir together the eggs, milk, vanilla and lemon zest. Add the wet ingredients to the dry ingredients and stir until well combined.
2. Spritz the baking pan with cooking spray and line with parchment paper, pressing it into place. Spray the parchment paper with cooking spray. Pour the batter into the pan and spread it out evenly. Sprinkle the blueberries evenly over the top.
3. Slide the baking pan into Rack Position 1, select Convection Bake, set temperature to 375ºF (190ºC) and set time to 10 minutes.
4. When cooking is complete, the cake should be pulling away from the edges of the pan and the top should be just starting to turn golden brown.
5. Let the cake rest for a minute before cutting into 16 squares. Serve immediately.

Chocolate Banana Bread

Prep time: 10 minutes | Cook time: 30 minutes | Serves 4

¼ cup cocoa powder
6 tablespoons plus 2 teaspoons all-purpose flour, divided
½ teaspoon kosher salt
¼ teaspoon baking soda
1½ ripe bananas
1 large egg, whisked
¼ cup vegetable oil

½ cup sugar
3 tablespoons buttermilk or plain yogurt (not Greek)
½ teaspoon vanilla extract
6 tablespoons chopped white chocolate
6 tablespoons chopped walnuts

1. Mix together the cocoa powder, 6 tablespoons of the flour, salt, and baking soda in a medium bowl.
2. Mash the bananas with a fork in another medium bowl until smooth. Fold in the egg, oil, sugar, buttermilk, and vanilla, and whisk until thoroughly combined. Add the wet mixture to the dry mixture and stir until well incorporated.
3. Combine the white chocolate, walnuts, and the remaining 2 tablespoons of flour in a third bowl and toss to coat. Add this mixture to the batter and stir until well incorporated. Pour the batter into the baking pan and smooth the top with a spatula.
4. Slide the baking pan into Rack Position 1, select Convection Bake, set temperature to 310ºF (154ºC) and set time to 30 minutes.
5. When done, a toothpick inserted into the center of the bread should come out clean.
6. Remove from the oven and allow to cool on a wire rack for 10 minutes before serving.

Spinach with Scrambled Eggs

Prep time: 10 minutes | Cook time: 10 minutes | Serves 2

2 tablespoons olive oil
4 eggs, whisked
5 ounces (142 g) fresh spinach, chopped
1 medium tomato, chopped

1 teaspoon fresh lemon juice
½ teaspoon coarse salt
½ teaspoon ground black pepper
½ cup of fresh basil, roughly chopped

1. Preheat the air fryer oven to 280ºF (138ºC). Grease a baking pan with the oil.
2. In the pan, mix the remaining ingredients, except for the basil leaves, whisking well until everything is completely combined.
3. Slide the baking pan into Rack Position 1, select Convection Bake and set time to 10 minutes.
4. Top with fresh basil leaves before serving.

Golden Avocado Tempura

Prep time: 5 minutes | Cook time: 10 minutes | Serves 4

½ cup bread crumbs
½ teaspoons salt
1 Haas avocado, pitted, peeled and

sliced
Liquid from 1 can white beans

1. Preheat the air fryer oven to 350ºF (177ºC).
2. Mix the bread crumbs and salt in a shallow bowl until well incorporated.
3. Dip the avocado slices in the bean liquid, then into the bread crumbs.
4. Arrange the avocado slices in the air fryer basket in a single layer.
5. Place the air fryer basket onto the baking pan and slide into Rack Position 2, select Air Fry and set time to 10 minutes, shaking the basket halfway through.
6. Serve immediately.

Baked Avocado with Eggs

Prep time: 5 minutes | Cook time: 9 minutes | Serves 2

1 large avocado, halved and pitted
2 large eggs
2 tomato slices, divided

½ cup nonfat Cottage cheese, divided
½ teaspoon fresh cilantro, for garnish

1. Line the baking pan with aluminium foil.
2. Slice a thin piece from the bottom of each avocado half so they sit flat. Remove a small amount from each avocado half to make a bigger hole to hold the egg.
3. Arrange the avocado halves on the pan, hollow-side up. Break 1 egg into each half. Top each half with 1 tomato slice and ¼ cup of the Cottage cheese.
4. Slide the baking pan into Rack Position 1, select Convection Bake, set temperature to 425ºF (220ºC) and set time to 9 minutes.
5. When cooking is complete, remove the pan from the oven. Garnish with the fresh cilantro and serve.

Mini Cinnamon Rolls

Prep time: 5 minutes | Cook time: 25 minutes | Makes 18 rolls

$\frac{1}{3}$ cup light brown sugar
2 teaspoons cinnamon
1 (9-by-9-inch) frozen puff pastry

sheet, thawed
All-purpose flour, for dusting
6 teaspoons unsalted butter, melted, divided

1. In a small bowl, stir together the brown sugar and cinnamon.
2. On a clean work surface, lightly dust with the flour and lay the puff pastry sheet. Using a rolling pin, press the folds together and roll the dough out in one direction so that it measures about 9 by 11 inches. Cut it in half to form two squat rectangles of about 5½ by 9 inches.
3. Brush 2 teaspoons of the butter over each pastry half. Sprinkle with 2 tablespoons of the cinnamon sugar. Pat it down lightly with the palm of your hand to help it adhere to the butter.
4. Starting with the 9-inch side of one rectangle. Using your hands, carefully roll the dough into a cylinder. Repeat with the other rectangle. To make slicing easier, refrigerate the rolls for 10 to 20 minutes.
5. Using a sharp knife, slice each roll into nine 1-inch pieces. Transfer the rolls to the center of the baking pan. They should be very close to each other, but not quite touching. Drizzle the remaining 2 teaspoons of the butter over the rolls and sprinkle with the remaining cinnamon sugar.
6. Slide the baking pan into Rack Position 1, select Convection Bake, set temperature to 350ºF (180ºC) and set time to 25 minutes.
7. When cooking is complete, remove the pan and check the rolls. They should be puffed up and golden brown.
8. Let the rolls rest for 5 minutes and transfer them to a wire rack to cool completely. Serve.

Egg Florentine with Spinach

Prep time: 10 minutes | Cook time: 15 minutes | Serves 4

3 cups frozen spinach, thawed and drained
2 tablespoons heavy cream
¼ teaspoon kosher salt
⅛ teaspoon freshly ground black pepper
4 ounces (113 g)

Ricotta cheese
2 garlic cloves, minced
½ cup panko bread crumbs
3 tablespoons grated Parmesan cheese
2 teaspoons unsalted butter, melted
4 large eggs

1. In a medium bowl, whisk together the spinach, heavy cream, salt, pepper, Ricotta cheese and garlic.
2. In a small bowl, whisk together the bread crumbs, Parmesan cheese and butter. Set aside.
3. Spoon the spinach mixture into the baking pan and form four even circles.
4. Slide the baking pan into Rack Position 2, select Roast, set temperature to 375ºF (190ºC) and set time to 15 minutes.
5. After 8 minutes, remove the pan. The spinach should be bubbling. With the back of a large spoon, make indentations in the spinach for the eggs. Crack the eggs into the indentations and sprinkle the panko mixture over the surface of the eggs.
6. Return the pan to the oven and continue cooking.
7. When cooking is complete, remove the pan from the oven. Serve hot.

French Toast Casserole

Prep time: 5 minutes | Cook time: 12 minutes | Serves 6

3 large eggs, beaten
1 cup whole milk
1 tablespoon pure maple syrup
1 teaspoon vanilla extract
¼ teaspoon cinnamon

¼ teaspoon kosher salt
3 cups stale bread cubes
1 tablespoon unsalted butter, at room temperature

1. In a medium bowl, whisk together the eggs, milk, maple syrup, vanilla extract, cinnamon and salt. Stir in the bread cubes to coat well.
2. Grease the bottom of the baking pan with the butter. Spread the bread mixture into the pan in an even layer.
3. Slide the baking pan into Rack Position 2, select Roast, set temperature to 350ºF (180ºC) and set time to 12 minutes.
4. After about 10 minutes, remove the pan and check the casserole. The top should be browned and the middle of the casserole just set. If more time is needed, return the pan to the oven and continue cooking.
5. When cooking is complete, serve warm.

Banana Bread

Prep time: 10 minutes | Cook time: 22 minutes | Makes 3 loaves

3 ripe bananas, mashed
1 cup sugar
1 large egg
4 tablespoons (½ stick) unsalted

butter, melted
1½ cups all-purpose flour
1 teaspoon baking soda
1 teaspoon salt

1. Preheat the air fryer oven to 310ºF (154ºC).
2. Coat the insides of 3 mini loaf pans with cooking spray.
3. In a large mixing bowl, mix the bananas and sugar.
4. In a separate large mixing bowl, combine the egg, butter, flour, baking soda, and salt and mix well.
5. Add the banana mixture to the egg and flour mixture. Mix well.
6. Divide the batter evenly among the prepared pans.
7. Slide the pans into Rack Position 1, select Convection Bake and set time to 22 minutes. Insert a toothpick into the center of each loaf; if it comes out clean, they are done.
8. When the loaves are cooked through, remove the pans from the oven. Turn out the loaves onto a wire rack to cool.
9. Serve warm.

Cashew Granola with Cranberries

Prep time: 5 minutes | Cook time: 12 minutes | Serves 6

3 cups old-fashioned rolled oats
2 cups raw cashews
1 cup unsweetened coconut chips
½ cup honey
¼ cup vegetable oil
⅓ cup packed light brown sugar
¼ teaspoon kosher salt
1 cup dried cranberries

1. In a large bowl, stir together all the ingredients, except for the cranberries. Spread the mixture in the baking pan in an even layer.
2. Slide the baking pan into Rack Position 1, select Convection Bake, set temperature to 325ºF (163ºC) and set time to 12 minutes.
3. After 5 to 6 minutes, remove the pan and stir the granola. Return the pan to the oven and continue cooking.
4. When cooking is complete, remove the pan. Let the granola cool to room temperature. Stir in the cranberries before serving.

Avocado Quesadillas

Prep time: 10 minutes | Cook time: 11 minutes | Serves 4

4 eggs
2 tablespoons skim milk
Salt and ground black pepper, to taste
Cooking spray
4 flour tortillas
4 tablespoons salsa
2 ounces (57 g) Cheddar cheese, grated
½ small avocado, peeled and thinly sliced

1. Preheat the air fryer oven to 270ºF (132ºC).
2. Beat together the eggs, milk, salt, and pepper.
3. Spray a baking pan lightly with cooking spray and add egg mixture.
4. Slide the baking pan into Rack Position 1, select Convection Bake and set time to 8 minutes, stirring every 1 to 2 minutes, or until eggs are scrambled to the liking. Remove and set aside.
5. Spray one side of each tortilla with cooking spray. Flip over.
6. Divide eggs, salsa, cheese, and avocado among the tortillas, covering only half of each tortilla.
7. Fold each tortilla in half and press down lightly. Increase the temperature to 390ºF (199ºC). Put the tortillas in air fryer basket.
8. Place the air fryer basket onto the baking pan and slide into Rack Position 2, select Air Fry and set time to 3 minutes, or until cheese melts and outside feels slightly crispy.
9. Cut each cooked tortilla into halves. Serve warm.

Kale and Potato Nuggets

Prep time: 10 minutes | Cook time: 18 minutes | Serves 4

1 teaspoon extra virgin olive oil
1 clove garlic, minced
4 cups kale, rinsed and chopped
2 cups potatoes,
boiled and mashed
⅛ cup milk
Salt and ground black pepper, to taste
Cooking spray

1. Preheat the air fryer oven to 390ºF (199ºC).
2. In a skillet over medium heat, sauté the garlic in the olive oil, until it turns golden brown. Sauté with the kale for an additional 3 minutes and remove from the heat.
3. Mix the mashed potatoes, kale and garlic in a bowl. Pour in the milk and sprinkle with salt and pepper.
4. Shape the mixture into nuggets and spritz with cooking spray. Put them in the air fryer basket.
5. Place the air fryer basket onto the baking pan and slide into Rack Position 2, select Air Fry and set time to 15 minutes, flipping the nuggets halfway through to make sure the nuggets fry evenly.
6. Serve immediately.

Soufflé

Prep time: 10 minutes | Cook time: 22 minutes | Serves 4

1/3 cup butter, melted
1/4 cup flour
1 cup milk
1 ounce (28 g) sugar
4 egg yolks
1 teaspoon vanilla

extract
6 egg whites
1 teaspoon cream of tartar
Cooking spray

1. In a bowl, mix the butter and flour until a smooth consistency is achieved.
2. Pour the milk into a saucepan over medium-low heat. Add the sugar and allow to dissolve before raising the heat to boil the milk.
3. Pour in the flour and butter mixture and stir rigorously for 7 minutes to eliminate any lumps. Make sure the mixture thickens. Take off the heat and allow to cool for 15 minutes.
4. Preheat the air fryer oven to 320ºF (160ºC). Spritz 6 soufflé dishes with cooking spray.
5. Put the egg yolks and vanilla extract in a separate bowl and beat them together with a fork. Pour in the milk and combine well to incorporate everything.
6. In a smaller bowl, mix the egg whites and cream of tartar with a fork. Fold into the egg yolks-milk mixture before adding in the flour mixture. Transfer equal amounts to the 6 soufflé dishes.
7. Place the dishes into Rack Position 1, select Convection Bake and set time to 15 minutes.
8. Serve warm.

Blueberry Muffins

Prep time: 10 minutes | Cook time: 12 minutes | Makes 8 muffins

1 1/3 cups flour
1/2 cup sugar
2 teaspoons baking powder
1/4 teaspoon salt
1/3 cup canola oil

1 egg
1/2 cup milk
2/3 cup blueberries, fresh or frozen and thawed

1. Preheat the air fryer oven to 330ºF (166ºC).
2. In a medium bowl, stir together flour, sugar, baking powder, and salt.
3. In a separate bowl, combine oil, egg, and milk and mix well.
4. Add egg mixture to dry ingredients and stir just until moistened.
5. Gently stir in the blueberries.
6. Spoon batter evenly into parchment paper-lined muffin cups. Place the muffin cups in a baking pan.
7. Slide the baking pan into Rack Position 1, select Convection Bake and set time to 12 minutes, or until tops spring back when touched lightly.
8. Serve immediately.

Mushroom and Squash Toast

Prep time: 10 minutes | Cook time: 10 minutes | Serves 4

1 tablespoon olive oil
1 red bell pepper, cut into strips
2 green onions, sliced
1 cup sliced button or cremini mushrooms

1 small yellow squash, sliced
2 tablespoons softened butter
4 slices bread
1/2 cup soft goat cheese

1. Preheat the air fryer oven to 350ºF (177ºC). Grease the air fryer basket with the olive oil.
2. Put the red pepper, green onions, mushrooms, and squash in the air fryer basket, stirring well.
3. Place the air fryer basket onto the baking pan and slide into Rack Position 2, select Air Fry and set time to 7 minutes, or the vegetables are tender, shaking the basket once throughout the cooking time.
4. Remove the vegetables and set them aside.
5. Spread the butter on the slices of bread and transfer to the air fryer basket, butter-side up.
6. Return to the oven and air fry for 3 minutes more.
7. Remove the toast and top with goat cheese and vegetables. Serve warm.

Scotch Eggs

Prep time: 5 minutes | Cook time: 25 minutes | Serves 4

4 large hard boiled eggs
1 (12-ounce / 340-g) package pork

sausage
8 slices thick-cut bacon

Special Equipment:
4 wooden toothpicks, soaked in water for at least 30 minutes

1. Slice the sausage into four parts and place each part into a large circle.
2. Put an egg into each circle and wrap it in the sausage. Put in the refrigerator for 1 hour.
3. Preheat the air fryer oven to 450°F (235°C).
4. Make a cross with two pieces of thick-cut bacon. Put a wrapped egg in the center, fold the bacon over top of the egg, and secure with a toothpick. Transfer to the air fryer basket.
5. Place the air fryer basket onto the baking pan and slide into Rack Position 2, select Air Fry and set time to 25 minutes.
6. Serve immediately.

English Pumpkin Egg Bake

Prep time: 10 minutes | Cook time: 10 minutes | Serves 2

2 eggs
½ cup milk
2 cups flour
2 tablespoons cider vinegar
2 teaspoons baking powder

1 tablespoon sugar
1 cup pumpkin purée
1 teaspoon cinnamon powder
1 teaspoon baking soda
1 tablespoon olive oil

1. Preheat the air fryer oven to 300°F (149°C).
2. Crack the eggs into a bowl and beat with a whisk. Combine with the milk, flour, cider vinegar, baking powder, sugar, pumpkin purée, cinnamon powder, and baking soda, mixing well.
3. Grease a baking tray with oil and add the mixture.

4. Place the baking tray into Rack Position 1, select Convection Bake and set time to 10 minutes.
5. Serve warm.

Potato Bread Rolls

Prep time: 15 minutes | Cook time: 20 minutes | Serves 5

5 large potatoes, boiled and mashed
Salt and ground black pepper, to taste
½ teaspoon mustard seeds
1 tablespoon olive oil
2 small onions, chopped

2 sprigs curry leaves
½ teaspoon turmeric powder
2 green chilis, seeded and chopped
1 bunch coriander, chopped
8 slices bread, brown sides discarded

1. Put the mashed potatoes in a bowl and sprinkle on salt and pepper. Set to one side.
2. Fry the mustard seeds in olive oil over a medium-low heat in a skillet, stirring continuously, until they sputter.
3. Add the onions and cook until they turn translucent. Add the curry leaves and turmeric powder and stir. Cook for a further 2 minutes until fragrant.
4. Remove the pan from the heat and combine with the potatoes. Mix in the green chilies and coriander.
5. Preheat the air fryer oven to 400°F (204°C).
6. Wet the bread slightly and drain of any excess liquid.
7. Spoon a small amount of the potato mixture into the center of the bread and enclose the bread around the filling, sealing it entirely. Continue until the rest of the bread and filling is used up. Brush each bread roll with some oil and transfer to the air fryer basket.
8. Place the air fryer basket onto the baking pan and slide into Rack Position 2, select Air Fry and set time to 15 minutes, gently shaking the basket halfway through to ensure each roll is cooked evenly.
9. Serve immediately.

Creamy Cinnamon Rolls

Prep time: 10 minutes | Cook time: 9 minutes | Serves 8

1 pound (454 g) frozen bread dough, thawed	4 ounces (113 g) cream cheese, softened
¼ cup butter, melted	2 tablespoons butter, softened
¾ cup brown sugar	1¼ cups powdered sugar
1½ tablespoons ground cinnamon	½ teaspoon vanilla extract
Cream Cheese Glaze:	

1. Let the bread dough come to room temperature on the counter. On a lightly floured surface, roll the dough into a 13-inch by 11-inch rectangle. Position the rectangle so the 13-inch side is facing you. Brush the melted butter all over the dough, leaving a 1-inch border uncovered along the edge farthest away from you.
2. Combine the brown sugar and cinnamon in a small bowl. Sprinkle the mixture evenly over the buttered dough, keeping the 1-inch border uncovered. Roll the dough into a log, starting with the edge closest to you. Roll the dough tightly, rolling evenly, and push out any air pockets. When you get to the uncovered edge of the dough, press the dough onto the roll to seal it together.
3. Cut the log into 8 pieces, slicing slowly with a sawing motion so you don't flatten the dough. Turn the slices on their sides and cover with a clean kitchen towel. Let the rolls sit in the warmest part of the kitchen for 1½ to 2 hours to rise.
4. To make the glaze, place the cream cheese and butter in a microwave-safe bowl. Soften the mixture in the microwave for 30 seconds at a time until it is easy to stir. Gradually add the powdered sugar and stir to combine. Add the vanilla extract and whisk until smooth. Set aside.
5. When the rolls have risen, preheat the air fryer oven to 350ºF (177ºC).
6. Transfer the rolls to the air fryer basket.
7. Place the air fryer basket onto the baking pan and slide into Rack Position 2, select Air Fry and set time to 5 minutes.
8. Turn the rolls over and air fry for another 4 minutes.
9. Let the rolls cool for 2 minutes before glazing. Spread large dollops of cream cheese glaze on top of the warm cinnamon rolls, allowing some glaze to drip down the side of the rolls. Serve warm.

Nut and Seed Muffins

Prep time: 15 minutes | Cook time: 10 minutes | Makes 8 muffins

½ cup whole-wheat flour, plus 2 tablespoons	2 tablespoons melted butter
¼ cup oat bran	1 egg
2 tablespoons flaxseed meal	½ teaspoon pure vanilla extract
¼ cup brown sugar	½ cup grated carrots
½ teaspoon baking soda	¼ cup chopped pecans
½ teaspoon baking powder	¼ cup chopped walnuts
¼ teaspoon salt	1 tablespoon pumpkin seeds
½ teaspoon cinnamon	1 tablespoon sunflower seeds
½ cup buttermilk	Cooking spray

Special Equipment:
16 foil muffin cups, paper liners removed

1. Preheat the air fryer oven to 330ºF (166ºC).
2. In a large bowl, stir together the flour, bran, flaxseed meal, sugar, baking soda, baking powder, salt, and cinnamon.
3. In a medium bowl, beat together the buttermilk, butter, egg, and vanilla. Pour into flour mixture and stir just until dry ingredients moisten. Do not beat.
4. Gently stir in carrots, nuts, and seeds.
5. Double up the foil cups so you have 8 total and spritz with cooking spray.
6. Divide the batter among the 8 foil cups. Place the cups in a baking pan.
7. Slide the baking pan into Rack Position 1, select Convection Bake and set time to 10 minutes, or until a toothpick inserted in center comes out clean.
8. Serve warm.

Posh Orange Rolls

Prep time: 15 minutes | Cook time: 8 minutes | Makes 8 rolls

3 ounces (85 g) low-fat cream cheese
1 tablespoon low-fat sour cream or plain yogurt
2 teaspoons sugar
¼ teaspoon pure vanilla extract
¼ teaspoon orange extract
1 can (8 count) organic crescent roll dough
¼ cup chopped walnuts
¼ cup dried cranberries
¼ cup shredded, sweetened coconut
Butter-flavored cooking spray

Orange Glaze:

½ cup powdered sugar
1 tablespoon orange juice
¼ teaspoon orange extract
Dash of salt

1. Cut a circular piece of parchment paper slightly smaller than the bottom of the air fryer basket. Set aside.
2. In a small bowl, combine the cream cheese, sour cream or yogurt, sugar, and vanilla and orange extracts. Stir until smooth.
3. Preheat the air fryer oven to 300ºF (149ºC).
4. Separate crescent roll dough into 8 triangles and divide cream cheese mixture among them. Starting at wide end, spread cheese mixture to within 1 inch of point.
5. Sprinkle nuts and cranberries evenly over cheese mixture.
6. Starting at wide end, roll up triangles, then sprinkle with coconut, pressing in lightly to make it stick. Spray tops of rolls with butter-flavored cooking spray.
7. Put parchment paper in the air fryer basket, and place the rolls on top, spaced evenly.
8. Place the air fryer basket onto the baking pan and slide into Rack Position 2, select Air Fry and set time to 8 minutes, or until rolls are golden brown and cooked through.
9. In a small bowl, stir together ingredients for glaze and drizzle over warm rolls. Serve warm.

Grit and Ham Fritters

Prep time: 15 minutes | Cook time: 20 minutes | Serves 6 to 8

4 cups water
1 cup quick-cooking grits
¼ teaspoon salt
2 tablespoons butter
2 cups grated Cheddar cheese, divided
1 cup finely diced ham
1 tablespoon chopped chives
Salt and freshly ground black pepper, to taste
1 egg, beaten
2 cups panko bread crumbs
Cooking spray

1. Bring the water to a boil in a saucepan. Whisk in the grits and ¼ teaspoon of salt, and cook for 7 minutes until the grits are soft. Remove the pan from the heat and stir in the butter and 1 cup of the grated Cheddar cheese. Transfer the grits to a bowl and let them cool for 10 to 15 minutes.
2. Stir the ham, chives and the rest of the cheese into the grits and season with salt and pepper to taste. Add the beaten egg and refrigerate the mixture for 30 minutes.
3. Put the panko bread crumbs in a shallow dish. Measure out ¼-cup portions of the grits mixture and shape them into patties. Coat all sides of the patties with the panko bread crumbs, patting them with the hands so the crumbs adhere to the patties. You should have about 16 patties. Spritz both sides of the patties with cooking spray.
4. Preheat the air fryer oven to 400ºF (204ºC).
5. Working in batches, arrange the patties in the air fryer basket.
6. Place the air fryer basket onto the baking pan and slide into Rack Position 2, select Air Fry and set time to 8 minutes.
7. Using a flat spatula, flip the fritters over and air fry for another 4 minutes.
8. Serve hot.

Lush Vegetable Omelet

Prep time: 10 minutes | Cook time: 13 minutes | Serves 2

2 teaspoons canola oil
4 eggs, whisked
3 tablespoons plain milk
1 teaspoon melted butter
1 red bell pepper, seeded and chopped
1 green bell pepper, seeded and chopped
1 white onion, finely chopped
½ cup baby spinach leaves, roughly chopped
½ cup Halloumi cheese, shaved
Kosher salt and freshly ground black pepper, to taste

1. Preheat the air fryer oven to 350ºF (177ºC).
2. Grease a baking pan with canola oil.
3. Put the remaining ingredients in the baking pan and stir well.
4. Slide the baking pan into Rack Position 1, select Convection Bake and set time to 13 minutes.
5. Serve warm.

Ham and Corn Muffins

Prep time: 10 minutes | Cook time: 6 minutes | Makes 8 muffins

¾ cup yellow cornmeal
¼ cup flour
1½ teaspoons baking powder
¼ teaspoon salt
1 egg, beaten
2 tablespoons canola oil
½ cup milk
½ cup shredded sharp Cheddar cheese
½ cup diced ham

1. Preheat the air fryer oven to 390ºF (199ºC).
2. In a medium bowl, stir together the cornmeal, flour, baking powder, and salt.
3. Add the egg, oil, and milk to dry ingredients and mix well.
4. Stir in shredded cheese and diced ham.
5. Divide batter among 8 parchment paper-lined muffin cups. Place the muffin cups in a baking pan.
6. Slide the baking pan into Rack Position 1, select Convection Bake and set time to 5 minutes.

7. Reduce the temperature to 330ºF (166ºC) and bake for 1 minute, or until a toothpick inserted in the center of the muffin comes out clean.
8. Serve warm.

Apple and Walnut Muffins

Prep time: 15 minutes | Cook time: 10 minutes | Makes 8 muffins

1 cup flour
$1/_3$ cup sugar
1 teaspoon baking powder
¼ teaspoon baking soda
¼ teaspoon salt
1 teaspoon cinnamon
¼ teaspoon ginger
¼ teaspoon nutmeg
1 egg
2 tablespoons
pancake syrup, plus 2 teaspoons
2 tablespoons melted butter, plus 2 teaspoons
¾ cup unsweetened applesauce
½ teaspoon vanilla extract
¼ cup chopped walnuts
¼ cup diced apple

1. Preheat the air fryer oven to 330ºF (166ºC).
2. In a large bowl, stir together the flour, sugar, baking powder, baking soda, salt, cinnamon, ginger, and nutmeg.
3. In a small bowl, beat egg until frothy. Add syrup, butter, applesauce, and vanilla and mix well.
4. Pour egg mixture into dry ingredients and stir just until moistened.
5. Gently stir in nuts and diced apple.
6. Divide batter among 8 parchment paper-lined muffin cups. Place the muffin cups in a baking pan.
7. Slide the baking pan into Rack Position 1, select Convection Bake and set time to 10 minutes, or until a toothpick inserted in the center comes out clean.
8. Serve warm.

Chapter 2 Vegetables

Zucchini Crisps

Prep time: 5 minutes | Cook time: 14 minutes | Serves 4

2 zucchini, sliced into ¼- to ½-inch-thick rounds (about 2 cups)
¼ teaspoon garlic granules
⅛ teaspoon sea salt
Freshly ground black pepper, to taste (optional)
Cooking spray

1. Spritz the air fryer basket with cooking spray.
2. Put the zucchini rounds in the basket, spreading them out as much as possible. Top with a sprinkle of garlic granules, sea salt, and black pepper (if desired). Spritz the zucchini rounds with cooking spray.
3. Put the air fryer basket on the baking pan and slide into Rack Position 2, select Roast, set temperature to 392ºF (200ºC), and set time to 14 minutes.
4. Flip the zucchini rounds halfway through.
5. When cooking is complete, the zucchini rounds should be crisp-tender. Remove from the oven. Let them rest for 5 minutes and serve.

Green Beans with Shallot

Prep time: 10 minutes | Cook time: 10 minutes | Serves 4

1½ pounds (680 g) French green beans, stems removed and blanched
1 tablespoon salt
½ pound (227 g)
shallots, peeled and cut into quarters
½ teaspoon ground white pepper
2 tablespoons olive oil

1. Preheat the air fryer oven to 400ºF (204ºC).
2. Coat the vegetables with the rest of the ingredients in a bowl. Transfer to the air fryer basket.
3. Place the air fryer basket onto the baking pan and slide into Rack Position 2, select Air Fry and set time to 10 minutes, making sure the green beans achieve a light brown color.
4. Serve hot.

Mediterranean Air Fried Veggies

Prep time: 10 minutes | Cook time: 6 minutes | Serves 4

1 large zucchini, sliced
1 cup cherry tomatoes, halved
1 parsnip, sliced
1 green pepper, sliced
1 carrot, sliced
1 teaspoon mixed
herbs
1 teaspoon mustard
1 teaspoon garlic purée
6 tablespoons olive oil
Salt and ground black pepper, to taste

1. Preheat the air fryer oven to 400ºF (204ºC).
2. Combine all the ingredients in a bowl, making sure to coat the vegetables well. Transfer to the air fryer basket.
3. Place the air fryer basket onto the baking pan and slide into Rack Position 2, select Air Fry and set time to 6 minutes, ensuring the vegetables are tender and browned.
4. Serve immediately.

Potatoes with Zucchinis

Prep time: 10 minutes | Cook time: 45 minutes | Serves 4

2 potatoes, peeled and cubed
4 carrots, cut into chunks
1 head broccoli, cut into florets
4 zucchinis, sliced
thickly
Salt and ground black pepper, to taste
¼ cup olive oil
1 tablespoon dry onion powder

1. Preheat the air fryer oven to 400ºF (204ºC).
2. In a baking dish, add all the ingredients and combine well.
3. Place the baking dish into Rack Position 1, select Convection Bake and set time to 45 minutes, or until the vegetables are soft and the sides have browned. Serve warm.

Cinnamon Celery Roots

Prep time: 10 minutes | Cook time: 20 minutes | Serves 4

2 celery roots, peeled and diced
1 teaspoon extra-virgin olive oil
1 teaspoon butter, melted
½ teaspoon ground cinnamon
Sea salt and freshly ground black pepper, to taste

1. Line the baking pan with aluminum foil.
2. Toss the celery roots with the olive oil in a large bowl until well coated. Transfer them to the prepared baking pan.
3. Slide the baking pan into Rack Position 2, select Roast, set temperature to 350ºF (180ºC), and set time to 20 minutes.
4. When done, the celery roots should be very tender. Remove from the oven to a serving bowl. Stir in the butter and cinnamon and mash them with a potato masher until fluffy.
5. Season with salt and pepper to taste. Serve immediately.

Lemony Wax Beans

Prep time: 5 minutes | Cook time: 12 minutes | Serves 4

2 pounds (907 g) wax beans
2 tablespoons extra-virgin olive oil
Salt and freshly
ground black pepper, to taste
Juice of ½ lemon, for serving

1. Line the air fryer basket with aluminum foil.
2. Toss the wax beans with the olive oil in a large bowl. Lightly season with salt and pepper.
3. Spread out the wax beans in the basket.
4. Put the air fryer basket on the baking pan and slide into Rack Position 2, select Roast, set temperature to 400ºF (205ºC), and set time to 12 minutes.
5. When done, the beans will be caramelized and tender. Remove from the oven to a plate and serve sprinkled with the lemon juice.

Tortellini with Veggies and Parmesan

Prep time: 10 minutes | Cook time: 16 minutes | Serves 4

8 ounces (227 g) sugar snap peas, trimmed
½ pound (227 g) asparagus, trimmed and cut into 1-inch pieces
2 teaspoons kosher salt or 1 teaspoon fine salt, divided
1 tablespoon extra-virgin olive oil
1½ cups water
1 (20-ounce / 340-g) package frozen cheese tortellini
2 garlic cloves, minced
1 cup heavy (whipping) cream
1 cup cherry tomatoes, halved
½ cup grated Parmesan cheese
¼ cup chopped fresh parsley or basil

1. Add the peas and asparagus to a large bowl. Add ½ teaspoon of kosher salt and the olive oil and toss until well coated. Place the veggies in the baking pan.
2. Slide the baking pan into Rack Position 1, select Convection Bake, set the temperature to 450ºF (235ºC), and set the time for 4 minutes.
3. Meanwhile, dissolve 1 teaspoon of kosher salt in the water.
4. Once cooking is complete, remove the pan from the oven and place the tortellini in the pan. Pour the salted water over the tortellini. Put the pan back to the oven.
5. Slide the baking pan into Rack Position 1, select Convection Bake, set temperature to 450ºF (235ºC), and set time for 7 minutes.
6. Meantime, stir together the garlic, heavy cream, and remaining ½ teaspoon of kosher salt in a small bowl.
7. Once cooking is complete, remove the pan from the oven. Blot off any remaining water with a paper towel. Gently stir the ingredients. Drizzle the cream over and top with the tomatoes.
8. Slide the baking pan into Rack Position 2, select Roast, set the temperature to 375ºF (190ºC), and set the time for 5 minutes.
9. After 4 minutes, remove from the oven.
10. Add the Parmesan cheese and stir until the cheese is melted
11. Serve topped with the parsley.

Lemony Brussels Sprouts and Tomatoes

Prep time: 15 minutes | Cook time: 20 minutes | Serves 4

1 pound (454 g) Brussels sprouts, trimmed and halved
1 tablespoon extra-virgin olive oil
Sea Salt and freshly ground black pepper, to taste
½ cup sun-dried tomatoes, chopped
2 tablespoons freshly squeezed lemon juice
1 teaspoon lemon zest

1. Line the air fryer basket with aluminum foil.
2. Toss the Brussels sprouts with the olive oil in a large bowl. Sprinkle with salt and black pepper.
3. Spread the Brussels sprouts in a single layer in the basket.
4. Put the air fryer basket on the baking pan and slide into Rack Position 2, select Roast, set temperature to 400ºF (205ºC), and set time to 20 minutes.
5. When done, the Brussels sprouts should be caramelized. Remove from the oven to a serving bowl, along with the tomatoes, lemon juice, and lemon zest. Toss to combine. Serve immediately.

Spicy Kung Pao Tofu

Prep time: 10 minutes | Cook time: 10 minutes | Serves 4

⅓ cup Asian-Style sauce
1 teaspoon cornstarch
½ teaspoon red pepper flakes, or more to taste
1 pound (454 g) firm or extra-firm tofu, cut into 1-inch cubes
1 small carrot, peeled and cut into ¼-inch-thick coins
1 small green bell pepper, cut into bite-size pieces
3 scallions, sliced, whites and green parts separated
3 tablespoons roasted unsalted peanuts

1. In a large bowl, whisk together the sauce, cornstarch, and red pepper flakes. Fold in the tofu, carrot, pepper, and the white parts of the scallions and toss to coat. Spread the mixture evenly in the baking pan.

2. Slide the baking pan into Rack Position 2, select Roast, set temperature to 375ºF (190ºC), and set time to 10 minutes.
3. Stir the ingredients once halfway through the cooking time.
4. When done, remove from the oven. Serve sprinkled with the peanuts and scallion greens.

Sweet and Spicy Broccoli

Prep time: 10 minutes | Cook time: 15 to 20 minutes | Serves 4

½ teaspoon olive oil, plus more for greasing
1 pound (454 g) fresh broccoli, cut into florets
½ tablespoon minced garlic
Salt, to taste
Sauce:
1½ tablespoons soy sauce
2 teaspoons hot sauce or sriracha
1½ teaspoons honey
1 teaspoon white vinegar
Freshly ground black pepper, to taste

1. Grease the air fryer basket with olive oil.
2. Add the broccoli florets, ½ teaspoon of olive oil, and garlic to a large bowl and toss well. Season with salt to taste.
3. Put the broccoli in the basket in a single layer.
4. Put the air fryer basket on the baking pan and slide into Rack Position 2, select Air Fry, set temperature to 400ºF (205ºC), and set time to 15 minutes.
5. Stir the broccoli florets three times during cooking.
6. Meanwhile, whisk together all the ingredients for the sauce in a small bowl until well incorporated. If the honey doesn't incorporate well, microwave the sauce for 10 to 20 seconds until the honey is melted.
7. When cooking is complete, the broccoli should be lightly browned and crispy. Continue cooking for 5 minutes, if desired. Remove from the oven to a serving bowl. Pour over the sauce and toss to combine. Add more salt and pepper, if needed. Serve warm.

Roasted Vegetables with Basil

Prep time: 15 minutes | Cook time: 20 minutes | Serves 2

1 small eggplant, halved and sliced
1 yellow bell pepper, cut into thick strips
1 red bell pepper, cut into thick strips
2 garlic cloves, quartered
1 red onion, sliced
1 tablespoon extra-virgin olive oil
Salt and freshly ground black pepper, to taste
½ cup chopped fresh basil, for garnish
Cooking spray

1. Grease the baking pan with cooking spray.
2. Place the eggplant, bell peppers, garlic, and red onion in the greased baking pan. Drizzle with the olive oil and toss to coat well. Spritz any uncoated surfaces with cooking spray.
3. Slide the baking pan into Rack Position 1, select Convection Bake, set temperature to 350ºF (180ºC), and set time to 20 minutes.
4. Flip the vegetables halfway through the cooking time.
5. When done, remove from the oven and sprinkle with salt and pepper.
6. Sprinkle the basil on top for garnish and serve.

Roasted Asparagus with Eggs and Tomatoes

Prep time: 10 minutes | Cook time: 12 minutes | Serves 4

2 pounds (907 g) asparagus, trimmed
3 tablespoons extra-virgin olive oil, divided
1 teaspoon kosher salt, divided
1 pint cherry tomatoes
4 large eggs
¼ teaspoon freshly ground black pepper

1. Put the asparagus in the baking pan and drizzle with 2 tablespoons of olive oil, tossing to coat. Season with ½ teaspoon of kosher salt.
2. Slide the baking pan into Rack Position 2, select Roast, set temperature to 375ºF (190ºC), and set time to 12 minutes.
3. Meanwhile, toss the cherry tomatoes with the remaining 1 tablespoon of olive oil in a medium bowl until well coated.
4. After 6 minutes, remove the pan and toss the asparagus. Evenly spread the asparagus in the middle of the pan. Add the tomatoes around the perimeter of the pan. Return the pan to the oven and continue cooking.
5. After 2 minutes, remove from the oven.
6. Carefully crack the eggs, one at a time, over the asparagus, spacing them out. Season with the remaining ½ teaspoon of kosher salt and the pepper. Return the pan to the oven and continue cooking. Cook for an additional 3 to 7 minutes, or until the eggs are cooked to your desired doneness.
7. When done, divide the asparagus and eggs among four plates. Top each plate evenly with the tomatoes and serve.

Maple and Pecan Granola

Prep time: 5 minutes | Cook time: 20 minutes | Serves 4

1½ cups rolled oats
¼ cup maple syrup
¼ cup pecan pieces
1 teaspoon vanilla
extract
½ teaspoon ground cinnamon

1. Line a baking sheet with parchment paper.
2. Mix together the oats, maple syrup, pecan pieces, vanilla, and cinnamon in a large bowl and stir until the oats and pecan pieces are completely coated. Spread the mixture evenly in the baking pan.
3. Slide the baking pan into Rack Position 1, select Convection Bake, set temperature to 300ºF (150ºC), and set time to 20 minutes.
4. Stir once halfway through the cooking time.
5. When done, remove from the oven and cool for 30 minutes before serving. The granola may still be a bit soft right after removing, but it will gradually firm up as it cools.

Cauliflower, Chickpea, and Avocado Mash

Prep time: 10 minutes | Cook time: 25 minutes | Serves 4

1 medium head cauliflower, cut into florets
1 can chickpeas, drained and rinsed
1 tablespoon extra-virgin olive oil
2 tablespoons lemon juice
Salt and ground black pepper, to taste
4 flatbreads, toasted
2 ripe avocados, mashed

1. Preheat the air fryer oven to 425°F (218°C).
2. In a bowl, mix the chickpeas, cauliflower, lemon juice and olive oil. Sprinkle salt and pepper as desired. Transfer to the air fryer basket.
3. Place the air fryer basket onto the baking pan and slide into Rack Position 2, select Air Fry and set time to 25 minutes.
4. Spread on top of the flatbread along with the mashed avocado. Sprinkle with more pepper and salt and serve.

Mushroom and Pepper Pizza Squares

Prep time: 10 minutes | Cook time: 10 minutes | Serves 10

1 pizza dough, cut into squares
1 cup chopped oyster mushrooms
1 shallot, chopped
¼ red bell pepper, chopped
2 tablespoons parsley
Salt and ground black pepper, to taste

1. Preheat the air fryer oven to 400°F (204°C).
2. In a bowl, combine the oyster mushrooms, shallot, bell pepper and parsley. Sprinkle some salt and pepper as desired.
3. Spread this mixture on top of the pizza squares, then transfer to a baking pan.
4. Slide the baking pan into Rack Position 1, select Convection Bake and set time to 10 minutes.
5. Serve warm.

Balsamic Brussels Sprouts

Prep time: 5 minutes | Cook time: 13 minutes | Serves 2

2 cups Brussels sprouts, halved
1 tablespoon olive oil
1 tablespoon balsamic vinegar
1 tablespoon maple syrup
¼ teaspoon sea salt

1. Preheat the air fryer oven to 375°F (191°C).
2. Evenly coat the Brussels sprouts with the olive oil, balsamic vinegar, maple syrup, and salt. Transfer to the air fryer basket.
3. Place the air fryer basket onto the baking pan and slide into Rack Position 2, select Air Fry and set time to 5 minutes.
4. Give the basket a good shake, increase the temperature to 400°F (204°C) and continue to air fry for another 8 minutes.
5. Serve hot.

Basmati Risotto

Prep time: 10 minutes | Cook time: 30 minutes | Serves 2

1 onion, diced
1 small carrot, diced
2 cups vegetable broth, boiling
½ cup grated Cheddar cheese
1 clove garlic, minced
¾ cup long-grain basmati rice
1 tablespoon olive oil
1 tablespoon unsalted butter

1. Preheat the air fryer oven to 390°F (199°C).
2. Grease a baking tin with oil and stir in the butter, garlic, carrot, and onion.
3. Place the baking tin into Rack Position 1, select Convection Bake and set time to 4 minutes.
4. Pour in the rice and bake for a further 4 minutes, stirring three times during cooking.
5. Reduce the temperature to 320°F (160°C).
6. Add the vegetable broth and give the dish a gentle stir. Bake, uncovered, for 22 minutes.
7. Pour in the cheese, stir once more and serve.

Spicy Thai-Style Vegetables

Prep time: 10 minutes | Cook time: 8 minutes | Serves 4

1 small head Napa cabbage, shredded, divided
1 medium carrot, cut into thin coins
8 ounces (227 g) snow peas
1 red or green bell pepper, sliced into thin strips
1 tablespoon vegetable oil
2 tablespoons soy sauce
1 tablespoon sesame oil

2 tablespoons brown sugar
2 tablespoons freshly squeezed lime juice
2 teaspoons red or green Thai curry paste
1 serrano chile, deseeded and minced
1 cup frozen mango slices, thawed
½ cup chopped roasted peanuts or cashews

1. Put half the Napa cabbage in a large bowl, along with the carrot, snow peas, and bell pepper. Drizzle with the vegetable oil and toss to coat. Spread them evenly in the air fryer basket.
2. Put the air fryer basket on the baking pan and slide into Rack Position 2, select Roast, set temperature to 375ºF (190ºC), and set time to 8 minutes.
3. Meanwhile, whisk together the soy sauce, sesame oil, brown sugar, lime juice, and curry paste in a small bowl.
4. When done, the vegetables should be tender and crisp. Remove from the oven and put the vegetables back into the bowl. Add the chile, mango slices, and the remaining cabbage. Pour over the dressing and toss to coat. Top with the roasted nuts and serve.

Paprika Cauliflower

Prep time: 10 minutes | Cook time: 20 minutes | Serves 4

1 large head cauliflower, broken into small florets
2 teaspoons smoked paprika
1 teaspoon garlic

powder
Salt and freshly ground black pepper, to taste
Cooking spray

1. Spray the air fryer basket with cooking spray.
2. In a medium bowl, toss the cauliflower florets with the smoked paprika and garlic powder until evenly coated. Sprinkle with salt and pepper.
3. Place the cauliflower florets in the basket and lightly mist with cooking spray.
4. Put the air fryer basket on the baking pan and slide into Rack Position 2, select Air Fry, set temperature to 400ºF (205ºC), and set time to 20 minutes.
5. Stir the cauliflower four times during cooking.
6. Remove the cauliflower from the oven and serve hot.

Cheesy Broccoli Tots

Prep time: 20 minutes | Cook time: 15 minutes | Serves 4

12 ounces (340 g) frozen broccoli, thawed, drained, and patted dry
1 large egg, lightly beaten
½ cup seasoned whole-wheat bread crumbs
¼ cup shredded

reduced-fat sharp Cheddar cheese
¼ cup grated Parmesan cheese
1½ teaspoons minced garlic
Salt and freshly ground black pepper, to taste
Cooking spray

1. Spritz the air fryer basket lightly with cooking spray.
2. Place the remaining ingredients into a food processor and process until the mixture resembles a coarse meal. Transfer the mixture to a bowl.
3. Using a tablespoon, scoop out the broccoli mixture and form into 24 oval "tater tot" shapes with your hands.
4. Put the tots in the prepared basket in a single layer, spacing them 1 inch apart. Mist the tots lightly with cooking spray.
5. Put the air fryer basket on the baking pan and slide into Rack Position 2, select Air Fry, set temperature to 375ºF (190ºC), and set time to 15 minutes.
6. Flip the tots halfway through the cooking time.
7. When done, the tots will be lightly browned and crispy. Remove from the oven and serve on a plate.

Herbed Broccoli with Cheese

Prep time: 5 minutes | Cook time: 18 minutes | Serves 4

1 large-sized head broccoli, stemmed and cut into small florets
2½ tablespoons canola oil
2 teaspoons dried basil

2 teaspoons dried rosemary
Salt and ground black pepper, to taste
⅓ cup grated yellow cheese

1. Bring a pot of lightly salted water to a boil. Add the broccoli florets to the boiling water and let boil for about 3 minutes.
2. Drain the broccoli florets well and transfer to a large bowl. Add the canola oil, basil, rosemary, salt, and black pepper to the bowl and toss until the broccoli is fully coated. Place the broccoli in the air fryer basket.
3. Put the air fryer basket on the baking pan and slide into Rack Position 2, select Air Fry, set temperature to 390ºF (199ºC), and set time to 15 minutes.
4. Stir the broccoli halfway through the cooking time.
5. When cooking is complete, the broccoli should be crisp. Serve the broccoli warm with grated cheese sprinkled on top.

Bean, Salsa, and Cheese Tacos

Prep time: 12 minutes | Cook time: 7 minutes | Serves 4

1 (15-ounce / 425-g) can black beans, drained and rinsed
½ cup prepared salsa
1½ teaspoons chili powder
4 ounces (113 g) grated Monterey Jack cheese

2 tablespoons minced onion
8 (6-inch) flour tortillas
2 tablespoons vegetable or extra-virgin olive oil
Shredded lettuce, for serving

1. In a medium bowl, add the beans, salsa and chili powder. Coarsely mash them with a potato masher. Fold in the cheese and onion and stir until combined.

2. Arrange the flour tortillas on a cutting board and spoon 2 to 3 tablespoons of the filling into each tortilla. Fold the tortillas over, pressing lightly to even out the filling. Brush the tacos on one side with half the olive oil and put them, oiled side down, in the air fryer basket. Brush the top side with the remaining olive oil.
3. Put the air fryer basket on the baking pan and slide into Rack Position 2, select Air Fry, set temperature to 400ºF (205ºC), and set time to 7 minutes.
4. Flip the tacos halfway through the cooking time.
5. Remove from the oven and allow to cool for 5 minutes. Serve with the shredded lettuce on the side.

Sesame-Thyme Whole Maitake Mushrooms

Prep time: 5 minutes | Cook time: 15 minutes | Serves 2

1 tablespoon soy sauce
2 teaspoons toasted sesame oil
3 teaspoons vegetable oil, divided
1 garlic clove, minced
7 ounces (198 g)

maitake (hen of the woods) mushrooms
½ teaspoon flaky sea salt
½ teaspoon sesame seeds
½ teaspoon finely chopped fresh thyme leaves

1. Whisk together the soy sauce, sesame oil, 1 teaspoon of vegetable oil, and garlic in a small bowl.
2. Arrange the mushrooms in the air fryer basket in a single layer. Drizzle the soy sauce mixture over the mushrooms.
3. Put the air fryer basket on the baking pan and slide into Rack Position 2, select Roast, set temperature to 300ºF (150ºC), and set time to 15 minutes.
4. After 10 minutes, remove from the oven. Flip the mushrooms and sprinkle the sea salt, sesame seeds, and thyme leaves on top. Drizzle the remaining 2 teaspoons of vegetable oil all over. Return to the oven and continue roasting for an additional 5 minutes.
5. When cooking is complete, remove the mushrooms from the oven to a plate and serve hot.

Ratatouille

Prep time: 10 minutes | Cook time: 12 minutes | Serves 6

1 medium zucchini, sliced ½-inch thick
1 small eggplant, peeled and sliced ½-inch thick
2 teaspoons kosher salt, divided
4 tablespoons extra-virgin olive oil, divided
3 garlic cloves, minced
1 small onion, chopped
1 small red bell pepper, cut into ½-inch chunks
1 small green bell pepper, cut into ½-inch chunks
½ teaspoon dried oregano
¼ teaspoon freshly ground black pepper
1 pint cherry tomatoes
2 tablespoons minced fresh basil
1 cup panko bread crumbs
½ cup grated Parmesan cheese (optional)

1. Season one side of the zucchini and eggplant slices with ¾ teaspoon of salt. Put the slices, salted side down, on a rack set over a baking sheet. Sprinkle the other sides with ¾ teaspoon of salt. Allow to sit for 10 minutes, or until the slices begin to exude water. When ready, rinse and dry them. Cut the zucchini slices into quarters and the eggplant slices into eighths.
2. Pour the zucchini and eggplant into a large bowl, along with 2 tablespoons of olive oil, garlic, onion, bell peppers, oregano, and black pepper. Toss to coat well. Arrange the vegetables in the air fryer basket.
3. Put the air fryer basket on the baking pan and slide into Rack Position 2, select Roast, set temperature to 375ºF (190ºC), and set time to 12 minutes.
4. Meanwhile, add the tomatoes and basil to the large bowl. Sprinkle with the remaining ½ teaspoon of salt and 1 tablespoon of olive oil. Toss well and set aside.
5. Stir together the remaining 1 tablespoon of olive oil, panko, and Parmesan cheese (if desired) in a small bowl.
6. After 6 minutes, remove from the oven and add the tomato mixture and stir to mix well. Scatter the panko mixture on top. Return to the oven and continue cooking for 6 minutes, or until the vegetables are softened and the topping is golden brown.
7. Cool for 5 minutes before serving.

Chermoula Beet

Prep time: 15 minutes | Cook time: 25 minutes | Serves 4

Chermoula:
1 cup packed fresh cilantro leaves
½ cup packed fresh parsley leaves
6 cloves garlic, peeled
2 teaspoons smoked paprika
2 teaspoons ground cumin
1 teaspoon ground coriander
½ to 1 teaspoon cayenne pepper
Pinch of crushed saffron (optional)
½ cup extra-virgin olive oil
Kosher salt, to taste

Beets:
3 medium beets, trimmed, peeled, and cut into 1-inch chunks
2 tablespoons chopped fresh cilantro
2 tablespoons chopped fresh parsley

1. In a food processor, combine the cilantro, parsley, garlic, paprika, cumin, coriander, and cayenne. Pulse until coarsely chopped. Add the saffron, if using, and process until combined. With the food processor running, slowly add the olive oil in a steady stream; process until the sauce is uniform. Season with salt.
2. Preheat the air fryer oven to 375ºF (191ºC).
3. In a large bowl, drizzle the beets with ½ cup of the chermoula to coat. Arrange the beets in the air fryer basket.
4. Place the air fryer basket onto the baking pan and slide into Rack Position 2, select Air Fry and set time to 25 minutes, or until the beets are tender.
5. Transfer the beets to a serving platter. Sprinkle with the chopped cilantro and parsley and serve.

Vegetable and Cheese Stuffed Tomatoes

Prep time: 10 minutes | Cook time: 18 minutes | Serves 4

4 medium beefsteak tomatoes, rinsed
½ cup grated carrot
1 medium onion, chopped
1 garlic clove, minced

2 teaspoons olive oil
2 cups fresh baby spinach
¼ cup crumbled low-sodium feta cheese
½ teaspoon dried basil

1. On your cutting board, cut a thin slice off the top of each tomato. Scoop out a ¼- to ½-inch-thick tomato pulp and place the tomatoes upside down on paper towels to drain. Set aside.
2. Stir together the carrot, onion, garlic, and olive oil in the baking pan.
3. Slide the baking pan into Rack Position 1, select Convection Bake, set temperature to 350ºF (180ºC) and set time to 5 minutes.
4. Stir the vegetables halfway through.
5. When cooking is complete, the carrot should be crisp-tender.
6. Remove from the oven and stir in the spinach, feta cheese, and basil.
7. Spoon ¼ of the vegetable mixture into each tomato and transfer the stuffed tomatoes to the oven. Set time to 13 minutes.
8. When cooking is complete, the filling should be hot and the tomatoes should be lightly caramelized.
9. Let the tomatoes cool for 5 minutes and serve.

Cheesy Cabbage Wedges

Prep time: 5 minutes | Cook time: 20 minutes | Serves 4

4 tablespoons melted butter
1 head cabbage, cut into wedges
1 cup shredded

Parmesan cheese
Salt and black pepper, to taste
½ cup shredded Mozzarella cheese

1. Brush the melted butter over the cut sides of cabbage wedges and sprinkle both sides with the Parmesan cheese. Season with salt and pepper to taste.
2. Place the cabbage wedges in the air fryer basket.
3. Put the air fryer basket on the baking pan and slide into Rack Position 2, select Air Fry, set temperature to 380ºF (193ºC), and set time to 20 minutes.
4. Flip the cabbage halfway through the cooking time.
5. When cooking is complete, the cabbage wedges should be lightly browned. Transfer the cabbage wedges to a plate and serve with the Mozzarella cheese sprinkled on top.

Roasted Veggie Salad

Prep time: 5 minutes | Cook time: 20 minutes | Serves 2

1 potato, chopped
1 carrot, sliced diagonally
1 cup cherry tomatoes
½ small beetroot, sliced
¼ onion, sliced
½ teaspoon turmeric
½ teaspoon cumin
¼ teaspoon sea salt

2 tablespoons olive oil, divided
A handful of arugula
A handful of baby spinach
Juice of 1 lemon
3 tablespoons canned chickpeas, for serving
Parmesan shavings, for serving

1. Combine the potato, carrot, cherry tomatoes, beetroot, onion, turmeric, cumin, salt, and 1 tablespoon of olive oil in a large bowl and toss until well coated.
2. Arrange the veggies in the air fryer basket.
3. Put the air fryer basket on the baking pan and slide into Rack Position 2, select Roast, set temperature to 370ºF (188ºC) and set time to 20 minutes.
4. Stir the vegetables halfway through.
5. When cooking is complete, the potatoes should be golden brown.
6. Let the veggies cool for 5 to 10 minutes in the oven.
7. Put the arugula, baby spinach, lemon juice, and remaining 1 tablespoon of olive oil in a salad bowl and stir to combine. Mix in the roasted veggies and toss well.
8. Scatter the chickpeas and Parmesan shavings on top and serve immediately.

Balsamic Asparagus

Prep time: 15 minutes | Cook time: 10 minutes | Serves 4

4 tablespoons olive oil, plus more for greasing	asparagus spears, trimmed
4 tablespoons balsamic vinegar	Salt and freshly ground black pepper, to taste
1½ pounds (680 g)	

1. Grease the air fryer basket with olive oil.
2. In a shallow bowl, stir together the 4 tablespoons of olive oil and balsamic vinegar to make a marinade.
3. Put the asparagus spears in the bowl so they are thoroughly covered by the marinade and allow to marinate for 5 minutes.
4. Put the asparagus in the greased basket in a single layer and season with salt and pepper.
5. Put the air fryer basket on the baking pan and slide into Rack Position 2, select Air Fry, set temperature to 350°F (180°C), and set time to 10 minutes.
6. Flip the asparagus halfway through the cooking time.
7. When done, the asparagus should be tender and lightly browned. Cool for 5 minutes before serving.

Mediterranean Baked Eggs with Spinach

Prep time: 10 minutes | Cook time: 10 minutes | Serves 2

2 tablespoons olive oil	lemon juice
4 eggs, whisked	½ teaspoon ground black pepper
5 ounces (142 g) fresh spinach, chopped	½ teaspoon coarse salt
1 medium-sized tomato, chopped	½ cup roughly chopped fresh basil leaves, for garnish
1 teaspoon fresh	

1. Generously grease the baking pan with olive oil.
2. Stir together the remaining ingredients except the basil leaves in the greased baking pan until well incorporated.

3. Slide the baking pan into Rack Position 1, select Convection Bake, set temperature to 280°F (137°C), and set time to 10 minutes.
4. When cooking is complete, the eggs should be completely set and the vegetables should be tender. Remove from the oven and serve garnished with the fresh basil leaves.

Sweet Potatoes with Zucchini

Prep time: 20 minutes | Cook time: 20 minutes | Serves 4

2 large-sized sweet potatoes, peeled and quartered	maple syrup
	½ teaspoon porcini powder
1 medium zucchini, sliced	¼ teaspoon mustard powder
1 Serrano pepper, deseeded and thinly sliced	½ teaspoon fennel seeds
1 bell pepper, deseeded and thinly sliced	1 tablespoon garlic powder
1 to 2 carrots, cut into matchsticks	½ teaspoon fine sea salt
¼ cup olive oil	¼ teaspoon ground black pepper
1½ tablespoons	Tomato ketchup, for serving

1. Preheat the air fryer oven to 350°F (177°C).
2. Put the sweet potatoes, zucchini, peppers, and the carrot into the air fryer basket. Coat with a drizzling of olive oil.
3. Place the air fryer basket onto the baking pan and slide into Rack Position 2, select Air Fry and set time to 15 minutes.
4. In the meantime, prepare the sauce by vigorously combining the other ingredients, except for the tomato ketchup, with a whisk.
5. Lightly grease a baking dish.
6. Transfer the cooked vegetables to the baking dish, pour over the sauce and coat the vegetables well.
7. Increase the temperature to 390°F (199°C) and air fry the vegetables for an additional 5 minutes.
8. Serve warm with a side of ketchup.

Spicy Cauliflower

Prep time: 15 minutes | Cook time: 20 minutes | Serves 4

Cauliflower:

5 cups cauliflower florets
3 tablespoons vegetable oil
½ teaspoon ground

cumin
½ teaspoon ground coriander
½ teaspoon kosher salt

Sauce:

½ cup Greek yogurt or sour cream
¼ cup chopped fresh cilantro
1 jalapeño, coarsely chopped

4 cloves garlic, peeled
½ teaspoon kosher salt
2 tablespoons water

1. Preheat the air fryer oven to 400°F (204°C).
2. In a large bowl, combine the cauliflower, oil, cumin, coriander, and salt. Toss to coat.
3. Put the cauliflower in the air fryer basket. Place the air fryer basket onto the baking pan and slide into Rack Position 2, select Air Fry and set time to 20 minutes, stirring halfway through the cooking time.
4. Meanwhile, in a blender, combine the yogurt, cilantro, jalapeño, garlic, and salt. Blend, adding the water as needed to keep the blades moving and to thin the sauce.
5. Transfer the cauliflower to a large serving bowl. Pour the sauce over and toss gently to coat. Serve immediately.

Creamy and Cheesy Spinach

Prep time: 10 minutes | Cook time: 15 minutes | Serves 4

Vegetable oil spray
1 (10-ounce / 283-g) package frozen spinach, thawed and squeezed dry
½ cup chopped onion
2 cloves garlic, minced
4 ounces (113 g)

cream cheese, diced
½ teaspoon ground nutmeg
1 teaspoon kosher salt
1 teaspoon black pepper
½ cup grated Parmesan cheese

1. Preheat the air fryer oven to 350°F (177°C). Spray a heatproof pan with vegetable oil spray.
2. In a medium bowl, combine the spinach, onion, garlic, cream cheese, nutmeg, salt, and pepper. Transfer to the prepared pan.
3. Slide the pan into Rack Position 1, select Convection Bake and set time to 10 minutes.
4. Stir, sprinkle the Parmesan cheese on top, and bake for 5 minutes, or until the cheese has melted and browned.
5. Serve hot.

Blistered Shishito Peppers

Prep time: 10 minutes | Cook time: 6 minutes | Serves 4

Dipping Sauce:

1 cup sour cream
2 tablespoons fresh lemon juice
1 clove garlic,

minced
1 green onion (white and green parts), finely chopped

Peppers:

8 ounces (227 g) shishito peppers
1 tablespoon vegetable oil
1 teaspoon toasted sesame oil

Kosher salt and black pepper, to taste
¼ to ½ teaspoon red pepper flakes
½ teaspoon toasted sesame seeds

1. In a small bowl, stir all the ingredients for the dipping sauce to combine. Cover and refrigerate for at least an hour.
2. Preheat the air fryer oven to 400°F (204°C).
3. In a medium bowl, toss the peppers with the vegetable oil. Put the peppers in the air fryer basket.
4. Place the air fryer basket onto the baking pan and slide into Rack Position 2, select Air Fry and set time to 6 minutes, or until peppers are lightly charred in spots, stirring the peppers halfway through the cooking time.
5. Transfer the peppers to a serving bowl. Drizzle with the sesame oil and toss to coat. Season with salt and pepper. Sprinkle with the red pepper and sesame seeds and toss again.
6. Serve immediately with the dipping sauce.

Cheesy Rice and Olives Stuffed Peppers

Prep time: 5 minutes | Cook time: 16 to 17 minutes | Serves 4

4 red bell peppers, tops sliced off
2 cups cooked rice
1 cup crumbled feta cheese
1 onion, chopped
¼ cup sliced kalamata olives
¾ cup tomato sauce
1 tablespoon Greek seasoning
Salt and black pepper, to taste
2 tablespoons chopped fresh dill, for serving

1. Microwave the red bell peppers for 1 to 2 minutes until tender.
2. When ready, transfer the red bell peppers to a plate to cool.
3. Mix the cooked rice, feta cheese, onion, kalamata olives, tomato sauce, Greek seasoning, salt, and pepper in a medium bowl and stir until well combined.
4. Divide the rice mixture among the red bell peppers and transfer to a greased baking pan.
5. Slide the baking pan into Rack Position 1, select Convection Bake, set temperature to 360ºF (182ºC) and set time to 15 minutes.
6. When cooking is complete, the rice should be heated through and the vegetables should be soft.
7. Remove from the oven and serve with the dill sprinkled on top.

Stuffed Portobello Mushrooms with Vegetables

Prep time: 5 minutes | Cook time: 8 minutes | Serves 4

4 portobello mushrooms, stem removed
1 tablespoon olive oil
1 tomato, diced
½ green bell pepper, diced
½ small red onion, diced
½ teaspoon garlic powder
Salt and black pepper, to taste
½ cup grated Mozzarella cheese

1. Using a spoon to scoop out the gills of the mushrooms and discard them. Brush the mushrooms with the olive oil.
2. In a mixing bowl, stir together the remaining ingredients except the Mozzarella cheese. Using a spoon to stuff each mushroom with the filling and scatter the Mozzarella cheese on top.
3. Arrange the mushrooms in the air fryer basket.
4. Put the air fryer basket on the baking pan and slide into Rack Position 2, select Roast, set temperature to 330ºF (166ºC) and set time to 8 minutes.
5. When cooking is complete, the cheese should be melted.
6. Serve warm.

Ratatouille

Prep time: 20 minutes | Cook time: 25 minutes | Serves 4

1 sprig basil
1 sprig flat-leaf parsley
1 sprig mint
1 tablespoon coriander powder
1 teaspoon capers
½ lemon, juiced
Salt and ground black pepper, to taste
2 eggplants, sliced crosswise
2 red onions, chopped
4 cloves garlic, minced
2 red peppers, sliced crosswise
1 fennel bulb, sliced crosswise
3 large zucchinis, sliced crosswise
5 tablespoons olive oil
4 large tomatoes, chopped
2 teaspoons herbs de Provence

1. Blend the basil, parsley, coriander, mint, lemon juice and capers, with a little salt and pepper. Make sure all ingredients are well incorporated.
2. Preheat the air fryer oven to 400ºF (204ºC).
3. Coat the eggplant, onions, garlic, peppers, fennel, and zucchini with olive oil.
4. Transfer the vegetables into a baking dish and top with the tomatoes and herb purée. Sprinkle with more salt and pepper, and the herbs de Provence.
5. Place the baking dish into Rack Position 1, select Convection Bake and set time to 25 minutes.
6. Serve immediately.

Honey-Glazed Roasted Veggies

Prep time: 15 minutes | Cook time: 20 minutes | Makes 3 cups

Glaze:

2 tablespoons raw honey

2 teaspoons minced garlic

¼ teaspoon dried marjoram

¼ teaspoon dried basil

¼ teaspoon dried oregano

⅛ teaspoon dried sage

⅛ teaspoon dried rosemary

⅛ teaspoon dried thyme

½ teaspoon salt

¼ teaspoon ground black pepper

Veggies:

3 to 4 medium red potatoes, cut into 1- to 2-inch pieces

1 small zucchini, cut into 1- to 2-inch pieces

1 small carrot, sliced into ¼-inch rounds

1 (10.5-ounce / 298-g) package cherry tomatoes, halved

1 cup sliced mushrooms

3 tablespoons olive oil

1. Combine the honey, garlic, marjoram, basil, oregano, sage, rosemary, thyme, salt, and pepper in a small bowl and stir to mix well. Set aside.
2. Place the red potatoes, zucchini, carrot, cherry tomatoes, and mushroom in a large bowl. Drizzle with the olive oil and toss to coat.
3. Pour the veggies into the baking pan.
4. Slide the baking pan into Rack Position 2, select Roast, set temperature to 380°F (193°C) and set time to 15 minutes.
5. Stir the veggies halfway through.
6. When cooking is complete, the vegetables should be tender.
7. When ready, transfer the roasted veggies to the large bowl. Pour the honey mixture over the veggies, tossing to coat.
8. Spread out the veggies in the baking pan.
9. Increase the temperature to 390°F (199°C) and set time to 5 minutes on Roast.
10. When cooking is complete, the veggies should be tender and glazed. Serve warm.

Stuffed Peppers with Beans and Rice

Prep time: 10 minutes | Cook time: 18 minutes | Serves 4

4 medium red, green, or yellow bell peppers, halved and deseeded

4 tablespoons extra-virgin olive oil, divided

½ teaspoon kosher salt, divided

1 (15-ounce / 425-g) can chickpeas

1½ cups cooked white rice

½ cup diced roasted red peppers

¼ cup chopped parsley

½ small onion, finely chopped

3 garlic cloves, minced

½ teaspoon cumin

¼ teaspoon freshly ground black pepper

¾ cup panko bread crumbs

1. Brush the peppers inside and out with 1 tablespoon of olive oil. Season the insides with ¼ teaspoon of kosher salt. Arrange the peppers in the air fryer basket, cut side up.
2. Place the chickpeas with their liquid into a large bowl. Lightly mash the beans with a potato masher. Sprinkle with the remaining ¼ teaspoon of kosher salt and 1 tablespoon of olive oil. Add the rice, red peppers, parsley, onion, garlic, cumin, and black pepper to the bowl and stir to incorporate.
3. Divide the mixture among the bell pepper halves.
4. Stir together the remaining 2 tablespoons of olive oil and panko in a small bowl. Top the pepper halves with the panko mixture.
5. Put the air fryer basket on the baking pan and slide into Rack Position 2, select Roast, set temperature to 375°F (190°C), and set time to 18 minutes.
6. When done, the peppers should be slightly wrinkled, and the panko should be golden brown.
7. Remove from the oven and serve on a plate.

Garlic Stuffed Mushrooms

Prep time: 5 minutes | Cook time: 12 minutes | Serves 2

18 medium-sized white mushrooms
1 small onion, peeled and chopped
4 garlic cloves, peeled and minced
2 tablespoons olive oil

2 teaspoons cumin powder
A pinch ground allspice
Fine sea salt and freshly ground black pepper, to taste

1. On a clean work surface, remove the mushroom stems. Using a spoon, scoop out the mushroom gills and discard.
2. Thoroughly combine the onion, garlic, olive oil, cumin powder, allspice, salt, and pepper in a mixing bowl. Stuff the mushrooms evenly with the mixture.
3. Place the stuffed mushrooms in the air fryer basket.
4. Put the air fryer basket on the baking pan and slide into Rack Position 2, select Roast, set temperature to 345ºF (174ºC) and set time to 12 minutes.
5. When cooking is complete, the mushroom should be browned.
6. Cool for 5 minutes before serving.

Beef Stuffed Bell Peppers

Prep time: 10 minutes | Cook time: 30 minutes | Serves 4

1 pound (454 g) ground beef
1 tablespoon taco seasoning mix
1 can diced tomatoes

and green chilis
4 green bell peppers
1 cup shredded Monterey jack cheese, divided

1. Preheat the air fryer oven to 350ºF (177ºC).
2. Place a skillet over a high heat and cook the ground beef for 8 minutes. Make sure it is cooked through and browned all over. Drain the fat.
3. Stir in the taco seasoning mix, and the diced tomatoes and green chilis. Allow the mixture to cook for a further 4 minutes.

4. In the meantime, slice the tops off the green peppers and remove the seeds and membranes.
5. When the meat mixture is fully cooked, spoon equal amounts of it into the peppers and top with the Monterey jack cheese. Arrange the peppers in the air fryer basket.
6. Place the air fryer basket onto the baking pan and slide into Rack Position 2, select Air Fry and set time to 15 minutes.
7. The peppers are ready when they are soft, and the cheese is bubbling and brown. Serve warm.

Rice and Eggplant Bowl

Prep time: 15 minutes | Cook time: 10 minutes | Serves 4

¼ cup sliced cucumber
1 teaspoon salt
1 tablespoon sugar
7 tablespoons Japanese rice vinegar
3 medium eggplants, sliced

3 tablespoons sweet white miso paste
1 tablespoon mirin rice wine
4 cups cooked sushi rice
4 spring onions
1 tablespoon toasted sesame seeds

1. Coat the cucumber slices with the rice wine vinegar, salt, and sugar.
2. Put a dish on top of the bowl to weight it down completely.
3. In a bowl, mix the eggplants, mirin rice wine, and miso paste. Allow to marinate for half an hour.
4. Preheat the air fryer oven to 400ºF (204ºC).
5. Put the eggplant slices in the air fryer basket.
6. Place the air fryer basket onto the baking pan and slide into Rack Position 2, select Air Fry and set time to 10 minutes.
7. Fill the bottom of a serving bowl with rice and top with the eggplants and pickled cucumbers.
8. Add the spring onions and sesame seeds for garnish. Serve immediately.

Cream Cheese Stuffed Bell Peppers

Prep time: 5 minutes | Cook time: 15 minutes | Serves 2

2 bell peppers, tops and seeds removed
Salt and pepper, to taste
⅔ cup cream cheese
2 tablespoons

mayonnaise
1 tablespoon chopped fresh celery stalks
Cooking spray

1. Spritz the air fryer basket with cooking spray.
2. Place the peppers in the air fryer basket.
3. Put the air fryer basket on the baking pan and slide into Rack Position 2, select Roast, set temperature to 400ºF (205ºC) and set time to 10 minutes.
4. Flip the peppers halfway through.
5. When cooking is complete, the peppers should be crisp-tender.
6. Remove from the oven to a plate and season with salt and pepper.
7. Mix the cream cheese, mayo, and celery in a small bowl and stir to incorporate. Evenly stuff the roasted peppers with the cream cheese mixture with a spoon. Serve immediately.

Cheese-Walnut Stuffed Mushrooms

Prep time: 5 minutes | Cook time: 10 minutes | Serves 4

4 large portobello mushrooms
1 tablespoon canola oil
½ cup shredded Mozzarella cheese

⅓ cup minced walnuts
2 tablespoons chopped fresh parsley
Cooking spray

1. Spritz the air fryer basket with cooking spray.
2. On a clean work surface, remove the mushroom stems. Scoop out the gills with a spoon and discard. Coat the mushrooms with canola oil. Top each mushroom evenly with the shredded Mozzarella cheese, followed by the minced walnuts.

3. Arrange the mushrooms in the basket.
4. Put the air fryer basket on the baking pan and slide into Rack Position 2, select Roast, set temperature to 350ºF (180ºC) and set time to 10 minutes.
5. When cooking is complete, the mushroom should be golden brown.
6. Transfer the mushrooms to a plate and sprinkle the parsley on top for garnish before serving.

Gorgonzola Mushrooms with Horseradish Mayo

Prep time: 15 minutes | Cook time: 10 minutes | Serves 5

½ cup bread crumbs
2 cloves garlic, pressed
2 tablespoons chopped fresh coriander
⅓ teaspoon kosher salt
½ teaspoon crushed red pepper flakes
1½ tablespoons olive oil
20 medium

mushrooms, stems removed
½ cup grated Gorgonzola cheese
¼ cup low-fat mayonnaise
1 teaspoon prepared horseradish, well-drained
1 tablespoon finely chopped fresh parsley

1. Preheat the air fryer oven to 380ºF (193ºC).
2. Combine the bread crumbs together with the garlic, coriander, salt, red pepper, and olive oil.
3. Take equal-sized amounts of the bread crumb mixture and use them to stuff the mushroom caps. Add the grated Gorgonzola on top of each. Put the mushrooms in the air fryer basket.
4. Place the air fryer basket onto the baking pan and slide into Rack Position 2, select Air Fry and set time to 10 minutes, or until cooked through.
5. In the meantime, prepare the horseradish mayo. Mix the mayonnaise, horseradish and parsley.
6. When the mushrooms are ready, serve with the mayo.

Kidney Beans Oatmeal in Peppers

Prep time: 15 minutes | Cook time: 6 minutes | Serves 2 to 4

2 large bell peppers, halved lengthwise, deseeded
2 tablespoons cooked kidney beans
2 tablespoons cooked chick peas
2 cups cooked oatmeal
1 teaspoon ground cumin
½ teaspoon paprika
½ teaspoon salt or to taste
¼ teaspoon black pepper powder
¼ cup yogurt

1. Preheat the air fryer oven to 355ºF (179ºC).
2. Put the bell peppers, cut side down, in the air fryer basket.
3. Place the air fryer basket onto the baking pan and slide into Rack Position 2, select Air Fry and set time to 2 minutes.
4. Remove from the oven and let cool.
5. In a bowl, combine the rest of the ingredients.
6. Divide the mixture evenly and use each portion to stuff a pepper.
7. Return the stuffed peppers to the oven and continue to air fry for 4 minutes.
8. Serve hot.

Ricotta Potatoes

Prep time: 15 minutes | Cook time: 15 minutes | Serves 4

4 potatoes
2 tablespoons olive oil
½ cup Ricotta cheese, at room temperature
2 tablespoons chopped scallions
1 tablespoon roughly chopped fresh parsley
1 tablespoon minced coriander
2 ounces (57 g) Cheddar cheese, preferably freshly grated
1 teaspoon celery seeds
½ teaspoon salt
½ teaspoon garlic pepper

1. Preheat the air fryer oven to 350ºF (177ºC).
2. Pierce the skin of the potatoes with a knife, then transfer to the air fryer basket.

3. Place the air fryer basket onto the baking pan and slide into Rack Position 2, select Air Fry and set time to 13 minutes. If they are not cooked through by this time, leave for 2 to 3 minutes longer.
4. In the meantime, make the stuffing by combining all the other ingredients.
5. Cut halfway into the cooked potatoes to open them.
6. Spoon equal amounts of the stuffing into each potato and serve hot.

Sweet Potatoes with Tofu

Prep time: 15 minutes | Cook time: 35 minutes | Serves 8

8 sweet potatoes, scrubbed
2 tablespoons olive oil
1 large onion, chopped
2 green chilies, deseeded and chopped
8 ounces (227 g)
tofu, crumbled
2 tablespoons Cajun seasoning
1 cup chopped tomatoes
1 can kidney beans, drained and rinsed
Salt and ground black pepper, to taste

1. Preheat the air fryer oven to 400ºF (204ºC).
2. With a knife, pierce the skin of the sweet potatoes and transfer to the air fryer basket.
3. Place the air fryer basket onto the baking pan and slide into Rack Position 2, select Air Fry and set time to 30 minutes, or until soft.
4. Remove from the oven, halve each potato, and set to one side.
5. Over a medium heat, fry the onions and chilies in the olive oil in a skillet for 2 minutes until fragrant.
6. Add the tofu and Cajun seasoning and air fry for a further 3 minutes before incorporating the kidney beans and tomatoes. Sprinkle some salt and pepper as desire.
7. Top each sweet potato halve with a spoonful of the tofu mixture and serve.

Jalapeño Poppers

Prep time: 5 minutes | Cook time: 33 minutes | Serves 4

8 medium jalapeño peppers
5 ounces (142 g) cream cheese
¼ cup grated

Mozzarella cheese
½ teaspoon Italian seasoning mix
8 slices bacon

1. Preheat the air fryer oven to 400°F (204°C).
2. Cut the jalapeños in half.
3. Use a spoon to scrape out the insides of the peppers.
4. In a bowl, add together the cream cheese, Mozzarella cheese and Italian seasoning.
5. Pack the cream cheese mixture into the jalapeño halves and place the other halves on top.
6. Wrap each pepper in 1 slice of bacon, starting from the bottom and working up. Put the peppers in the air fryer basket.
7. Place the air fryer basket onto the baking pan and slide into Rack Position 2, select Air Fry and set time to 33 minutes.
8. Serve!

Golden Garlicky Mushrooms

Prep time: 10 minutes | Cook time: 10 minutes | Serves 4

6 small mushrooms
1 tablespoon bread crumbs
1 tablespoon olive oil
1 ounce (28 g) onion, peeled and diced

1 teaspoon parsley
1 teaspoon garlic purée
Salt and ground black pepper, to taste

1. Preheat the air fryer oven to 350°F (177°C).
2. Combine the bread crumbs, oil, onion, parsley, salt, pepper and garlic in a bowl. Cut out the mushrooms' stalks and stuff each cap with the crumb mixture. Transfer to the air fryer basket.
3. Place the air fryer basket onto the baking pan and slide into Rack Position 2, select Air Fry and set time to 10 minutes.
4. Serve hot.

Marinara Pepperoni Mushroom Pizza

Prep time: 5 minutes | Cook time: 18 minutes | Serves 4

4 large portobello mushrooms, stems removed
4 teaspoons olive oil
1 cup marinara

sauce
1 cup shredded Mozzarella cheese
10 slices sugar-free pepperoni

1. Preheat the air fryer oven to 375°F (191°C).
2. Brush each mushroom cap with the olive oil, one teaspoon for each cap. Put them stem-side down in a baking pan.
3. Slide the baking pan into Rack Position 1, select Convection Bake and set time to 8 minutes.
4. Remove from the oven and divide the marinara sauce, Mozzarella cheese and pepperoni evenly among the caps.
5. Return to the oven and bake for another 10 minutes until browned.
6. Serve hot.

Cashew Stuffed Mushrooms

Prep time: 10 minutes | Cook time: 15 minutes | Serves 6

1 cup basil
½ cup cashew, soaked overnight
½ cup nutritional yeast
1 tablespoon lemon juice

2 cloves garlic
1 tablespoon olive oil
Salt, to taste
1 pound (454 g) baby Bella mushroom, stems removed

1. Preheat the air fryer oven to 400°F (204°C).
2. Prepare the pesto. In a food processor, blend the basil, cashew nuts, nutritional yeast, lemon juice, garlic and olive oil to combine well. Sprinkle with salt as desired.
3. Turn the mushrooms cap-side down and spread the pesto on the underside of each cap. Transfer to the air fryer basket.
4. Place the air fryer basket onto the baking pan and slide into Rack Position 2, select Air Fry and set time to 15 minutes.
5. Serve warm.

Stuffed Portobellos with Peppers and Cheese

Prep time: 15 minutes | Cook time: 15 minutes | Serves 4

4 tablespoons sherry vinegar or white wine vinegar
6 garlic cloves, minced, divided
1 tablespoon fresh thyme leaves
1 teaspoon Dijon mustard
1 teaspoon kosher salt, divided
¼ cup plus 3¼ teaspoons extra-virgin olive oil, divided
8 portobello mushroom caps,

each about 3 inches across, patted dry
1 small red or yellow bell pepper, thinly sliced
1 small green bell pepper, thinly sliced
1 small onion, thinly sliced
¼ teaspoon red pepper flakes
Freshly ground black pepper, to taste
4 ounces (113 g) shredded Fontina cheese

1. Stir together the vinegar, 4 minced garlic cloves, thyme, mustard, and ½ teaspoon of kosher salt in a small bowl. Slowly pour in ¼ cup of olive oil, whisking constantly, or until an emulsion is formed. Reserve 2 tablespoons of the marinade and set aside.
2. Put the mushrooms in a resealable plastic bag and pour in the marinade. Seal and shake the bag, coating the mushrooms in the marinade. Transfer the mushrooms to the baking pan, gill-side down.
3. Put the remaining 2 minced garlic cloves, bell peppers, onion, red pepper flakes, remaining ½ teaspoon of salt, and black pepper in a medium bowl. Drizzle with the remaining 3¼ teaspoons of olive oil and toss well. Transfer the bell pepper mixture to the pan.
4. Slide the baking pan into Rack Position 2, select Roast, set temperature to 375ºF (190ºC), and set time to 12 minutes.
5. After 7 minutes, remove the pan and stir the peppers and flip the mushrooms. Return the pan to the oven and continue cooking for 5 minutes.
6. Remove from the oven and place the pepper mixture onto a cutting board and coarsely chop.
7. Brush both sides of the mushrooms with the reserved 2 tablespoons marinade. Stuff the caps evenly with the pepper mixture. Scatter the cheese on top.
8. Select Convection Broil, set temperature to High, and set time to 3 minutes.
9. When done, the mushrooms should be tender and the cheese should be melted.
10. Serve warm.

Mascarpone Mushrooms

Prep time: 10 minutes | Cook time: 15 minutes | Serves 4

Vegetable oil spray
4 cups sliced mushrooms
1 medium yellow onion, chopped
2 cloves garlic, minced
¼ cup heavy whipping cream or half-and-half
8 ounces (227 g) mascarpone cheese

1 teaspoon dried thyme
1 teaspoon kosher salt
1 teaspoon black pepper
½ teaspoon red pepper flakes
4 cups cooked konjac noodles, for serving
½ cup grated Parmesan cheese

1. Preheat the air fryer oven to 350ºF (177ºC). Spray a heatproof pan with vegetable oil spray.
2. In a medium bowl, combine the mushrooms, onion, garlic, cream, mascarpone, thyme, salt, black pepper, and red pepper flakes. Stir to combine. Transfer the mixture to the prepared pan.
3. Slide the pan into Rack Position 1, select Convection Bake and set time to 15 minutes, stirring halfway through the baking time.
4. Divide the pasta among four shallow bowls. Spoon the mushroom mixture evenly over the pasta. Sprinkle with Parmesan cheese and serve.

Lush Summer Rolls

Prep time: 15 minutes | Cook time: 15 minutes | Serves 4

1 cup shiitake mushroom, sliced thinly
1 celery stalk, chopped
1 medium carrot, shredded
½ teaspoon finely chopped ginger

1 teaspoon sugar
1 tablespoon soy sauce
1 teaspoon nutritional yeast
8 spring roll sheets
1 teaspoon corn starch
2 tablespoons water

1. Preheat the air fryer oven to 400ºF (204ºC).
2. In a bowl, combine the ginger, soy sauce, nutritional yeast, carrots, celery, mushroom, and sugar.
3. Mix the cornstarch and water to create an adhesive for the spring rolls.
4. Scoop a tablespoonful of the vegetable mixture into the middle of the spring roll sheets. Brush the edges of the sheets with the cornstarch adhesive and enclose around the filling to make spring rolls. Arrange the rolls in the air fryer basket.
5. Place the air fryer basket onto the baking pan and slide into Rack Position 2, select Air Fry and set time to 15 minutes, or until crisp.
6. Serve hot.

Potato and Broccoli with Tofu Scramble

Prep time: 15 minutes | Cook time: 30 minutes | Serves 3

2½ cups chopped red potato
2 tablespoons olive oil, divided
1 block tofu, chopped finely
2 tablespoons tamari
1 teaspoon turmeric

powder
½ teaspoon onion powder
½ teaspoon garlic powder
½ cup chopped onion
4 cups broccoli florets

1. Preheat the air fryer oven to 400ºF (204ºC).
2. Toss together the potatoes and 1 tablespoon of the olive oil, then transfer to a baking dish.

3. Place the baking dish into Rack Position 1, select Convection Bake and set time to 15 minutes. Stir the potatoes once during cooking.
4. Combine the tofu, the remaining 1 tablespoon of the olive oil, turmeric, onion powder, tamari, and garlic powder together, stirring in the onions, followed by the broccoli.
5. Top the potatoes with the tofu mixture and bake for an additional 15 minutes. Serve warm.

Prosciutto Mini Mushroom Pizza

Prep time: 10 minutes | Cook time: 5 minutes | Serves 3

3 portobello mushroom caps, cleaned and scooped
3 tablespoons olive oil
Pinch of salt
Pinch of dried Italian

seasonings
3 tablespoons tomato sauce
3 tablespoons shredded Mozzarella cheese
12 slices prosciutto

1. Preheat the air fryer oven to 330ºF (166ºC).
2. Season both sides of the portobello mushrooms with a drizzle of olive oil, then sprinkle salt and the Italian seasonings on the insides.
3. With a knife, spread the tomato sauce evenly over the mushroom, before adding the Mozzarella on top. Put the portobello in the air fryer basket.
4. Place the air fryer basket onto the baking pan and slide into Rack Position 2, select Air Fry and set time to 1 minute.
5. Put the prosciutto slices on top and air fry for another 4 minutes.
6. Serve warm.

Black Bean and Tomato Chili

Prep time: 15 minutes | Cook time: 23 minutes | Serves 6

1 tablespoon olive oil
1 medium onion, diced
3 garlic cloves, minced
1 cup vegetable broth
3 cans black beans, drained and rinsed
2 cans diced tomatoes

2 chipotle peppers, chopped
2 teaspoons cumin
2 teaspoons chili powder
1 teaspoon dried oregano
½ teaspoon salt

1. Over a medium heat, fry the garlic and onions in the olive oil for 3 minutes.
2. Add the remaining ingredients, stirring constantly and scraping the bottom to prevent sticking.
3. Preheat the air fryer oven to 400ºF (204ºC).
4. Take a dish and place the mixture inside. Put a sheet of aluminum foil on top.
5. Place the dish into Rack Position 1, select Convection Bake and set time to 20 minutes.
6. Serve immediately.

Air Fried Vegetables

Prep time: 15 minutes | Cook time: 20 minutes | Serves 6

1⅓ cups small parsnips, peeled and cubed
1⅓ cups celery
2 red onions, sliced
1⅓ cups small butternut squash, cut in half,

deseeded and cubed
1 tablespoon fresh thyme
1 tablespoon olive oil
Salt and ground black pepper, to taste

1. Preheat the air fryer oven to 390ºF (199ºC).
2. Combine the vegetables with the thyme, olive oil, salt and pepper. Put the vegetables in the air fryer basket.
3. Place the air fryer basket onto the baking pan and slide into Rack Position 2, select Air Fry and set time to 20 minutes, stirring once during cooking, until the vegetables are nicely browned and cooked through.
4. Serve warm.

Super Veg Rolls

Prep time: 20 minutes | Cook time: 10 minutes | Serves 6

2 potatoes, mashed
¼ cup peas
¼ cup mashed carrots
1 small cabbage, sliced
¼ cups beans

2 tablespoons sweetcorn
1 small onion, chopped
½ cup bread crumbs
1 packet spring roll sheets
½ cup cornstarch slurry

1. Preheat the air fryer oven to 390ºF (199ºC).
2. Boil all the vegetables in water over a low heat. Rinse and allow to dry.
3. Unroll the spring roll sheets and spoon equal amounts of vegetable onto the center of each one. Fold into spring rolls and coat each one with the slurry and bread crumbs. Transfer to the air fryer basket.
4. Place the air fryer basket onto the baking pan and slide into Rack Position 2, select Air Fry and set time to 10 minutes.
5. Serve warm.

Chapter 3 Fish and Seafood

Homemade Fish Sticks

Prep time: 10 minutes | Cook time: 8 minutes | Makes 8 fish sticks

8 ounces (227 g) fish fillets (pollock or cod), cut into ½×3-inch strips Salt, to taste	(optional) ½ cup plain bread crumbs Cooking spray

1. Season the fish strips with salt to taste, if desired.
2. Place the bread crumbs on a plate. Roll the fish strips in the bread crumbs to coat. Spritz the fish strips with cooking spray.
3. Arrange the fish strips in the air fryer basket in a single layer.
4. Put the air fryer basket on the baking pan and slide into Rack Position 2, select Air Fry, set temperature to 390ºF (199ºC), and set time to 8 minutes.
5. When cooking is complete, they should be golden brown. Remove from the oven and cool for 5 minutes before serving.

Coconut Chili Fish Curry

Prep time: 10 minutes | Cook time: 22 minutes | Serves 4

2 tablespoons sunflower oil, divided 1 pound (454 g) fish, chopped 1 ripe tomato, pureéd 2 red chilies, chopped 1 shallot, minced 1 garlic clove,	minced 1 cup coconut milk 1 tablespoon coriander powder 1 teaspoon red curry paste ½ teaspoon fenugreek seeds Salt and white pepper, to taste

1. Coat the air fryer basket with 1 tablespoon of sunflower oil. Place the fish in the basket.
2. Put the air fryer basket on the baking pan and slide into Rack Position 2, select Air Fry, set temperature to 380ºF (193ºC), and set time to 10 minutes.

3. Flip the fish halfway through the cooking time.
4. When cooking is complete, transfer the cooked fish to the baking pan greased with the remaining 1 tablespoon of sunflower oil. Stir in the remaining ingredients.
5. Put the air fryer basket on the baking pan and slide into Rack Position 2, select Air Fry, set temperature to 350ºF (180ºC), and set time to 12 minutes.
6. When cooking is complete, they should be heated through. Cool for 5 to 8 minutes before serving.

Fired Shrimp with Mayonnaise Sauce

Prep time: 5 minutes | Cook time: 7 minutes | Serves 4

Shrimp

12 jumbo shrimp ½ teaspoon garlic salt	¼ teaspoon freshly cracked mixed peppercorns

Sauce:

4 tablespoons mayonnaise 1 teaspoon grated lemon rind 1 teaspoon Dijon	mustard 1 teaspoon chipotle powder ½ teaspoon cumin powder

1. In a medium bowl, season the shrimp with garlic salt and cracked mixed peppercorns.
2. Place the shrimp in the air fryer basket.
3. Put the air fryer basket on the baking pan and slide into Rack Position 2, select Air Fry, set temperature to 395ºF (202ºC), and set time to 7 minutes.
4. After 5 minutes, remove from the oven and flip the shrimp. Return to the oven and continue cooking for 2 minutes more, or until they are pink and no longer opaque.
5. Meanwhile, stir together all the ingredients for the sauce in a small bowl until well mixed.
6. When cooking is complete, remove the shrimp from the oven and serve alongside the sauce.

Baked Flounder Fillets

Prep time: 8 minutes | Cook time: 12 minutes | Serves 2

2 flounder fillets, patted dry
1 egg
½ teaspoon Worcestershire sauce
¼ cup almond flour
¼ cup coconut flour
½ teaspoon coarse sea salt
½ teaspoon lemon pepper
¼ teaspoon chili powder
Cooking spray

1. In a shallow bowl, beat together the egg with Worcestershire sauce until well incorporated.
2. In another bowl, thoroughly combine the almond flour, coconut flour, sea salt, lemon pepper, and chili powder.
3. Dredge the fillets in the egg mixture, shaking off any excess, then roll in the flour mixture to coat well.
4. Spritz the baking pan with cooking spray. Place the fillets in the pan.
5. Slide the baking pan into Rack Position 1, select Convection Bake, set temperature to 390ºF (199ºC), and set time to 12 minutes.
6. After 7 minutes, remove from the oven and flip the fillets and spray with cooking spray. Return the pan to the oven and continue cooking for 5 minutes, or until the fish is flaky.
7. When cooking is complete, remove from the oven and serve warm.

Parmesan Fish Fillets

Prep time: 8 minutes | Cook time: 17 minutes | Serves 4

1/3 cup grated Parmesan cheese
½ teaspoon fennel seed
½ teaspoon tarragon
1/3 teaspoon mixed peppercorns
2 eggs, beaten
4 (4-ounce / 113-g) fish fillets, halved
2 tablespoons dry white wine
1 teaspoon seasoned salt

1. Place the grated Parmesan cheese, fennel seed, tarragon, and mixed peppercorns in a food processor and pulse for about 20 seconds until well combined. Transfer the cheese mixture to a shallow dish.
2. Place the beaten eggs in another shallow dish.
3. Drizzle the dry white wine over the top of fish fillets. Dredge each fillet in the beaten eggs on both sides, shaking off any excess, then roll them in the cheese mixture until fully coated. Season with the salt.
4. Arrange the fillets in the air fryer basket.
5. Put the air fryer basket on the baking pan and slide into Rack Position 2, select Air Fry, set temperature to 345ºF (174ºC), and set time to 17 minutes.
6. Flip the fillets once halfway through the cooking time.
7. When cooking is complete, the fish should be cooked through no longer translucent. Remove from the oven and cool for 5 minutes before serving.

Goat Cheese Shrimp

Prep time: 15 minutes | Cook time: 8 minutes | Serves 2

1 pound (454 g) shrimp, deveined
1½ tablespoons olive oil
1½ tablespoons balsamic vinegar
1 tablespoon coconut aminos
½ tablespoon fresh parsley, roughly chopped
Sea salt flakes, to taste
1 teaspoon Dijon mustard
½ teaspoon smoked cayenne pepper
½ teaspoon garlic powder
Salt and ground black peppercorns, to taste
1 cup shredded goat cheese

1. Except for the cheese, stir together all the ingredients in a large bowl until the shrimp are evenly coated.
2. Place the shrimp in the air fryer basket.
3. Put the air fryer basket on the baking pan and slide into Rack Position 2, select Roast, set temperature to 385ºF (196ºC), and set time to 8 minutes.
4. When cooking is complete, the shrimp should be pink and cooked through. Remove from the oven and serve with the shredded goat cheese sprinkled on top.

Crab Cakes with Sriracha Mayonnaise

Prep time: 15 minutes | Cook time: 10 minutes | Serves 4

Sriracha Mayonnaise:

1 cup mayonnaise
1 tablespoon sriracha
1½ teaspoons

freshly squeezed lemon juice

Crab Cakes:

1 teaspoon extra-virgin olive oil
¼ cup finely diced red bell pepper
¼ cup diced onion
¼ cup diced celery
1 pound (454 g) lump crab meat
1 teaspoon Old Bay seasoning

1 egg
1½ teaspoons freshly squeezed lemon juice
1¾ cups panko bread crumbs, divided
Vegetable oil, for spraying

1. Mix the mayonnaise, sriracha, and lemon juice in a small bowl. Place ²/₃ cup of the mixture in a separate bowl to form the base of the crab cakes. Cover the remaining sriracha mayonnaise and refrigerate. (This will become dipping sauce for the crab cakes once they are cooked.)
2. Heat the olive oil in a heavy-bottomed, medium skillet over medium-high heat. Add the bell pepper, onion, and celery and sauté for 3 minutes. Transfer the vegetables to the bowl with the reserved ²/₃ cup of sriracha mayonnaise. Mix in the crab, Old Bay seasoning, egg, and lemon juice. Add 1 cup of the panko. Form the crab mixture into 8 cakes. Dredge the cakes in the remaining ¾ cup of panko, turning to coat. Place on a baking sheet. Cover and refrigerate for at least 1 hour and up to 8 hours.
3. Preheat the air fryer oven to 375ºF (191ºC). Spray a baking pan with oil.
4. Place the chilled crab cakes in a single layer in the baking pan. Spray the crab cakes with oil.
5. Slide the baking pan into Rack Position 1, select Convection Bake and set time to 10 minutes, turning halfway through cooking.
6. Serve the crab cakes immediately with sriracha mayonnaise dipping sauce.

Fish Croquettes with Lemon-Dill Aioli

Prep time: 15 minutes | Cook time: 10 minutes | Serves 4

Croquettes:

3 large eggs, divided
12 ounces (340 g) raw cod fillet, flaked apart with two forks
¼ cup 1% milk
½ cup boxed instant mashed potatoes
2 teaspoons olive oil
¹/₃ cup chopped fresh dill
1 shallot, minced
1 large garlic clove, minced

¾ cup plus 2 tablespoons bread crumbs, divided
1 teaspoon fresh lemon juice
1 teaspoon kosher salt
½ teaspoon dried thyme
¼ teaspoon freshly ground black pepper
Cooking spray

Lemon-Dill Aioli:

5 tablespoons mayonnaise
Juice of ½ lemon
1 tablespoon chopped fresh dill

1. For the croquettes: In a medium bowl, lightly beat 2 of the eggs. Add the fish, milk, instant mashed potatoes, olive oil, dill, shallot, garlic, 2 tablespoons of the bread crumbs, lemon juice, salt, thyme, and pepper. Mix to thoroughly combine. Place in the refrigerator for 30 minutes.
2. For the lemon-dill aioli: In a small bowl, combine the mayonnaise, lemon juice, and dill. Set aside.
3. Measure out about 3½ tablespoons of the fish mixture and gently roll in your hands to form a log about 3 inches long. Repeat to make a total of 12 logs.
4. Beat the remaining egg in a small bowl. Place the remaining ¾ cup bread crumbs in a separate bowl. Dip the croquettes in the egg, then coat in the bread crumbs, gently pressing to adhere. Place on a work surface and spray both sides with cooking spray.
5. Preheat the air fryer oven to 350ºF (177ºC).
6. Arrange a single layer of the croquettes in the air fryer basket.
7. Place the air fryer basket onto the baking pan and slide into Rack Position 2, select Air Fry and set time to 10 minutes, flipping halfway through, until golden.
8. Serve with the aioli for dipping.

Spicy Orange Shrimp

Prep time: 40 minutes | Cook time: 12 minutes | Serves 4

⅓ cup orange juice
3 teaspoons minced garlic
1 teaspoon Old Bay seasoning
¼ to ½ teaspoon cayenne pepper

1 pound (454 g) medium shrimp, thawed, deveined, peeled, with tails off, and patted dry
Cooking spray

1. Stir together the orange juice, garlic, Old Bay seasoning, and cayenne pepper in a medium bowl. Add the shrimp to the bowl and toss to coat well.
2. Cover the bowl with plastic wrap and marinate in the refrigerator for 30 minutes.
3. Spritz the air fryer basket with cooking spray. Place the shrimp in the pan and spray with cooking spray.
4. Put the air fryer basket on the baking pan and slide into Rack Position 2, select Air Fry, set temperature to 400ºF (205ºC), and set time to 12 minutes.
5. Flip the shrimp halfway through the cooking time.
6. When cooked, the shrimp should be opaque and crisp. Remove from the oven and serve hot.

Garlic Shrimp with Parsley

Prep time: 10 minutes | Cook time: 5 minutes | Serves 4

18 shrimp, shelled and deveined
2 garlic cloves, peeled and minced
2 tablespoons extra-virgin olive oil
2 tablespoons freshly squeezed lemon juice
½ cup fresh parsley,

coarsely chopped
1 teaspoon onion powder
1 teaspoon lemon-pepper seasoning
½ teaspoon hot paprika
½ teaspoon salt
¼ teaspoon cumin powder

1. Toss all the ingredients in a mixing bowl until the shrimp are well coated.
2. Cover and allow to marinate in the refrigerator for 30 minutes.
3. When ready, transfer the shrimp to the air fryer basket.

4. Put the air fryer basket on the baking pan and slide into Rack Position 2, select Air Fry, set temperature to 400ºF (205ºC), and set time to 5 minutes.
5. When cooking is complete, the shrimp should be pink on the outside and opaque in the center. Remove from the oven and serve warm.

Coconut-Crusted Prawns

Prep time: 15 minutes | Cook time: 8 minutes | Serves 4

12 prawns, cleaned and deveined
1 teaspoon fresh lemon juice
½ teaspoon cumin powder
Salt and ground black pepper, to taste
1 medium egg

⅓ cup beer
½ cup flour, divided
1 tablespoon curry powder
1 teaspoon baking powder
½ teaspoon grated fresh ginger
1 cup flaked coconut

1. In a large bowl, toss the prawns with the lemon juice, cumin powder, salt, and pepper until well coated. Set aside.
2. In a shallow bowl, whisk together the egg, beer, ¼ cup of flour, curry powder, baking powder, and ginger until combined.
3. In a separate shallow bowl, put the remaining ¼ cup of flour, and on a plate, place the flaked coconut.
4. Dip the prawns in the flour, then in the egg mixture, finally roll in the flaked coconut to coat well. Transfer the prawns to a baking sheet.
5. Put the air fryer basket on the baking pan and slide into Rack Position 2, select Air Fry, set temperature to 350ºF (180ºC), and set time to 8 minutes.
6. After 5 minutes, remove from the oven and flip the prawns. Return to the oven and continue cooking for 3 minutes more.
7. When cooking is complete, remove from the oven and serve warm.

Glazed Cod with Sesame Seeds

Prep time: 5 minutes | Cook time: 8 minutes | Makes 1 fillet

1 tablespoon reduced-sodium soy sauce
2 teaspoons honey
Cooking spray
6 ounces (170 g) fresh cod fillet
1 teaspoon sesame seeds

1. Preheat the air fryer oven to 360°F (182°C).
2. In a small bowl, combine the soy sauce and honey.
3. Spray the air fryer basket with cooking spray, then place the cod in the basket, brush with the soy mixture, and sprinkle sesame seeds on top.
4. Place the air fryer basket onto the baking pan and slide into Rack Position 2, select Air Fry and set time to 8 minutes, or until opaque.
5. Remove the fish and allow to cool on a wire rack for 5 minutes before serving.

Caesar Shrimp Salad

Prep time: 10 minutes | Cook time: 15 minutes | Serves 4

½ baguette, cut into 1-inch cubes (about 2½ cups)
4 tablespoons extra-virgin olive oil, divided
¼ teaspoon granulated garlic
¼ teaspoon kosher salt
¾ cup Caesar dressing, divided
2 romaine lettuce hearts, cut in half lengthwise and ends trimmed
1 pound (454 g) medium shrimp, peeled and deveined
2 ounces (57 g) Parmesan cheese, coarsely grated

1. Make the croutons: Put the bread cubes in a medium bowl and drizzle 3 tablespoons of olive oil over top. Season with granulated garlic and salt and toss to coat. Transfer to the air fryer basket in a single layer.
2. Put the air fryer basket on the baking pan and slide into Rack Position 2, select Air Fry, set temperature to 400°F (205°C), and set time to 4 minutes.
3. Toss the croutons halfway through the cooking time.
4. When done, remove from the oven and set aside.
5. Brush 2 tablespoons of Caesar dressing on the cut side of the lettuce. Set aside.
6. Toss the shrimp with the ¼ cup of Caesar dressing in a large bowl until well coated. Set aside.
7. Coat the baking pan with the remaining 1 tablespoon of olive oil. Arrange the romaine halves on the coated pan, cut side down. Brush the tops with the remaining 2 tablespoons of Caesar dressing.
8. Slide the baking pan into Rack Position 2, select Roast, set temperature to 375°F (190°C), and set time to 10 minutes.
9. After 5 minutes, remove from the oven and flip the romaine halves. Spoon the shrimp around the lettuce. Return the pan to the oven and continue cooking.
10. When done, remove from the oven. If they are not quite cooked through, roast for another 1 minute.
11. On each of four plates, put a romaine half. Divide the shrimp among the plates and top with croutons and grated Parmesan cheese. Serve immediately.

Paprika Shrimp

Prep time: 5 minutes | Cook time: 10 minutes | Serves 4

1 pound (454 g) tiger shrimp
2 tablespoons olive oil
½ tablespoon old bay seasoning
¼ tablespoon smoked paprika
¼ teaspoon cayenne pepper
A pinch of sea salt

1. Toss all the ingredients in a large bowl until the shrimp are evenly coated.
2. Arrange the shrimp in the air fryer basket.
3. Put the air fryer basket on the baking pan and slide into Rack Position 2, select Air Fry, set temperature to 380°F (193°C), and set time to 10 minutes.
4. When cooking is complete, the shrimp should be pink and cooked through. Remove from the oven and serve hot.

Shrimp and Vegetable Paella

Prep time: 5 minutes | Cook time: 16 minutes | Serves 4

1 (10-ounce / 284-g) package frozen cooked rice, thawed
1 (6-ounce / 170-g) jar artichoke hearts, drained and chopped
¼ cup vegetable broth
½ teaspoon dried thyme
½ teaspoon turmeric
1 cup frozen cooked small shrimp
½ cup frozen baby peas
1 tomato, diced

1. Mix together the cooked rice, chopped artichoke hearts, vegetable broth, thyme, and turmeric in the baking pan and stir to combine.
2. Slide the baking pan into Rack Position 1, select Convection Bake, set temperature to 340ºF (171ºC), and set time to 16 minutes.
3. After 9 minutes, remove from the oven and add the shrimp, baby peas, and diced tomato to the baking pan. Mix well. Return the pan to the oven and continue cooking for 7 minutes more, or until the shrimp are done and the paella is bubbling.
4. When cooking is complete, remove from the oven. Cool for 5 minutes before serving.

Shrimp and Cherry Tomato Kebabs

Prep time: 15 minutes | Cook time: 5 minutes | Serves 4

1½ pounds (680 g) jumbo shrimp, cleaned, shelled and deveined
1 pound (454 g) cherry tomatoes
2 tablespoons butter, melted
1 tablespoons Sriracha sauce
Sea salt and ground black pepper, to taste
1 teaspoon dried parsley flakes
½ teaspoon dried basil
½ teaspoon dried oregano
½ teaspoon mustard seeds
½ teaspoon marjoram

Special Equipment:
4 to 6 wooden skewers, soaked in water for 30 minutes

1. Put all the ingredients in a large bowl and toss to coat well.
2. Make the kebabs: Thread, alternating jumbo shrimp and cherry tomatoes, onto the wooden skewers. Place the kebabs in the air fryer basket.
3. Put the air fryer basket on the baking pan and slide into Rack Position 2, select Air Fry, set temperature to 400ºF (205ºC), and set time to 5 minutes.
4. When cooking is complete, the shrimp should be pink and the cherry tomatoes should be softened. Remove from the oven. Let the shrimp and cherry tomato kebabs cool for 5 minutes and serve hot.

Browned Shrimp Patties

Prep time: 15 minutes | Cook time: 12 minutes | Serves 4

½ pound (227 g) raw shrimp, shelled, deveined, and chopped finely
2 cups cooked sushi rice
¼ cup chopped red bell pepper
¼ cup chopped celery
¼ cup chopped
green onion
2 teaspoons Worcestershire sauce
½ teaspoon salt
½ teaspoon garlic powder
½ teaspoon Old Bay seasoning
½ cup plain bread crumbs
Cooking spray

1. Put all the ingredients except the bread crumbs and oil in a large bowl and stir to incorporate.
2. Scoop out the shrimp mixture and shape into 8 equal-sized patties with your hands, no more than ½-inch thick. Roll the patties in the bread crumbs on a plate and spray both sides with cooking spray. Place the patties in the air fryer basket.
3. Put the air fryer basket on the baking pan and slide into Rack Position 2, select Air Fry, set temperature to 390ºF (199ºC), and set time to 12 minutes.
4. Flip the patties halfway through the cooking time.
5. When cooking is complete, the outside should be crispy brown. Divide the patties among four plates and serve warm.

Lemony Shrimp

Prep time: 10 minutes | Cook time: 8 minutes | Serves 4

1 pound (454 g) shrimp, deveined	2 cloves garlic, finely minced
4 tablespoons olive oil	1 teaspoon crushed red pepper flakes, or more to taste
1½ tablespoons lemon juice	Garlic pepper, to taste
1½ tablespoons fresh parsley, roughly chopped	Sea salt flakes, to taste

1. Toss all the ingredients in a large bowl until the shrimp are coated on all sides.
2. Arrange the shrimp in the air fryer basket.
3. Put the air fryer basket on the baking pan and slide into Rack Position 2, select Air Fry, set temperature to 385ºF (196ºC), and set time to 8 minutes.
4. When cooking is complete, the shrimp should be pink and cooked through. Remove from the oven and serve warm.

Roasted Scallops with Snow Peas

Prep time: 10 minutes | Cook time: 8 minutes | Serves 4

1 pound (454 g) sea scallops	3 teaspoons vegetable oil, divided
3 tablespoons hoisin sauce	1 teaspoon soy sauce
½ cup toasted sesame seeds	1 teaspoon sesame oil
6 ounces (170 g) snow peas, trimmed	1 cup roasted mushrooms

1. Brush the scallops with the hoisin sauce. Put the sesame seeds in a shallow dish. Roll the scallops in the sesame seeds until evenly coated.
2. Combine the snow peas with 1 teaspoon of vegetable oil, the sesame oil, and soy sauce in a medium bowl and toss to coat.
3. Grease the baking pan with the remaining 2 teaspoons of vegetable oil. Put the scallops in the middle of the pan and arrange the snow peas around the scallops in a single layer.

4. Slide the baking pan into Rack Position 2, select Roast, set temperature to 375ºF (190ºC), and set time to 8 minutes.
5. After 5 minutes, remove the pan and flip the scallops. Fold in the mushrooms and stir well. Return the pan to the oven and continue cooking.
6. When done, remove from the oven and cool for 5 minutes. Serve warm.

Seasoned Breaded Shrimp

Prep time: 15 minutes | Cook time: 15 minutes | Serves 4

2 teaspoons Old Bay seasoning, divided	g) large shrimp, deveined, with tails on
½ teaspoon garlic powder	2 large eggs
½ teaspoon onion powder	½ cup whole-wheat panko bread crumbs
1 pound (454	Cooking spray

1. Preheat the air fryer oven to 380ºF (193ºC).
2. Spray the air fryer basket lightly with cooking spray.
3. In a medium bowl, mix together 1 teaspoon of Old Bay seasoning, garlic powder, and onion powder. Add the shrimp and toss with the seasoning mix to lightly coat.
4. In a separate small bowl, whisk the eggs with 1 teaspoon water.
5. In a shallow bowl, mix together the remaining 1 teaspoon Old Bay seasoning and the panko bread crumbs.
6. Dip each shrimp in the egg mixture and dredge in the bread crumb mixture to evenly coat.
7. Place the shrimp in the air fryer basket in a single layer. Lightly spray the shrimp with cooking spray. You many need to cook the shrimp in batches.
8. Place the air fryer basket onto the baking pan and slide into Rack Position 2, select Air Fry and set time to 15 minutes, or until the shrimp is cooked through and crispy, shaking the basket at 5-minute intervals to redistribute and evenly cook.
9. Serve immediately.

Crab Cakes with Bell Peppers

Prep time: 5 minutes | Cook time: 10 minutes | Serves 4

8 ounces (227 g) jumbo lump crab meat
1 egg, beaten
Juice of ½ lemon
⅓ cup bread crumbs
¼ cup diced green bell pepper
¼ cup diced red bell pepper
¼ cup mayonnaise
1 tablespoon Old Bay seasoning
1 teaspoon flour
Cooking spray

1. Make the crab cakes: Place all the ingredients except the flour and oil in a large bowl and stir until well incorporated.
2. Divide the crab mixture into four equal portions and shape each portion into a patty with your hands. Top each patty with a sprinkle of ¼ teaspoon of flour.
3. Arrange the crab cakes in the air fryer basket and spritz them with cooking spray.
4. Put the air fryer basket on the baking pan and slide into Rack Position 2, select Air Fry, set temperature to 375ºF (190ºC), and set time to 10 minutes.
5. Flip the crab cakes halfway through.
6. When cooking is complete, the cakes should be cooked through. Remove from the oven and divide the crab cakes among four plates and serve.

Garlic Butter Shrimp Scampi

Prep time: 5 minutes | Cook time: 8 minutes | Serves 4

Sauce:
¼ cup unsalted butter
2 tablespoons fish stock or chicken broth
2 cloves garlic, minced
2 tablespoons chopped fresh basil
Shrimp:
1 pound (454 g) large shrimp, peeled and deveined, tails
leaves
1 tablespoon lemon juice
1 tablespoon chopped fresh parsley, plus more for garnish
1 teaspoon red pepper flakes

removed
Fresh basil sprigs, for garnish

1. Put all the ingredients for the sauce in the baking pan and stir to incorporate.
2. Put the air fryer basket on the baking pan and slide into Rack Position 2, select Air Fry, set temperature to 350ºF (180ºC), and set time to 8 minutes.
3. After 3 minutes, remove from the oven and add the shrimp to the baking pan, flipping to coat in the sauce. Return to the oven and continue cooking for 5 minutes until the shrimp are pink and opaque. Stir the shrimp twice during cooking.
4. When cooking is complete, remove from the oven. Serve garnished with the parsley and basil sprigs.

Panko Crab Sticks with Mayo Sauce

Prep time: 5 minutes | Cook time: 12 minutes | Serves 4

Crab Sticks:
2 eggs
1 cup flour
⅓ cup panko bread crumbs
1 tablespoon old bay
Mayo Sauce:
½ cup mayonnaise
1 lime, juiced
seasoning
1 pound (454 g) crab sticks
Cooking spray

2 garlic cloves, minced

1. In a bowl, beat the eggs. In a shallow bowl, place the flour. In another shallow bowl, thoroughly combine the panko bread crumbs and old bay seasoning.
2. Dredge the crab sticks in the flour, shaking off any excess, then in the beaten eggs, finally press them in the bread crumb mixture to coat well.
3. Arrange the crab sticks in the air fryer basket and spray with cooking spray.
4. Put the air fryer basket on the baking pan and slide into Rack Position 2, select Air Fry, set temperature to 390ºF (199ºC), and set time to 12 minutes.
5. Flip the crab sticks halfway through the cooking time.
6. Meanwhile, make the sauce by whisking together the mayo, lime juice, and garlic in a small bowl.
7. When cooking is complete, remove from the oven. Serve the crab sticks with the mayo sauce on the side.

Seafood Spring Rolls

Prep time: 10 minutes | Cook time: 20 minutes | Serves 4

1 tablespoon olive oil	drained
2 teaspoons minced garlic	4 teaspoons soy sauce
1 cup matchstick cut carrots	Salt and freshly ground black pepper, to taste
2 cups finely sliced cabbage	16 square spring roll wrappers
2 (4-ounce / 113-g) cans tiny shrimp,	Cooking spray

1. Spray the air fryer basket with cooking spray. Set aside.
2. Heat the olive oil in a medium skillet over medium heat until it shimmers.
3. Add the garlic to the skillet and cook for 30 seconds. Stir in the cabbage and carrots and sauté for about 5 minutes, stirring occasionally, or until the vegetables are lightly tender.
4. Fold in the shrimp and soy sauce and sprinkle with salt and pepper, then stir to combine. Sauté for another 2 minutes, or until the moisture is evaporated. Remove from the heat and set aside to cool.
5. Put a spring roll wrapper on a work surface and spoon 1 tablespoon of the shrimp mixture onto the lower end of the wrapper.
6. Roll the wrapper away from you halfway, and then fold in the right and left sides, like an envelope. Continue to roll to the very end, using a little water to seal the edge. Repeat with the remaining wrappers and filling.
7. Place the spring rolls in the air fryer basket in a single layer, leaving space between each spring roll. Mist them lightly with cooking spray.
8. Put the air fryer basket on the baking pan and slide into Rack Position 2, select Air Fry, set temperature to 375ºF (190ºC), and set time to 10 minutes.
9. Flip the rolls halfway through the cooking time.
10. When cooking is complete, the spring rolls will be heated through and start to brown. If necessary, continue cooking for 5 minutes more. Remove from the oven and cool for a few minutes before serving.

Air Fried Spring Rolls

Prep time: 10 minutes | Cook time: 17 to 22 minutes | Serves 4

2 teaspoons minced garlic	4 teaspoons soy sauce
2 cups finely sliced cabbage	Salt and freshly ground black pepper, to taste
1 cup matchstick cut carrots	16 square spring roll wrappers
2 (4-ounce / 113-g) cans tiny shrimp, drained	Cooking spray

1. Preheat the air fryer oven to 370ºF (188ºC).
2. Spray the air fryer basket lightly with cooking spray. Spray a medium sauté pan with cooking spray.
3. Add the garlic to the sauté pan and cook over medium heat until fragrant, 30 to 45 seconds. Add the cabbage and carrots and sauté until the vegetables are slightly tender, about 5 minutes.
4. Add the shrimp and soy sauce and season with salt and pepper, then stir to combine. Sauté until the moisture has evaporated, 2 more minutes. Set aside to cool.
5. Place a spring roll wrapper on a work surface so it looks like a diamond. Place 1 tablespoon of the shrimp mixture on the lower end of the wrapper.
6. Roll the wrapper away from you halfway, then fold in the right and left sides, like an envelope. Continue to roll to the very end, using a little water to seal the edge. Repeat with the remaining wrappers and filling.
7. Place the spring rolls in the air fryer basket in a single layer, leaving room between each roll. Lightly spray with cooking spray. You may need to cook them in batches.
8. Place the air fryer basket onto the baking pan and slide into Rack Position 2, select Air Fry and set time to 5 minutes.
9. Turn the rolls over, lightly spray with cooking spray, and air fry until heated through and the rolls start to brown, 5 to 10 more minutes. Cool for 5 minutes before serving.

Breaded Calamari with Lemon

Prep time: 5 minutes | Cook time: 12 minutes | Serves 4

2 large eggs
2 garlic cloves, minced
½ cup cornstarch
1 cup bread crumbs
1 pound (454 g) calamari rings
Cooking spray
1 lemon, sliced

1. In a small bowl, whisk the eggs with minced garlic. Place the cornstarch and bread crumbs into separate shallow dishes.
2. Dredge the calamari rings in the cornstarch, then dip in the egg mixture, shaking off any excess, finally roll them in the bread crumbs to coat well. Let the calamari rings sit for 10 minutes in the refrigerator.
3. Spritz the air fryer basket with cooking spray. Transfer the calamari rings to the pan.
4. Put the air fryer basket on the baking pan and slide into Rack Position 2, select Air Fry, set temperature to 390ºF (199ºC), and set time to 12 minutes.
5. Stir the calamari rings once halfway through the cooking time.
6. When cooking is complete, remove from the oven. Serve the calamari rings with the lemon slices sprinkled on top.

Easy Scallops

Prep time: 5 minutes | Cook time: 4 minutes | Serves 2

12 medium sea scallops, rinsed and patted dry
1 teaspoon fine sea salt
¾ teaspoon ground
black pepper, plus more for garnish
Fresh thyme leaves, for garnish (optional)
Avocado oil spray

1. Coat the air fryer basket with avocado oil spray.
2. Place the scallops in a medium bowl and spritz with avocado oil spray. Sprinkle the salt and pepper to season.
3. Transfer the seasoned scallops to the basket, spacing them apart.

4. Put the air fryer basket on the baking pan and slide into Rack Position 2, select Air Fry, set temperature to 390ºF (199ºC), and set time to 4 minutes.
5. Flip the scallops halfway through the cooking time.
6. When cooking is complete, the scallops should reach an internal temperature of just 145ºF (63ºC) on a meat thermometer. Sprinkle the pepper and thyme leaves on top for garnish, if desired. Serve immediately.

Air-Fried Scallops

Prep time: 10 minutes | Cook time: 12 minutes | Serves 2

⅓ cup shallots, chopped
1½ tablespoons olive oil
1½ tablespoons coconut aminos
1 tablespoon Mediterranean seasoning mix
½ tablespoon
balsamic vinegar
½ teaspoon ginger, grated
1 clove garlic, chopped
1 pound (454 g) scallops, cleaned
Cooking spray
Belgian endive, for garnish

1. Place all the ingredients except the scallops and Belgian endive in a small skillet over medium heat and stir to combine. Let this mixture simmer for about 2 minutes.
2. Remove the mixture from the skillet to a large bowl and set aside to cool.
3. Add the scallops, coating them all over, then transfer to the refrigerator to marinate for at least 2 hours.
4. When ready, place the scallops in the air fryer basket in a single layer and spray with cooking spray.
5. Put the air fryer basket on the baking pan and slide into Rack Position 2, select Air Fry, set temperature to 345ºF (174ºC), and set time to 10 minutes.
6. Flip the scallops halfway through the cooking time.
7. When cooking is complete, the scallops should be tender and opaque. Remove from the oven and serve garnished with the Belgian endive.

Piri-Piri King Prawns

Prep time: 10 minutes | Cook time: 8 minutes | Serves 2

12 king prawns, rinsed	1 teaspoon garlic paste
1 tablespoon coconut oil	1 teaspoon curry powder
Salt and ground black pepper, to taste	½ teaspoon piri piri powder
1 teaspoon onion powder	½ teaspoon cumin powder

1. Combine all the ingredients in a large bowl and toss until the prawns are completely coated. Place the prawns in the air fryer basket.
2. Put the air fryer basket on the baking pan and slide into Rack Position 2, select Air Fry, set temperature to 360ºF (182ºC), and set time to 8 minutes.
3. Flip the prawns halfway through the cooking time.
4. When cooking is complete, the prawns will turn pink. Remove from the oven and serve hot.

Chili Prawns

Prep time: 10 minutes | Cook time: 8 minutes | Serves 2

8 prawns, cleaned	powder
Salt and black pepper, to taste	½ teaspoon ground cumin
½ teaspoon ground cayenne pepper	½ teaspoon red chili flakes
½ teaspoon garlic	Cooking spray

1. Spritz the air fryer basket with cooking spray.
2. Toss the remaining ingredients in a large bowl until the prawns are well coated.
3. Spread the coated prawns evenly in the basket and spray them with cooking spray.
4. Put the air fryer basket on the baking pan and slide into Rack Position 2, select Air Fry, set temperature to 340ºF (171ºC), and set time to 8 minutes.
5. Flip the prawns halfway through the cooking time.

6. When cooking is complete, the prawns should be pink. Remove the prawns from the oven to a plate.

Crispy Crab and Fish Cakes

Prep time: 20 minutes | Cook time: 12 minutes | Serves 4

8 ounces (227 g) imitation crab meat	saltine cracker crumbs
4 ounces (113 g) leftover cooked fish (such as cod, pollock, or haddock)	2 teaspoons dried parsley flakes
2 tablespoons minced celery	1 teaspoon prepared yellow mustard
2 tablespoons minced green onion	½ teaspoon garlic powder
2 tablespoons light mayonnaise	½ teaspoon dried dill weed, crushed
1 tablespoon plus 2 teaspoons Worcestershire sauce	½ teaspoon Old Bay seasoning
¾ cup crushed	½ cup panko bread crumbs
	Cooking spray

1. Pulse the crab meat and fish in a food processor until finely chopped.
2. Transfer the meat mixture to a large bowl, along with the celery, green onion, mayo, Worcestershire sauce, cracker crumbs, parsley flakes, mustard, garlic powder, dill weed, and Old Bay seasoning. Stir to mix well.
3. Scoop out the meat mixture and form into 8 equal-sized patties with your hands.
4. Place the panko bread crumbs on a plate. Roll the patties in the bread crumbs until they are evenly coated on both sides. Put the patties in the baking pan and spritz them with cooking spray.
5. Slide the baking pan into Rack Position 1, select Convection Bake, set temperature to 390ºF (199ºC), and set time to 12 minutes.
6. Flip the patties halfway through the cooking time.
7. When cooking is complete, they should be golden brown and cooked through. Remove the pan from the oven. Divide the patties among four plates and serve.

Herbed Scallops with Vegetables

Prep time: 15 minutes | Cook time: 9 minutes | Serves 4

1 cup frozen peas
1 cup green beans
1 cup frozen chopped broccoli
2 teaspoons olive oil
½ teaspoon dried oregano
½ teaspoon dried basil
12 ounces (340 g) sea scallops, rinsed and patted dry

1. Put the peas, green beans, and broccoli in a large bowl. Drizzle with the olive oil and toss to coat well. Transfer the vegetables to the air fryer basket.
2. Put the air fryer basket on the baking pan and slide into Rack Position 2, select Air Fry, set temperature to 400°F (205°C), and set time to 5 minutes.
3. When cooking is complete, the vegetables should be fork-tender. Transfer the vegetables to a serving bowl. Scatter with the oregano and basil and set aside.
4. Place the scallops in the basket.
5. Put the air fryer basket on the baking pan and slide into Rack Position 2, select Air Fry, set temperature to 400°F (205°C), and set time to 4 minutes.
6. When cooking is complete, the scallops should be firm and just opaque in the center. Remove from the oven to the bowl of vegetables and toss well. Serve warm.

Salmon Patty Bites

Prep time: 15 minutes | Cook time: 15 minutes | Serves 4

4 (5-ounce / 142-g) cans pink salmon, skinless, boneless in water, drained
2 eggs, beaten
1 cup whole-wheat panko bread crumbs
4 tablespoons finely
minced red bell pepper
2 tablespoons parsley flakes
2 teaspoons Old Bay seasoning
Cooking spray

1. Preheat the air fryer oven to 360°F (182°C).
2. Spray the air fryer basket lightly with cooking spray.
3. In a medium bowl, mix the salmon, eggs, panko bread crumbs, red bell pepper, parsley flakes, and Old Bay seasoning.
4. Using a small cookie scoop, form the mixture into 20 balls.
5. Place the salmon bites in the air fryer basket in a single layer and spray lightly with cooking spray.
6. Place the air fryer basket onto the baking pan and slide into Rack Position 2, select Air Fry and set time to 15 minutes, shaking the basket a couple of times for even cooking.
7. Serve immediately.

Cajun-Style Salmon Burgers

Prep time: 10 minutes | Cook time: 12 to 15 minutes | Serves 4

4 (5-ounce / 142-g) cans pink salmon in water, any skin and bones removed, drained
2 eggs, beaten
1 cup whole-wheat bread crumbs
4 tablespoons light mayonnaise
2 teaspoons Cajun seasoning
2 teaspoons dry mustard
4 whole-wheat buns
Cooking spray

1. In a medium bowl, mix the salmon, egg, bread crumbs, mayonnaise, Cajun seasoning, and dry mustard. Cover with plastic wrap and refrigerate for 30 minutes.
2. Preheat the air fryer oven to 360°F (182°C). Spray the air fryer basket lightly with cooking spray.
3. Shape the mixture into four ½-inch-thick patties about the same size as the buns.
4. Place the salmon patties in the air fryer basket in a single layer and lightly spray the tops with cooking spray.
5. Place the air fryer basket onto the baking pan and slide into Rack Position 2, select Air Fry and set time to 8 minutes.
6. Turn the patties over and lightly spray with cooking spray. Air fry until crispy on the outside, 4 to 7 more minutes.
7. Serve on whole-wheat buns.

Almond Crusted Fish

Prep time: 10 minutes | Cook time: 8 minutes | Serves 4

½ cup raw whole almonds
1 scallion, finely chopped
Grated zest and juice of 1 lemon
½ tablespoon extra-virgin olive oil
¾ teaspoon kosher

salt, divided
Freshly ground black pepper, to taste
4 (6 ounces / 170 g each) skinless fish fillets
Cooking spray
1 teaspoon Dijon mustard

1. In a food processor, pulse the almonds to coarsely chop. Transfer to a small bowl and add the scallion, lemon zest, and olive oil. Season with ¼ teaspoon of the salt and pepper to taste and mix to combine.
2. Spray the top of the fish with oil and squeeze the lemon juice over the fish. Season with the remaining ½ teaspoon salt and pepper to taste. Spread the mustard on top of the fish. Dividing evenly, press the almond mixture onto the top of the fillets to adhere.
3. Preheat the air fryer oven to 375ºF (191ºC).
4. Place the fillets in the air fryer basket in a single layer.
5. Place the air fryer basket onto the baking pan and slide into Rack Position 2, select Air Fry and set time to 8 minutes, until the crumbs start to brown and the fish is cooked through.
6. Serve immediately.

Breaded Scallops

Prep time: 5 minutes | Cook time: 7 minutes | Serves 4

1 egg
3 tablespoons flour
1 cup bread crumbs
1 pound (454 g) fresh scallops

2 tablespoons olive oil
Salt and black pepper, to taste

1. In a bowl, lightly beat the egg. Place the flour and bread crumbs into separate shallow dishes.
2. Dredge the scallops in the flour and shake off any excess. Dip the flour-coated scallops in the beaten egg and roll in the bread crumbs.
3. Brush the scallops generously with olive oil and season with salt and pepper, to taste. Transfer the scallops to the air fryer basket.
4. Put the air fryer basket on the baking pan and slide into Rack Position 2, select Air Fry, set temperature to 360ºF (182ºC), and set time to 7 minutes.
5. Flip the scallops halfway through the cooking time.
6. When cooking is complete, the scallops should reach an internal temperature of just 145ºF (63ºC) on a meat thermometer. Remove from the oven. Let the scallops cool for 5 minutes and serve.

Bacon-Wrapped Scallops

Prep time: 5 minutes | Cook time: 10 minutes | Serves 4

8 slices bacon, cut in half
16 sea scallops, patted dry
Cooking spray
Salt and freshly

ground black pepper, to taste
16 toothpicks, soaked in water for at least 30 minutes

1. On a clean work surface, wrap half of a slice of bacon around each scallop and secure with a toothpick.
2. Lay the bacon-wrapped scallops in the air fryer basket in a single layer.
3. Spritz the scallops with cooking spray and sprinkle the salt and pepper to season.
4. Put the air fryer basket on the baking pan and slide into Rack Position 2, select Air Fry, set temperature to 370ºF (188ºC), and set time to 10 minutes.
5. Flip the scallops halfway through the cooking time.
6. When cooking is complete, the bacon should be cooked through and the scallops should be firm. Remove the scallops from the oven to a plate Serve warm.

Crispy Cod Cakes with Salad Greens

Prep time: 15 minutes | Cook time: 12 minutes | Serves 4

1 pound (454 g) cod fillets, cut into chunks
1/3 cup packed fresh basil leaves
3 cloves garlic, crushed
1/2 teaspoon smoked paprika
1/4 teaspoon salt
1/4 teaspoon pepper
1 large egg, beaten
1 cup panko bread crumbs
Cooking spray
Salad greens, for serving

1. In a food processor, pulse cod, basil, garlic, smoked paprika, salt, and pepper until cod is finely chopped, stirring occasionally. Form into 8 patties, about 2 inches in diameter. Dip each first into the egg, then into the panko, patting to adhere. Spray with oil on one side.
2. Preheat the air fryer oven to 400ºF (204ºC).
3. Place the cakes in the air fryer basket, oil-side down; spray with oil.
4. Place the air fryer basket onto the baking pan and slide into Rack Position 2, select Air Fry and set time to 12 minutes, until golden brown and cooked through.
5. Serve cod cakes with salad greens.

Crispy Coconut Shrimp

Prep time: 15 minutes | Cook time: 8 minutes | Serves 4

Sweet Chili Mayo:
3 tablespoons mayonnaise
3 tablespoons Thai sweet chili sauce
1 tablespoon Sriracha sauce
Shrimp:
2/3 cup sweetened shredded coconut
2/3 cup panko bread crumbs
Kosher salt, to taste
2 tablespoons all-purpose or gluten-free flour
2 large eggs
24 extra-jumbo shrimp (about 1 pound / 454 g), peeled and deveined
Cooking spray

1. In a medium bowl, combine the mayonnaise, Thai sweet chili sauce, and Sriracha and mix well.
2. In a medium bowl, combine the coconut, panko, and 1/4 teaspoon salt. Place the flour in a shallow bowl. Whisk the eggs in another shallow bowl.
3. Season the shrimp with 1/8 teaspoon salt. Dip the shrimp in the flour, shaking off any excess, then into the egg. Coat in the coconut-panko mixture, gently pressing to adhere, then transfer to a large plate. Spray both sides of the shrimp with oil.
4. Preheat the air fryer oven to 360ºF (182ºC).
5. Working in batches, arrange a single layer of the shrimp in the air fryer basket.
6. Place the air fryer basket onto the baking pan and slide into Rack Position 2, select Air Fry and set time to 8 minutes, flipping halfway through, or until the crust is golden brown and the shrimp are cooked through.
7. Serve with the sweet chili mayo for dipping.

Garlic-Lemon Tilapia

Prep time: 5 minutes | Cook time: 15 minutes | Serves 4

1 tablespoon lemon juice
1 tablespoon olive oil
1 teaspoon minced garlic
1/2 teaspoon chili powder
4 (6-ounce / 170-g) tilapia fillets

1. Preheat the air fryer oven to 380ºF (193ºC). Line the air fryer basket with parchment paper.
2. In a large, shallow bowl, mix together the lemon juice, olive oil, garlic, and chili powder to make a marinade. Place the tilapia fillets in the bowl and coat evenly.
3. Place the fillets in the basket in a single layer, leaving space between each fillet.
4. Place the air fryer basket onto the baking pan and slide into Rack Position 2, select Air Fry and set time to 15 minutes, until the fish is cooked and flakes easily with a fork.
5. Serve hot.

Salmon Burgers

Prep time: 15 minutes | Cook time: 12 minutes | Serves 5

Lemon-Caper Rémoulade:

½ cup mayonnaise
2 tablespoons minced drained capers
2 tablespoons

chopped fresh parsley
2 teaspoons fresh lemon juice

Salmon Patties:

1 pound (454 g) wild salmon fillet, skinned and pin bones removed
6 tablespoons panko bread crumbs
¼ cup minced red onion plus ¼ cup slivered for serving
1 garlic clove, minced

1 large egg, lightly beaten
1 tablespoon Dijon mustard
1 teaspoon fresh lemon juice
1 tablespoon chopped fresh parsley
½ teaspoon kosher salt

For Serving:

5 whole wheat potato buns or gluten-free buns

10 butter lettuce leaves

1. For the lemon-caper rémoulade: In a small bowl, combine the mayonnaise, capers, parsley, and lemon juice and mix well.
2. For the salmon patties: Cut off a 4-ounce / 113-g piece of the salmon and transfer to a food processor. Pulse until it becomes pasty. With a sharp knife, chop the remaining salmon into small cubes.
3. In a medium bowl, combine the chopped and processed salmon with the panko, minced red onion, garlic, egg, mustard, lemon juice, parsley, and salt. Toss gently to combine. Form the mixture into 5 patties about ¾ inch thick. Refrigerate for at least 30 minutes.
4. Preheat the air fryer oven to 400ºF (204ºC).
5. Place the patties in the air fryer basket.
6. Place the air fryer basket onto the baking pan and slide into Rack Position 2, select Air Fry and set time to 12 minutes, gently flipping halfway through, until golden and cooked through.
7. To serve, transfer each patty to a bun. Top each with 2 lettuce leaves, 2 tablespoons of the rémoulade, and the slivered red onions.

Garlic-Butter Shrimp with Vegetables

Prep time: 10 minutes | Cook time: 15 minutes | Serves 4

1 pound (454 g) small red potatoes, halved
2 ears corn, shucked and cut into rounds, 1 to 1½ inches thick
2 tablespoons Old Bay or similar seasoning
½ cup unsalted butter, melted

1 (12- to 13-ounce / 340- to 369-g) package kielbasa or other smoked sausages
3 garlic cloves, minced
1 pound (454 g) medium shrimp, peeled and deveined

1. Place the potatoes and corn in a large bowl.
2. Stir together the butter and Old Bay seasoning in a small bowl. Drizzle half the butter mixture over the potatoes and corn, tossing to coat. Spread out the vegetables in the baking pan.
3. Slide the baking pan into Rack Position 2, select Roast, set temperature to 350ºF (180ºC), and set time to 15 minutes.
4. Meanwhile, cut the sausages into 2-inch lengths, then cut each piece in half lengthwise. Put the sausages and shrimp in a medium bowl and set aside.
5. Add the garlic to the bowl of remaining butter mixture and stir well.
6. After 10 minutes, remove the pan and pour the vegetables into the large bowl. Drizzle with the garlic butter and toss until well coated. Arrange the vegetables, sausages, and shrimp in the pan.
7. Return to the oven and continue cooking. After 5 minutes, check the shrimp for doneness. The shrimp should be pink and opaque. If they are not quite cooked through, roast for an additional 1 minute.
8. When done, remove from the oven and serve on a plate.

Garlic Scallops

Prep time: 10 minutes | Cook time: 10 to 15 minutes | Serves 4

2 teaspoons olive oil
1 packet dry zesty Italian dressing mix
1 teaspoon minced garlic

16 ounces (454 g) small scallops, patted dry
Cooking spray

1. Preheat the air fryer oven to 400°F (204°C).
2. Spray the air fryer basket lightly with cooking spray.
3. In a large zip-top plastic bag, combine the olive oil, Italian dressing mix, and garlic.
4. Add the scallops, seal the zip-top bag, and coat the scallops in the seasoning mixture.
5. Place the scallops in the air fryer basket and lightly spray with cooking spray.
6. Place the air fryer basket onto the baking pan and slide into Rack Position 2, select Air Fry and set time to 5 minutes.
7. Shake the basket and air fry for 5 to 10 more minutes, or until the scallops reach an internal temperature of 120°F (49°C).
8. Serve immediately.

Spanish Garlic Shrimp

Prep time: 10 minutes | Cook time: 10 to 15 minutes | Serves 4

2 teaspoons minced garlic
2 teaspoons lemon juice
2 teaspoons olive oil
½ to 1 teaspoon

crushed red pepper
12 ounces (340 g) medium shrimp, deveined, with tails on
Cooking spray

1. In a medium bowl, mix together the garlic, lemon juice, olive oil, and crushed red pepper to make a marinade.
2. Add the shrimp and toss to coat in the marinade. Cover with plastic wrap and place the bowl in the refrigerator for 30 minutes.
3. Preheat the air fryer oven to 400°F (204°C). Spray the air fryer basket lightly with cooking spray.
4. Place the shrimp in the air fryer basket.

5. Place the air fryer basket onto the baking pan and slide into Rack Position 2, select Air Fry and set time to 5 minutes.
6. Shake the basket and air fry until the shrimp are cooked through and nicely browned, an additional 5 to 10 minutes.
7. Cool for 5 minutes before serving.

Classic Shrimp Empanadas

Prep time: 10 minutes | Cook time: 8 minutes | Serves 5

½ pound (227g) raw shrimp, peeled, deveined and chopped
¼ cup chopped red onion
1 scallion, chopped
2 garlic cloves, minced
2 tablespoons minced red bell pepper
2 tablespoons chopped fresh cilantro

½ tablespoon fresh lime juice
¼ teaspoon sweet paprika
⅛ teaspoon kosher salt
⅛ teaspoon crushed red pepper flakes (optional)
1 large egg, beaten
10 frozen Goya Empanada Discos, thawed
Cooking spray

1. In a medium bowl, combine the shrimp, red onion, scallion, garlic, bell pepper, cilantro, lime juice, paprika, salt, and pepper flakes (if using).
2. In a small bowl, beat the egg with 1 teaspoon water until smooth.
3. Place an empanada disc on a work surface and put 2 tablespoons of the shrimp mixture in the center. Brush the outer edges of the disc with the egg wash. Fold the disc over and gently press the edges to seal. Use a fork and press around the edges to crimp and seal completely. Brush the tops of the empanadas with the egg wash.
4. Preheat the air fryer oven to 380°F (193°C). Spray the air fryer basket with cooking spray.
5. Arrange a single layer of the empanadas in the air fryer basket.
6. Place the air fryer basket onto the baking pan and slide into Rack Position 2, select Air Fry and set time to 8 minutes, flipping halfway through, or until golden brown and crispy. Serve hot.

Cajun-Style Fish Tacos

Prep time: 5 minutes | Cook time: 15 minutes | Serves 6

2 teaspoons avocado oil	g) package coleslaw mix
1 tablespoon Cajun seasoning	12 corn tortillas
4 tilapia fillets	2 limes, cut into wedges
1 (14-ounce / 397-	

1. Preheat the air fryer oven to 380°F (193°C). Line the air fryer basket with parchment paper.
2. In a medium, shallow bowl, mix the avocado oil and the Cajun seasoning to make a marinade. Add the tilapia fillets and coat evenly.
3. Place the fillets in the basket in a single layer, leaving room between each fillet.
4. Place the air fryer basket onto the baking pan and slide into Rack Position 2, select Air Fry and set time to 15 minutes, or until the fish is cooked and easily flakes with a fork.
5. Assemble the tacos by placing some of the coleslaw mix in each tortilla. Add ⅓ of a tilapia fillet to each tortilla. Squeeze some lime juice over the top of each taco and serve.

Blackened Shrimp Tacos

Prep time: 10 minutes | Cook time: 10 to 15 minutes | Serves 4

12 ounces (340 g) medium shrimp, deveined, with tails off	8 corn tortillas, warmed
1 teaspoon olive oil	1 (14-ounce / 397-g) bag coleslaw mix
1 to 2 teaspoons Blackened seasoning	2 limes, cut in half
	Cooking spray

1. Preheat the air fryer oven to 400°F (204°C).
2. Spray the air fryer basket lightly with cooking spray.
3. Dry the shrimp with a paper towel to remove excess water.
4. In a medium bowl, toss the shrimp with olive oil and Blackened seasoning.
5. Place the shrimp in the air fryer basket.

6. Place the air fryer basket onto the baking pan and slide into Rack Position 2, select Air Fry and set time to 5 minutes.
7. Shake the basket, lightly spray with cooking spray, and cook until the shrimp are cooked through and starting to brown, 5 to 10 more minutes.
8. Fill each tortilla with the coleslaw mix and top with the blackened shrimp. Squeeze fresh lime juice over top and serve.

Marinated Salmon Fillets

Prep time: 10 minutes | Cook time: 18 minutes | Serves 4

¼ cup soy sauce	ginger
¼ cup rice wine vinegar	½ teaspoon freshly ground black pepper
1 tablespoon brown sugar	½ teaspoon minced garlic
1 tablespoon olive oil	4 (6-ounce / 170-g) salmon fillets, skin-on
1 teaspoon mustard powder	
1 teaspoon ground	Cooking spray

1. In a small bowl, combine the soy sauce, rice wine vinegar, brown sugar, olive oil, mustard powder, ginger, black pepper, and garlic to make a marinade.
2. Place the fillets in a shallow baking dish and pour the marinade over them. Cover the baking dish and marinate for at least 1 hour in the refrigerator, turning the fillets occasionally to keep them coated in the marinade.
3. Preheat the air fryer oven to 370°F (188°C). Spray the air fryer basket lightly with cooking spray.
4. Shake off as much marinade as possible from the fillets and place them, skin-side down, in the air fryer basket in a single layer.
5. Place the air fryer basket onto the baking pan and slide into Rack Position 2, select Air Fry and set time to 18 minutes. The minimum internal temperature should be 145°F (63°C) at the thickest part of the fillets.
6. Serve hot.

Homemade Fish Sticks

Prep time: 15 minutes | Cook time: 13 to 15 minutes | Serves 4

4 fish fillets
½ cup whole-wheat flour
1 teaspoon seasoned salt
2 eggs
1½ cups whole-wheat panko bread crumbs
½ tablespoon dried parsley flakes
Cooking spray

1. Preheat the air fryer oven to 400ºF (204ºC). Spray the air fryer basket lightly with cooking spray.
2. Cut the fish fillets lengthwise into "sticks."
3. In a shallow bowl, mix the whole-wheat flour and seasoned salt.
4. In a small bowl, whisk the eggs with 1 teaspoon of water.
5. In another shallow bowl, mix the panko bread crumbs and parsley flakes.
6. Coat each fish stick in the seasoned flour, then in the egg mixture, and dredge them in the panko bread crumbs.
7. Place the fish sticks in the air fryer basket in a single layer and lightly spray the fish sticks with cooking spray.
8. Place the air fryer basket onto the baking pan and slide into Rack Position 2, select Air Fry and set time to 8 minutes.
9. Flip the fish sticks over and lightly spray with cooking spray. Air fry until golden brown and crispy, 5 to 7 more minutes.
10. Serve warm.

Spicy Orange Shrimp

Prep time: 20 minutes | Cook time: 10 to 15 minutes | Serves 4

⅓ cup orange juice
3 teaspoons minced garlic
1 teaspoon Old Bay seasoning
¼ to ½ teaspoon
cayenne pepper
1 pound (454 g) medium shrimp, peeled and deveined, with tails off
Cooking spray

1. In a medium bowl, combine the orange juice, garlic, Old Bay seasoning, and cayenne pepper.
2. Dry the shrimp with paper towels to remove excess water.

3. Add the shrimp to the marinade and stir to evenly coat. Cover with plastic wrap and place in the refrigerator for 30 minutes so the shrimp can soak up the marinade.
4. Preheat the air fryer oven to 400ºF (204ºC). Spray the air fryer basket lightly with cooking spray.
5. Place the shrimp into the air fryer basket.
6. Place the air fryer basket onto the baking pan and slide into Rack Position 2, select Air Fry and set time to 5 minutes.
7. Shake the basket and lightly spray with olive oil. Air fry until the shrimp are opaque and crisp, 5 to 10 more minutes.
8. Serve immediately.

Country Shrimp

Prep time: 10 minutes | Cook time: 15 minutes | Serves 4

1 pound (454 g) large shrimp, deveined, with tails on
1 pound (454 g) smoked turkey sausage, cut into thick slices
2 corn cobs, quartered
1 zucchini, cut into bite-sized pieces
1 red bell pepper, cut into chunks
1 tablespoon Old Bay seasoning
2 tablespoons olive oil
Cooking spray

1. Preheat the air fryer oven to 400ºF (204ºC). Spray the air fryer basket lightly with cooking spray.
2. In a large bowl, mix the shrimp, turkey sausage, corn, zucchini, bell pepper, and Old Bay seasoning, and toss to coat with the spices. Add the olive oil and toss again until evenly coated.
3. Spread the mixture in the air fryer basket in a single layer.
4. Place the air fryer basket onto the baking pan and slide into Rack Position 2, select Air Fry and set time to 15 minutes, or until cooked through, shaking the basket every 5 minutes for even cooking.
5. Serve immediately.

Tuna Patty Sliders

Prep time: 15 minutes | Cook time: 12 to 15 minutes | Serves 4

3 (5-ounce / 142-g) cans tuna, packed in water
²/₃ cup whole-wheat panko bread crumbs
¹/₃ cup shredded Parmesan cheese
1 tablespoon sriracha
¾ teaspoon black pepper
10 whole-wheat slider buns
Cooking spray

1. Preheat the air fryer oven to 350ºF (177ºC).
2. Spray the air fryer basket lightly with cooking spray.
3. In a medium bowl combine the tuna, bread crumbs, Parmesan cheese, sriracha, and black pepper and stir to combine.
4. Form the mixture into 10 patties.
5. Place the patties in the air fryer basket in a single layer. Spray the patties lightly with cooking spray.
6. Place the air fryer basket onto the baking pan and slide into Rack Position 2, select Air Fry and set time to 8 minutes.
7. Turn the patties over and lightly spray with cooking spray. Air fry until golden brown and crisp, another 4 to 7 more minutes. Serve warm.

Vegetable and Fish Tacos

Prep time: 10 minutes | Cook time: 10 minutes | Serves 4

1 pound (454 g) white fish fillets
2 teaspoons olive oil
3 tablespoons freshly squeezed lemon juice, divided
1½ cups chopped red cabbage
1 large carrot, grated
½ cup low-sodium salsa
¹/₃ cup low-fat Greek yogurt
4 soft low-sodium whole-wheat tortillas

1. Preheat the air fryer oven to 400ºF (204ºC).
2. Brush the fish with the olive oil and sprinkle with 1 tablespoon of lemon juice. Transfer to the air fryer basket.
3. Place the air fryer basket onto the baking pan and slide into Rack Position 2, select Air Fry and set time to 10 minutes, or

until the fish just flakes when tested with a fork.
4. Meanwhile, in a medium bowl, stir together the remaining 2 tablespoons of lemon juice, the red cabbage, carrot, salsa, and yogurt.
5. When the fish is cooked, remove it from the air fryer basket and break it up into large pieces.
6. Offer the fish, tortillas, and the cabbage mixture, and let each person assemble a taco. Serve immediately.

Sesame Glazed Salmon

Prep time: 5 minutes | Cook time: 16 minutes | Serves 4

3 tablespoons soy sauce
1 tablespoon rice wine or dry sherry
1 tablespoon brown sugar
1 tablespoon toasted sesame oil
1 teaspoon minced
garlic
¼ teaspoon minced ginger
4 (6-ounce / 170-g) salmon fillets, skin-on
½ tablespoon sesame seeds
Cooking spray

1. In a small bowl, mix the soy sauce, rice wine, brown sugar, toasted sesame oil, garlic, and ginger.
2. Place the salmon in a shallow baking dish and pour the marinade over the fillets. Cover and refrigerate for at least 1 hour, turning the fillets occasionally to coat in the marinade.
3. Preheat the air fryer oven to 370ºF (188ºC). Spray the air fryer basket lightly with cooking spray.
4. Shake off as much marinade as possible and place the fillets, skin-side down, in the air fryer basket in a single layer. Reserve the marinade.
5. Place the air fryer basket onto the baking pan and slide into Rack Position 2, select Air Fry and set time to 10 minutes.
6. Brush the tops of the salmon fillets with the reserved marinade and sprinkle with sesame seeds. Increase the temperature to 400ºF (204ºC) and air fry for 2 to 5 more minutes for medium, 1 to 3 minutes for medium rare, or 4 to 6 minutes for well done.
7. Serve warm.

Green Curry Shrimp

Prep time: 15 minutes | Cook time: 5 minutes | Serves 4

1 to 2 tablespoons Thai green curry paste
2 tablespoons coconut oil, melted
1 tablespoon half-and-half or coconut milk
1 teaspoon fish sauce
1 teaspoon soy sauce

1 teaspoon minced fresh ginger
1 clove garlic, minced
1 pound (454 g) jumbo raw shrimp, peeled and deveined
¼ cup chopped fresh Thai basil or sweet basil
¼ cup chopped fresh cilantro

1. In a baking pan, combine the curry paste, coconut oil, half-and-half, fish sauce, soy sauce, ginger, and garlic. Whisk until well combined.
2. Add the shrimp and toss until well coated. Marinate at room temperature for 15 to 30 minutes.
3. Preheat the air fryer oven to 400°F (204°C).
4. Slide the baking pan into Rack Position 1, select Convection Bake and set time to 5 minutes, stirring halfway through the cooking time.
5. Transfer the shrimp to a serving bowl or platter. Garnish with the basil and cilantro. Serve immediately.

Lime-Chili Shrimp Bowl

Prep time: 10 minutes | Cook time: 10 to 15 minutes | Serves 4

2 teaspoons lime juice
1 teaspoon olive oil
1 teaspoon honey
1 teaspoon minced garlic
1 teaspoon chili powder
Salt, to taste
12 ounces (340 g) medium shrimp,

peeled and deveined
2 cups cooked brown rice
1 (15-ounce / 425-g) can seasoned black beans, warmed
1 large avocado, chopped
1 cup sliced cherry tomatoes
Cooking spray

1. Preheat the air fryer oven to 400°F (204°C). Spray the air fryer basket lightly with cooking spray.
2. In a medium bowl, mix together the lime juice, olive oil, honey, garlic, chili powder, and salt to make a marinade.
3. Add the shrimp and toss to coat evenly in the marinade.
4. Place the shrimp in the air fryer basket.
5. Place the air fryer basket onto the baking pan and slide into Rack Position 2, select Air Fry and set time to 5 minutes.
6. Shake the basket and air fry until the shrimp are cooked through and starting to brown, an additional 5 to 10 minutes.
7. To assemble the bowls, spoon ¼ of the rice, black beans, avocado, and cherry tomatoes into each of four bowls. Top with the shrimp and serve.

Crispy Catfish Strips

Prep time: 5 minutes | Cook time: 16 to 18 minutes | Serves 4

1 cup buttermilk
5 catfish fillets, cut into 1½-inch strips
Cooking spray

1 cup cornmeal
1 tablespoon Creole, Cajun, or Old Bay seasoning

1. Pour the buttermilk into a shallow baking dish. Place the catfish in the dish and refrigerate for at least 1 hour to help remove any fishy taste.
2. Preheat the air fryer oven to 400°F (204°C). Spray the air fryer basket lightly with cooking spray.
3. In a shallow bowl, combine cornmeal and Creole seasoning.
4. Shake any excess buttermilk off the catfish. Place each strip in the cornmeal mixture and coat completely. Press the cornmeal into the catfish gently to help it stick.
5. Place the strips in the air fryer basket in a single layer. Lightly spray the catfish with cooking spray.
6. Place the air fryer basket onto the baking pan and slide into Rack Position 2, select Air Fry and set time to 8 minutes.
7. Turn the catfish strips over and lightly spray with cooking spray. Air fry until golden brown and crispy, 8 to 10 more minutes.
8. Serve warm.

Tortilla Shrimp Tacos

Prep time: 10 minutes | Cook time: 6 minutes | Serves 4

Spicy Mayo:

3 tablespoons mayonnaise
1 tablespoon

Louisiana-style hot pepper sauce

Cilantro-Lime Slaw:

2 cups shredded green cabbage
½ small red onion, thinly sliced
1 small jalapeño, thinly sliced

2 tablespoons chopped fresh cilantro
Juice of 1 lime
¼ teaspoon kosher salt

Shrimp:

1 large egg, beaten
1 cup crushed tortilla chips
24 jumbo shrimp (about 1 pound / 454 g), peeled and

deveined
⅛ teaspoon kosher salt
Cooking spray
8 corn tortillas, for serving

1. For the spicy mayo: In a small bowl, mix the mayonnaise and hot pepper sauce.
2. For the cilantro-lime slaw: In a large bowl, toss together the cabbage, onion, jalapeño, cilantro, lime juice, and salt to combine. Cover and refrigerate to chill.
3. For the shrimp: Place the egg in a shallow bowl and the crushed tortilla chips in another. Season the shrimp with the salt. Dip the shrimp in the egg, then in the crumbs, pressing gently to adhere. Place on a work surface and spray both sides with oil.
4. Preheat the air fryer oven to 360ºF (182ºC).
5. Working in batches, arrange a single layer of the shrimp in the air fryer basket.
6. Place the air fryer basket onto the baking pan and slide into Rack Position 2, select Air Fry and set time to 6 minutes, flipping halfway through, or until golden and cooked through in the center.
7. To serve, place 2 tortillas on each plate and top each with 3 shrimp. Top each taco with ¼ cup slaw, then drizzle with spicy mayo.

Crab Cake Sandwich

Prep time: 15 minutes | Cook time: 10 minutes | Serves 4

Crab Cakes:

½ cup panko bread crumbs
1 large egg, beaten
1 large egg white
1 tablespoon mayonnaise
1 teaspoon Dijon mustard
¼ cup minced fresh parsley
1 tablespoon fresh lemon juice

½ teaspoon Old Bay seasoning
⅛ teaspoon sweet paprika
⅛ teaspoon kosher salt
Freshly ground black pepper, to taste
10 ounces (283 g) lump crab meat
Cooking spray

Cajun Mayo:

¼ cup mayonnaise
1 tablespoon minced dill pickle
1 teaspoon fresh

lemon juice
¾ teaspoon Cajun seasoning

For Serving:

4 Boston lettuce leaves
4 whole wheat potato

buns or gluten-free buns

1. For the crab cakes: In a large bowl, combine the panko, whole egg, egg white, mayonnaise, mustard, parsley, lemon juice, Old Bay, paprika, salt, and pepper to taste and mix well. Fold in the crab meat, being careful not to over mix. Gently shape into 4 round patties, about ½ cup each, ¾ inch thick. Spray both sides with oil.
2. Preheat the air fryer oven to 370ºF (188ºC).
3. Place the crab cakes in the air fryer basket.
4. Place the air fryer basket onto the baking pan and slide into Rack Position 2, select Air Fry and set time to 10 minutes, flipping halfway through, until the edges are golden.
5. Meanwhile, for the Cajun mayo: In a small bowl, combine the mayonnaise, pickle, lemon juice, and Cajun seasoning.
6. Place a lettuce leaf on each bun bottom and top with a crab cake and a generous tablespoon of Cajun mayonnaise. Add the bun top and serve.

Blackened Salmon

Prep time: 10 minutes | Cook time: 6 minutes | Serves 4

Salmon:
1 tablespoon sweet paprika
½ teaspoon cayenne pepper
1 teaspoon garlic powder
1 teaspoon dried oregano
1 teaspoon dried thyme

¾ teaspoon kosher salt
⅛ teaspoon freshly ground black pepper
Cooking spray
4 (6 ounces / 170 g each) wild salmon fillets

Cucumber-Avocado Salsa:
2 tablespoons chopped red onion
1½ tablespoons fresh lemon juice
1 teaspoon extra-virgin olive oil
¼ teaspoon plus ⅛ teaspoon kosher salt

Freshly ground black pepper, to taste
4 Persian cucumbers, diced
6 ounces (170 g) Hass avocado, diced

1. For the salmon: In a small bowl, combine the paprika, cayenne, garlic powder, oregano, thyme, salt, and black pepper. Spray both sides of the fish with oil and rub all over. Coat the fish all over with the spices.
2. For the cucumber-avocado salsa: In a medium bowl, combine the red onion, lemon juice, olive oil, salt, and pepper. Let stand for 5 minutes, then add the cucumbers and avocado.
3. Preheat the air fryer oven to 400ºF (204ºC).
4. Arrange the salmon fillets skin-side down in the air fryer basket.
5. Place the air fryer basket onto the baking pan and slide into Rack Position 2, select Air Fry and set time to 6 minutes, or until the fish flakes easily with a fork, depending on the thickness of the fish.
6. Serve topped with the salsa.

Lemony Shrimp and Zucchini

Prep time: 15 minutes | Cook time: 8 minutes | Serves 4

1¼ pounds (567 g) extra-large raw shrimp, peeled and deveined
2 medium zucchini (about 8 ounces / 227 g each), halved lengthwise and cut into ½-inch-thick slices
1½ tablespoons olive oil
½ teaspoon garlic salt

1½ teaspoons dried oregano
⅛ teaspoon crushed red pepper flakes (optional)
Juice of ½ lemon
1 tablespoon chopped fresh mint
1 tablespoon chopped fresh dill

1. Preheat the air fryer oven to 350ºF (177ºC).
2. In a large bowl, combine the shrimp, zucchini, oil, garlic salt, oregano, and pepper flakes (if using) and toss to coat.
3. Working in batches, arrange a single layer of the shrimp and zucchini in the air fryer basket.
4. Place the air fryer basket onto the baking pan and slide into Rack Position 2, select Air Fry and set time to 8 minutes, shaking the basket halfway through, until the zucchini is golden and the shrimp are cooked through.
5. Transfer to a serving dish and tent with foil while you air fry the remaining shrimp and zucchini.
6. Top with the lemon juice, mint, and dill and serve.

Chapter 4 Poultry

Air Fried Chicken Wings

Prep time: 10 minutes | Cook time: 15 minutes | Serves 4

1 tablespoon olive oil
8 whole chicken wings
Chicken seasoning or rub, to taste
1 teaspoon garlic powder
Freshly ground black pepper, to taste

1. Grease the basket with olive oil.
2. On a clean work surface, rub the chicken wings with chicken seasoning and rub, garlic powder, and ground black pepper.
3. Arrange the well-coated chicken wings in the basket.
4. Put the air fryer basket on the baking pan and slide into Rack Position 2, select Air Fry, set temperature to 400ºF (205ºC) and set time to 15 minutes.
5. Flip the chicken wings halfway through.
6. When cooking is complete, the internal temperature of the chicken wings should reach at least 165ºF (74ºC).
7. Remove the chicken wings from the oven. Serve immediately.

Spanish Chicken and Pepper Baguette

Prep time: 10 minutes | Cook time: 20 minutes | Serves 2

1¼ pounds (567 g) assorted small chicken parts, breasts cut into halves
¼ teaspoon salt
¼ teaspoon ground black pepper
2 teaspoons olive oil
½ pound (227 g)
mini sweet peppers
¼ cup light mayonnaise
¼ teaspoon smoked paprika
½ clove garlic, crushed
Baguette, for serving
Cooking spray

1. Spritz the air fryer basket with cooking spray.
2. Toss the chicken with salt, ground black pepper, and olive oil in a large bowl.
3. Arrange the sweet peppers and chicken in the basket.

4. Put the air fryer basket on the baking pan and slide into Rack Position 2, select Air Fry, set temperature to 375ºF (190ºC) and set time to 20 minutes.
5. Flip the chicken and transfer the peppers on a plate halfway through.
6. When cooking is complete, the chicken should be well browned.
7. Meanwhile, combine the mayo, paprika, and garlic in a small bowl. Stir to mix well.
8. Assemble the baguette with chicken and sweet pepper, then spread with mayo mixture and serve.

Turkey and Cauliflower Meatloaf

Prep time: 15 minutes | Cook time: 50 minutes | Serves 6

2 pounds (907 g) lean ground turkey
1⅓ cups riced cauliflower
2 large eggs, lightly beaten
¼ cup almond flour
⅔ cup chopped yellow or white onion
1 teaspoon ground dried turmeric
1 teaspoon ground cumin
1 teaspoon ground coriander
1 tablespoon minced garlic
1 teaspoon salt
1 teaspoon ground black pepper
Cooking spray

1. Spritz the baking pan with cooking spray.
2. Combine all the ingredients in a large bowl. Stir to mix well. Pour half of the mixture in the prepared pan and press with a spatula to coat the bottom evenly. Spritz the mixture with cooking spray.
3. Slide the baking pan into Rack Position 1, select Convection Bake, set temperature to 350ºF (180ºC) and set time to 25 minutes.
4. When cooking is complete, the meat should be well browned and the internal temperature should reach at least 165ºF (74ºC).
5. Remove the pan from the oven and serve immediately.

Deep Fried Duck Leg Quarters

Prep time: 5 minutes | Cook time: 45 minutes | Serves 4

4 (½-pound / 227-g) skin-on duck leg quarters
2 medium garlic cloves, minced
½ teaspoon salt
½ teaspoon ground black pepper

1. Spritz the air fryer basket with cooking spray.
2. On a clean work surface, rub the duck leg quarters with garlic, salt, and black pepper.
3. Arrange the leg quarters in the basket and spritz with cooking spray.
4. Put the air fryer basket on the baking pan and slide into Rack Position 2, select Air Fry, set temperature to 300ºF (150ºC) and set time to 30 minutes.
5. After 30 minutes, remove from the oven. Flip the leg quarters. Increase temperature to 375ºF (190ºC) and set time to 15 minutes. Return to the oven and continue cooking.
6. When cooking is complete, the leg quarters should be well browned and crispy.
7. Remove the duck leg quarters from the oven and allow to cool for 10 minutes before serving.

Yakitori

Prep time: 10 minutes | Cook time: 15 minutes | Serves 4

½ cup mirin
¼ cup dry white wine
½ cup soy sauce
1 tablespoon light brown sugar
1½ pounds (680 g) boneless, skinless
chicken thighs, cut into 1½-inch pieces, fat trimmed
4 medium scallions, trimmed, cut into 1½-inch pieces
Cooking spray

Special Equipment:
4 (4-inch) bamboo skewers, soaked in water for at least 30 minutes

1. Combine the mirin, dry white wine, soy sauce, and brown sugar in a saucepan. Bring to a boil over medium heat. Keep stirring.
2. Boil for another 2 minutes or until it has a thick consistency. Turn off the heat.
3. Spritz the air fryer basket with cooking spray.
4. Run the bamboo skewers through the chicken pieces and scallions alternatively.
5. Arrange the skewers in the basket, then brush with mirin mixture on both sides. Spritz with cooking spray.
6. Put the air fryer basket on the baking pan and slide into Rack Position 2, select Air Fry, set temperature to 400ºF (205ºC) and set time to 10 minutes.
7. Flip the skewers halfway through.
8. When cooking is complete, the chicken and scallions should be glossy.
9. Serve immediately.

Thai Drumsticks with Green Beans

Prep time: 5 minutes | Cook time: 25 minutes | Serves 4

8 skin-on chicken drumsticks
1 teaspoon kosher salt, divided
1 pound (454 g) green beans, trimmed
2 garlic cloves, minced
2 tablespoons vegetable oil
⅓ cup Thai sweet chili sauce

1. Salt the drumsticks on all sides with ½ teaspoon of kosher salt. Let sit for a few minutes, then blot dry with a paper towel. Place in the baking pan.
2. Slide the baking pan into Rack Position 2, select Roast, set temperature to 375ºF (190ºC), and set time to 25 minutes.
3. While the chicken cooks, place the green beans in a large bowl. Add the remaining kosher salt, the garlic, and oil. Toss to coat.
4. After 15 minutes, remove from the oven. Brush the drumsticks with the sweet chili sauce. Place the green beans in the pan. Return the pan to the oven and continue cooking.
5. When cooking is complete, the green beans should be sizzling and browned in spots and the chicken cooked through, reading 165ºF (74ºC) on a meat thermometer. Serve the chicken with the green beans on the side.

Strawberry-Glazed Turkey

Prep time: 15 minutes | Cook time: 37 minutes | Serves 2

2 pounds (907 g) turkey breast
1 tablespoon olive oil
Salt and ground
black pepper, to taste
1 cup fresh strawberries

1. Rub the turkey bread with olive oil on a clean work surface, then sprinkle with salt and ground black pepper.
2. Transfer the turkey in the air fryer basket and spritz with cooking spray.
3. Put the air fryer basket on the baking pan and slide into Rack Position 2, select Air Fry, set temperature to 375ºF (190ºC) and set time to 30 minutes.
4. Flip the turkey breast halfway through.
5. Meanwhile, put the strawberries in a food processor and pulse until smooth.
6. When cooking is complete, spread the puréed strawberries over the turkey and fry for 7 more minutes.
7. Serve immediately.

Italian Chicken Breasts with Tomatoes

Prep time: 10 minutes | Cook time: 35 minutes | Serves 8

3 pounds (1.4 kg) chicken breasts, bone-in
1 teaspoon minced fresh basil
1 teaspoon minced fresh rosemary
2 tablespoons minced fresh parsley
1 teaspoon cayenne pepper
½ teaspoon salt
½ teaspoon freshly ground black pepper
4 medium Roma tomatoes, halved
Cooking spray

1. Spritz the air fryer basket with cooking spray.
2. Combine all the ingredients, except for the chicken breasts and tomatoes, in a large bowl. Stir to mix well.
3. Dunk the chicken breasts in the mixture and press to coat well.
4. Transfer the chicken breasts in the basket.
5. Put the air fryer basket on the baking pan and slide into Rack Position 2, select Air Fry, set temperature to 370ºF (188ºC) and set time to 20 minutes.
6. Flip the breasts halfway through the cooking time.
7. When cooking is complete, the internal temperature of the thickest part of the breasts should reach at least 165ºF (74ºC).
8. Remove the cooked chicken breasts from the oven and adjust the temperature to 350ºF (180ºC).
9. Place the tomatoes in the basket and spritz with cooking spray. Sprinkle with a touch of salt.
10. Set time to 10 minutes. Stir the tomatoes halfway through the cooking time.
11. When cooking is complete, the tomatoes should be tender.
12. Serve the tomatoes with chicken breasts on a large serving plate.

Pineapple Chicken

Prep time: 10 minutes | Cook time: 10 minutes | Serves 6

1½ pounds (680 g) boneless, skinless chicken breasts, cut into 1-inch chunks
¾ cup soy sauce
2 tablespoons ketchup
2 tablespoons brown sugar
2 tablespoons rice vinegar
1 red bell pepper, cut
into 1-inch chunks
1 green bell pepper, cut into 1-inch chunks
6 scallions, cut into 1-inch pieces
1 cup (¾-inch chunks) fresh pineapple, rinsed and drained
Cooking spray

1. Place the chicken in a large bowl. Add the soy sauce, ketchup, brown sugar, vinegar, red and green peppers, and scallions. Toss to coat.
2. Spritz the baking pan with cooking spray and place the chicken and vegetables on the pan.
3. Slide the baking pan into Rack Position 2, select Roast, set temperature to 375ºF (190ºC), and set time to 10 minutes.
4. After 6 minutes, remove from the oven. Add the pineapple chunks to the pan and stir. Return the pan to the oven and continue cooking.
5. When cooking is complete, remove from the oven. Serve with steamed rice, if desired.

Turkey and Mushroom Meatballs

Prep time: 10 minutes | Cook time: 15 minutes | Serves 6

Sauce:
2 tablespoons tamari
2 tablespoons tomato sauce
1 tablespoon lime juice
¼ teaspoon peeled and grated fresh ginger
1 clove garlic, smashed to a paste
½ cup chicken broth
⅓ cup sugar
2 tablespoons toasted sesame oil
Cooking spray

Meatballs:
2 pounds (907 g) ground turkey
¾ cup finely chopped button mushrooms
2 large eggs, beaten
1½ teaspoons tamari
¼ cup finely chopped green onions, plus more for garnish
2 teaspoons peeled and grated fresh ginger
1 clove garlic, smashed
2 teaspoons toasted sesame oil
2 tablespoons sugar

For Serving:
Lettuce leaves, for serving
Sliced red chiles, for garnish (optional)
Toasted sesame seeds, for garnish (optional)

1. Spritz the air fryer basket with cooking spray.
2. Combine the ingredients for the sauce in a small bowl. Stir to mix well. Set aside.
3. Combine the ingredients for the meatballs in a large bowl. Stir to mix well, then shape the mixture in twelve 1½-inch meatballs.
4. Arrange the meatballs in the basket, then baste with the sauce.
5. Put the air fryer basket on the baking pan and slide into Rack Position 2, select Air Fry, set temperature to 350ºF (180ºC) and set time to 15 minutes.
6. Flip the balls halfway through.
7. When cooking is complete, the meatballs should be golden brown.
8. Unfold the lettuce leaves on a large serving plate, then transfer the cooked meatballs on the leaves. Spread the red chiles and sesame seeds over the balls, then serve.

Glazed Duck with Cherry Sauce

Prep time: 20 minutes | Cook time: 32 minutes | Serves 12

1 whole duck (about 5 pounds / 2.3 kg in total), split in half, back and rib bones removed, fat trimmed
1 teaspoon olive oil
Salt and freshly ground black pepper, to taste

Cherry Sauce:
1 tablespoon butter
1 shallot, minced
½ cup sherry
1 cup chicken stock
1 teaspoon white wine vinegar
¾ cup cherry preserves
1 teaspoon fresh thyme leaves
Salt and freshly ground black pepper, to taste

1. On a clean work surface, rub the duck with olive oil, then sprinkle with salt and ground black pepper to season.
2. Place the duck in the air fryer basket, breast side up.
3. Put the air fryer basket on the baking pan and slide into Rack Position 2, select Air Fry, set temperature to 400ºF (205ºC) and set time to 25 minutes.
4. Flip the ducks halfway through the cooking time.
5. Meanwhile, make the cherry sauce: Heat the butter in a skillet over medium-high heat or until melted.
6. Add the shallot and sauté for 5 minutes or until lightly browned.
7. Add the sherry and simmer for 6 minutes or until it reduces in half.
8. Add the chicken stick, white wine vinegar, and cherry preserves. Stir to combine well. Simmer for 6 more minutes or until thickened.
9. Fold in the thyme leaves and sprinkle with salt and ground black pepper. Stir to mix well.
10. When the cooking of the duck is complete, glaze the duck with a quarter of the cherry sauce, then air fry for another 4 minutes.
11. Flip the duck and glaze with another quarter of the cherry sauce. Air fry for an additional 3 minutes.
12. Transfer the duck on a large plate and serve with remaining cherry sauce.

China Spicy Turkey Thighs

Prep time: 10 minutes | Cook time: 25 minutes | Serves 6

2 pounds (907 g) turkey thighs
1 teaspoon Chinese five-spice powder
¼ teaspoon Sichuan pepper
1 teaspoon pink Himalayan salt
1 tablespoon Chinese rice vinegar
1 tablespoon mustard
1 tablespoon chili sauce
2 tablespoons soy sauce
Cooking spray

1. Spritz the air fryer basket with cooking spray.
2. Rub the turkey thighs with five-spice powder, Sichuan pepper, and salt on a clean work surface.
3. Put the turkey thighs in the basket and spritz with cooking spray.
4. Put the air fryer basket on the baking pan and slide into Rack Position 2, select Air Fry, set temperature to 360ºF (182ºC) and set time to 22 minutes.
5. Flip the thighs at least three times during the cooking.
6. When cooking is complete, the thighs should be well browned.
7. Meanwhile, heat the remaining ingredients in a saucepan over medium-high heat. Cook for 3 minutes or until the sauce is thickened and reduces to two thirds.
8. Transfer the thighs onto a plate and baste with sauce before serving.

Rosemary Turkey Scotch Eggs

Prep time: 15 minutes | Cook time: 12 minutes | Serves 4

1 egg
1 cup panko bread crumbs
½ teaspoon rosemary
1 pound (454 g) ground turkey
4 hard-boiled eggs, peeled
Salt and ground black pepper, to taste
Cooking spray

1. Spritz the air fryer basket with cooking spray.
2. Whisk the egg with salt in a bowl. Combine the bread crumbs with rosemary in a shallow dish.
3. Stir the ground turkey with salt and ground black pepper in a separate large bowl, then divide the ground turkey into four portions.
4. Wrap each hard-boiled egg with a portion of ground turkey. Dredge in the whisked egg, then roll over the breadcrumb mixture.
5. Place the wrapped eggs in the basket and spritz with cooking spray.
6. Put the air fryer basket on the baking pan and slide into Rack Position 2, select Air Fry, set temperature to 400ºF (205ºC) and set time to 12 minutes.
7. Flip the eggs halfway through.
8. When cooking is complete, the scotch eggs should be golden brown and crunchy.
9. Serve immediately.

Duck Breasts with Balsamic Glaze

Prep time: 5 minutes | Cook time: 13 minutes | Serves 4

4 (6-ounce / 170-g) skin-on duck breasts
1 teaspoon salt
¼ cup orange marmalade
1 tablespoon white balsamic vinegar
¾ teaspoon ground black pepper

1. Cut 10 slits into the skin of the duck breasts, then sprinkle with salt on both sides.
2. Place the breasts in the air fryer basket, skin side up.
3. Put the air fryer basket on the baking pan and slide into Rack Position 2, select Air Fry, set temperature to 400ºF (205ºC) and set time to 10 minutes.
4. Meanwhile, combine the remaining ingredients in a small bowl. Stir to mix well.
5. When cooking is complete, brush the duck skin with the marmalade mixture. Flip the breast and air fry for 3 more minutes or until the skin is crispy and the breast is well browned.
6. Serve immediately.

Thai Game Hens with Cucumber Salad

Prep time: 25 minutes | Cook time: 25 minutes | Serves 6

2 (1¼-pound / 567-g) Cornish game hens, giblets discarded
1 tablespoon fish sauce
6 tablespoons chopped fresh cilantro
2 teaspoons lime zest
1 teaspoon ground coriander
2 garlic cloves, minced
2 tablespoons packed light brown sugar
2 teaspoons vegetable oil

Salt and ground black pepper, to taste
1 English cucumber, halved lengthwise and sliced thin
1 Thai chile, stemmed, deseeded, and minced
2 tablespoons chopped dry-roasted peanuts
1 small shallot, sliced thinly
1 tablespoon lime juice
Lime wedges, for serving
Cooking spray

1. Arrange a game hen on a clean work surface, remove the backbone with kitchen shears, then pound the hen breast to flat. Cut the breast in half. Repeat with the remaining game hen.
2. Loose the breast and thigh skin with your fingers, then pat the game hens dry and pierce about 10 holes into the fat deposits of the hens. Tuck the wings under the hens.
3. Combine 2 teaspoons of fish sauce, ¼ cup of cilantro, lime zest, coriander, garlic, 4 teaspoons of sugar, 1 teaspoon of vegetable oil, ½ teaspoon of salt, and ⅛ teaspoon of ground black pepper in a small bowl. Stir to mix well.
4. Rub the fish sauce mixture under the breast and thigh skin of the game hens, then let sit for 10 minutes to marinate.
5. Spritz the air fryer basket with cooking spray.
6. Arrange the marinated game hens in the basket, skin side down.
7. Put the air fryer basket on the baking pan and slide into Rack Position 2, select Air Fry, set temperature to 400°F (205°C) and set time to 25 minutes.
8. Flip the game hens halfway through the cooking time.
9. When cooking is complete, the hen skin should be golden brown and the internal temperature of the hens should read at least 165°F (74°C).
10. Meanwhile, combine all the remaining ingredients, except for the lime wedges, in a large bowl and sprinkle with salt and black pepper. Toss to mix well.
11. Transfer the fried hens on a large plate, then sit the salad aside and squeeze the lime wedges over before serving.

Peach and Cherry Chicken

Prep time: 8 minutes | Cook time: 15 minutes | Serves 4

⅓ cup peach preserves
1 teaspoon ground rosemary
½ teaspoon black pepper
½ teaspoon salt
½ teaspoon marjoram
1 teaspoon light

olive oil
1 pound (454 g) boneless chicken breasts, cut in 1½-inch chunks
1 (10-ounce / 284-g) package frozen dark cherries, thawed and drained
Cooking spray

1. In a medium bowl, mix peach preserves, rosemary, pepper, salt, marjoram, and olive oil.
2. Stir in chicken chunks and toss to coat well with the preserve mixture.
3. Spritz the baking pan with cooking spray and lay chicken chunks in the pan.
4. Slide the baking pan into Rack Position 1, select Convection Bake, set the temperature to 400°F (205°C) and set the time to 15 minutes.
5. After 7 minutes, remove from the oven and flip the chicken chunks. Return the pan to the oven and continue cooking.
6. When cooking is complete, the chicken should no longer pink and the juices should run clear.
7. Scatter the cherries over and cook for an additional minute to heat cherries.
8. Serve immediately.

Cheesy Turkey Burgers

Prep time: 10 minutes | Cook time: 25 minutes | Serves 4

2 medium yellow onions	mustard
1 tablespoon olive oil	2 teaspoons Worcestershire sauce
1½ teaspoons kosher salt, divided	4 slices sharp Cheddar cheese
1¼ pound (567 g) ground turkey	(about 4 ounces / 113 g in total)
⅓ cup mayonnaise	4 hamburger buns,
1 tablespoon Dijon	sliced

1. Trim the onions and cut them in half through the root. Cut one of the halves in half. Grate one quarter. Place the grated onion in a large bowl. Thinly slice the remaining onions and place in a medium bowl with the oil and ½ teaspoon of kosher salt. Toss to coat. Place the onions in a single layer in the baking pan.
2. Slide the baking pan into Rack Position 2, select Roast, set temperature to 350ºF (180ºC), and set time to 10 minutes.
3. While the onions are cooking, add the turkey to the grated onion. Add the remaining kosher salt, mayonnaise, mustard, and Worcestershire sauce. Mix just until combined, being careful not to overwork the turkey. Divide the mixture into 4 patties, each about ¾-inch thick.
4. When cooking is complete, remove from the oven. Move the onions to one side of the pan and place the burgers on the pan. Poke your finger into the center of each burger to make a deep indentation.
5. Select Convection Broil, set temperature to High, and set time to 12 minutes.
6. After 6 minutes, remove the pan. Turn the burgers and stir the onions. Return the pan to the oven and continue cooking. After about 4 minutes, remove the pan and place the cheese slices on the burgers. Return the pan to the oven and continue cooking for about 1 minute, or until the cheese is melted and the center of the burgers has reached at least 165ºF (74ºC) on a meat thermometer.
7. When cooking is complete, remove from the oven. Loosely cover the burgers with foil.
8. Lay out the buns, cut-side up, on the oven rack. Select Convection Broil; set temperature to High, and set time to 3 minutes. Check the buns after 2 minutes; they should be lightly browned.
9. Remove the buns from the oven. Assemble the burgers and serve.

Turkey and Bean Stuffed Peppers

Prep time: 20 minutes | Cook time: 15 minutes | Serves 4

½ pound (227 g) lean ground turkey	1 cup mild salsa
4 medium bell peppers	1¼ teaspoons chili powder
1 (15-ounce / 425-g) can black beans, drained and rinsed	1 teaspoon salt
	½ teaspoon ground cumin
1 cup shredded Cheddar cheese	½ teaspoon freshly ground black pepper
1 cup cooked long-grain brown rice	Chopped fresh cilantro, for garnish
	Cooking spray

1. In a large skillet over medium-high heat, cook the turkey, breaking it up with a spoon, until browned, about 5 minutes. Drain off any excess fat.
2. Cut about ½ inch off the tops of the peppers and then cut in half lengthwise. Remove and discard the seeds and set the peppers aside.
3. In a large bowl, combine the browned turkey, black beans, Cheddar cheese, rice, salsa, chili powder, salt, cumin, and black pepper. Spoon the mixture into the bell peppers.
4. Lightly spray the basket with cooking spray. Arrange the bell peppers in the pan.
5. Put the air fryer basket on the baking pan and slide into Rack Position 2, select Air Fry, set the temperature to 350ºF (180ºC) and set the time to 15 minutes.
6. When cooking is complete, the stuffed peppers should be lightly charred and wilted.
7. Allow to cool for a few minutes and garnish with cilantro before serving.

Chicken Thighs with Radish Slaw

Prep time: 10 minutes | Cook time: 27 minutes | Serves 4

4 bone-in, skin-on chicken thighs
1½ teaspoon kosher salt, divided
1 tablespoon smoked paprika
½ teaspoon granulated garlic
½ teaspoon dried oregano
¼ teaspoon freshly ground black pepper

3 cups shredded cabbage
½ small red onion, thinly sliced
4 large radishes, julienned
3 tablespoons red wine vinegar
2 tablespoons olive oil
Cooking spray

1. Salt the chicken thighs on both sides with 1 teaspoon of kosher salt. In a small bowl, combine the paprika, garlic, oregano, and black pepper. Sprinkle half this mixture over the skin sides of the thighs. Spritz the baking pan with cooking spray and place the thighs skin-side down in the pan. Sprinkle the remaining spice mixture over the other sides of the chicken pieces.
2. Slide the baking pan into Rack Position 2, select Roast, set temperature to 375ºF (190ºC), and set time to 27 minutes.
3. After 10 minutes, remove from the oven and turn over the chicken thighs. Return to the oven and continue cooking.
4. While the chicken cooks, place the cabbage, onion, and radishes in a large bowl. Sprinkle with the remaining kosher salt, vinegar, and olive oil. Toss to coat.
5. After another 9 to 10 minutes, remove from the oven and place the chicken thighs on a cutting board. Place the cabbage mixture in the pan and toss with the chicken fat and spices.
6. Spread the cabbage in an even layer on the pan and place the chicken on it, skin-side up. Return the pan to the oven and continue cooking. Roast for another 7 to 8 minutes.
7. When cooking is complete, the cabbage is just becoming tender. Remove from the oven. Taste and adjust the seasoning if necessary. Serve.

Chicken with Potatoes and Corn

Prep time: 10 minutes | Cook time: 25 minutes | Serves 4

4 bone-in, skin-on chicken thighs
2 teaspoons kosher salt, divided
1 cup Bisquick baking mix
½ cup butter, melted, divided
1 pound (454 g) small red potatoes,

quartered
3 ears corn, shucked and cut into rounds 1- to 1½-inches thick
1/3 cup heavy whipping cream
½ teaspoon freshly ground black pepper

1. Sprinkle the chicken on all sides with 1 teaspoon of kosher salt. Place the baking mix in a shallow dish. Brush the thighs on all sides with ¼ cup of butter, then dredge them in the baking mix, coating them all on sides. Place the chicken in the center of the baking pan.
2. Place the potatoes in a large bowl with 2 tablespoons of butter and toss to coat. Place them on one side of the chicken on the pan.
3. Place the corn in a medium bowl and drizzle with the remaining butter. Sprinkle with ¼ teaspoon of kosher salt and toss to coat. Place on the pan on the other side of the chicken.
4. Slide the baking pan into Rack Position 2, select Roast, set temperature to 375ºF (190ºC), and set time to 25 minutes.
5. After 20 minutes, remove from the oven and put the potatoes back to the bowl. Return the pan to oven and continue cooking.
6. As the chicken continues cooking, add the cream, black pepper, and remaining kosher salt to the potatoes. Lightly mash the potatoes with a potato masher.
7. When cooking is complete, the corn should be tender and the chicken cooked through, reading 165ºF (74ºC) on a meat thermometer. Remove from the oven. Serve the chicken with the smashed potatoes and corn on the side.

Nutty Chicken Tenders

Prep time: 5 minutes | Cook time: 12 minutes | Serves 4

1 pound (454 g) chicken tenders
1 teaspoon kosher salt
1 teaspoon black pepper
½ teaspoon smoked
paprika
¼ cup coarse mustard
2 tablespoons honey
1 cup finely crushed pecans

1. Preheat the air fryer oven to 350ºF (177ºC).
2. Place the chicken in a large bowl. Sprinkle with the salt, pepper, and paprika. Toss until the chicken is coated with the spices. Add the mustard and honey and toss until the chicken is coated.
3. Place the pecans on a plate. Working with one piece of chicken at a time, roll the chicken in the pecans until both sides are coated. Lightly brush off any loose pecans. Place the chicken in a baking pan.
4. Slide the baking pan into Rack Position 1, select Convection Bake and set time to 12 minutes, or until the chicken is cooked through and the pecans are golden brown.
5. Serve warm.

Balsamic Chicken Breast Roast

Prep time: 35 minutes | Cook time: 40 minutes | Serves 2

¼ cup balsamic vinegar
2 teaspoons dried oregano
2 garlic cloves, minced
1 tablespoon olive oil
⅛ teaspoon salt
½ teaspoon freshly ground black pepper
2 (4-ounce / 113-g) boneless, skinless, chicken-breast halves
Cooking spray

1. In a small bowl, add the vinegar, oregano, garlic, olive oil, salt, and pepper. Mix to combine.
2. Put the chicken in a resealable plastic bag. Pour the vinegar mixture in the bag with the chicken, seal the bag, and shake to coat the chicken. Refrigerate for 30 minutes to marinate.
3. Spritz the baking pan with cooking spray. Put the chicken in the prepared baking pan and pour the marinade over the chicken.
4. Slide the baking pan into Rack Position 1, select Convection Bake, set temperature to 400ºF (205ºC) and set time to 40 minutes.
5. After 20 minutes, remove the pan from the oven. Flip the chicken. Return the pan to the oven and continue cooking.
6. When cooking is complete, the internal temperature of the chicken should registers at least 165ºF (74ºC).
7. Let sit for 5 minutes, then serve.

Creole Hens

Prep time: 10 minutes | Cook time: 40 minutes | Serves 4

½ tablespoon Creole seasoning
½ tablespoon garlic powder
½ tablespoon onion powder
½ tablespoon freshly
ground black pepper
½ tablespoon paprika
2 tablespoons olive oil
2 Cornish hens
Cooking spray

1. Spritz the air fryer basket with cooking spray.
2. In a small bowl, mix the Creole seasoning, garlic powder, onion powder, pepper, and paprika.
3. Pat the Cornish hens dry and brush each hen all over with the olive oil. Rub each hen with the seasoning mixture. Place the Cornish hens in the basket.
4. Put the air fryer basket on the baking pan and slide into Rack Position 2, select Air Fry, set the temperature to 375ºF (190ºC) and set the time to 30 minutes.
5. After 15 minutes, remove from the oven. Flip the hens over and baste it with any drippings collected in the bottom drawer of the oven. Return to the oven and continue cooking.
6. When cooking is complete, a thermometer inserted into the thickest part of the hens should reach at least 165ºF (74ºC).
7. Let the hens rest for 10 minutes before carving.

Chicken Ciabatta Sandwiches

Prep time: 12 minutes | Cook time: 13 minutes | Serves 4

2 (8-ounce / 227-g) boneless, skinless chicken breasts
1 teaspoon kosher salt, divided
1 cup all-purpose flour
1 teaspoon Italian seasoning
2 large eggs
2 tablespoons plain yogurt
2 cups panko bread crumbs
1⅓ cups grated Parmesan cheese, divided
2 tablespoons olive oil
4 ciabatta rolls, split in half
½ cup marinara sauce
½ cup shredded Mozzarella cheese

1. Lay the chicken breasts on a cutting board and cut each one in half parallel to the board so you have 4 fairly even, flat fillets. Place a piece of plastic wrap over the chicken pieces and use a rolling pin to gently pound them to an even thickness, about ½-inch thick. Season the chicken on both sides with ½ teaspoon of kosher salt.
2. Place the flour on a plate and add the remaining kosher salt and the Italian seasoning. Mix with a fork to distribute evenly. In a wide bowl, whisk together the eggs with the yogurt. In a small bowl combine the panko, 1 cup of Parmesan cheese, and olive oil. Place this in a shallow bowl.
3. Lightly dredge both sides of the chicken pieces in the seasoned flour, and then dip them in the egg wash to coat completely, letting the excess drip off. Finally, dredge the chicken in the bread crumbs. Carefully place the breaded chicken pieces in the basket.
4. Put the air fryer basket on the baking pan and slide into Rack Position 2, select Air Fry, set temperature to 375°F (190°C), and set time to 10 minutes.
5. After 5 minutes, remove from the oven. Carefully turn the chicken over. Return to the oven and continue cooking. When cooking is complete, remove from the oven.
6. Unfold the rolls on the basket and spread each half with 1 tablespoon of marinara sauce. Place a chicken breast piece on the bottoms of the buns and sprinkle the remaining Parmesan cheese over the chicken pieces. Divide the Mozzarella among the top halves of the buns.
7. Select Convection Broil, set temperature to High, and set time to 3 minutes.
8. Check the sandwiches halfway through. When cooking is complete, the Mozzarella cheese should be melted and bubbly.
9. Remove from the oven and close the sandwiches and serve.

Glazed Chicken Drumsticks

Prep time: 5 minutes | Cook time: 20 minutes | Serves 2

4 chicken drumsticks
3 tablespoons soy sauce
2 tablespoons brown sugar
1 teaspoon minced garlic
1 teaspoon minced fresh ginger
1 teaspoon toasted sesame oil
½ teaspoon red pepper flakes
½ teaspoon kosher salt
½ teaspoon black pepper

1. Preheat the air fryer oven to 400°F (204°C).
2. Line a round baking pan with aluminum foil. (If you don't do this, you'll either end up scrubbing forever or throwing out the pan.) Arrange the drumsticks in the prepared pan.
3. In a medium bowl, stir together the soy sauce, brown sugar, garlic, ginger, sesame oil, red pepper flakes, salt, and black pepper. Pour the sauce over the drumsticks and toss to coat.
4. Slide the baking pan into Rack Position 1, select Convection Bake and set time to 20 minutes, turning the drumsticks halfway through the cooking time. Use a meat thermometer to ensure the chicken has reached an internal temperature of 165°F (74°C).
5. Cool for 5 minutes before serving.

Rosemary Turkey Breast

Prep time: 2 hours 20 minutes | Cook time: 30 minutes | Serves 6

½ teaspoon dried rosemary
2 minced garlic cloves
2 teaspoons salt
1 teaspoon ground black pepper
¼ cup olive oil
2½ pounds (1.1 kg) turkey breast
¼ cup pure maple syrup
1 tablespoon stone-ground brown mustard
1 tablespoon melted vegan butter

1. Combine the rosemary, garlic, salt, ground black pepper, and olive oil in a large bowl. Stir to mix well.
2. Dunk the turkey breast in the mixture and wrap the bowl in plastic. Refrigerate for 2 hours to marinate.
3. Remove the bowl from the refrigerator and let sit for half an hour before cooking.
4. Spritz the air fryer basket with cooking spray.
5. Remove the turkey from the marinade and place in the basket.
6. Put the air fryer basket on the baking pan and slide into Rack Position 2, select Air Fry, set temperature to 400ºF (205ºC) and set time to 20 minutes.
7. Flip the breast halfway through.
8. When cooking is complete, the breast should be well browned.
9. Meanwhile, combine the remaining ingredients in a small bowl. Stir to mix well.
10. Pour half of the butter mixture over the turkey breast in the oven and air fry for 10 more minutes. Flip the breast and pour the remaining half of butter mixture over halfway through.
11. Transfer the turkey on a plate and slice to serve.

Golden Chicken Fries

Prep time: 20 minutes | Cook time: 6 minutes | Serves 4 to 6

1 pound (454 g) chicken tenders, cut into about ½-inch-wide strips
Salt, to taste
¼ cup all-purpose flour
2 eggs
¾ cup panko bread crumbs
¾ cup crushed organic nacho cheese tortilla chips
Cooking spray

Seasonings:
½ teaspoon garlic powder
1 tablespoon chili powder
½ teaspoon onion powder
1 teaspoon ground cumin

1. Stir together all seasonings in a small bowl and set aside.
2. Sprinkle the chicken with salt. Place strips in a large bowl and sprinkle with 1 tablespoon of the seasoning mix. Stir well to distribute seasonings.
3. Add flour to chicken and stir well to coat all sides.
4. Beat eggs in a separate bowl.
5. In a shallow dish, combine the panko, crushed chips, and the remaining 2 teaspoons of seasoning mix.
6. Dip chicken strips in eggs, then roll in crumbs. Mist with oil or cooking spray. Arrange the chicken strips in a single layer in the basket.
7. Put the air fryer basket on the baking pan and slide into Rack Position 2, select Air Fry, set the temperature to 400ºF (205ºC) and set the time to 6 minutes.
8. After 4 minutes, remove from the oven. Flip the strips with tongs. Return to the oven and continue cooking.
9. When cooking is complete, the chicken should be crispy and its juices should be run clear.
10. Allow to cool under room temperature before serving.

Chicken Skewers with Corn Salad

Prep time: 17 minutes | Cook time: 10 minutes | Serves 4

1 pound (454 g) boneless, skinless chicken breast, cut into 1½-inch chunks
1 green bell pepper, deseeded and cut into 1-inch pieces
1 red bell pepper, deseeded and cut into 1-inch pieces
1 large onion, cut into large chunks
2 tablespoons fajita seasoning
3 tablespoons vegetable oil, divided
2 teaspoons kosher salt, divided
2 cups corn, drained
¼ teaspoon granulated garlic
1 teaspoon freshly squeezed lime juice
1 tablespoon mayonnaise
3 tablespoons grated Parmesan cheese

Special Equipment:
12 wooden skewers, soaked in water for at least 30 minutes

1. Place the chicken, bell peppers, and onion in a large bowl. Add the fajita seasoning, 2 tablespoons of vegetable oil, and 1½ teaspoons of kosher salt. Toss to coat evenly.
2. Alternate the chicken and vegetables on the skewers, making about 12 skewers.
3. Place the corn in a medium bowl and add the remaining vegetable oil. Add the remaining kosher salt and the garlic, and toss to coat. Place the corn in an even layer in the baking pan and place the skewers on top.
4. Slide the baking pan into Rack Position 2, select Roast, set temperature to 375ºF (190ºC), and set time to 10 minutes.
5. After about 5 minutes, remove from the oven and turn the skewers. Return to the oven and continue cooking.
6. When cooking is complete, remove from the oven. Place the skewers on a platter. Put the corn back to the bowl and combine with the lime juice, mayonnaise, and Parmesan cheese. Stir to mix well. Serve the skewers with the corn.

Braised Chicken with Hot Peppers

Prep time: 10 minutes | Cook time: 27 minutes | Serves 4

4 bone-in, skin-on chicken thighs (about 1½ pounds / 680 g)
1½ teaspoon kosher salt, divided
1 link sweet Italian sausage (about 4 ounces / 113 g), whole
8 ounces (227 g) miniature bell peppers, halved and deseeded
1 small onion, thinly sliced
2 garlic cloves, minced
1 tablespoon olive oil
4 hot pickled cherry peppers, deseeded and quartered, along with 2 tablespoons pickling liquid from the jar
¼ cup chicken stock
Cooking spray

1. Salt the chicken thighs on both sides with 1 teaspoon of kosher salt. Spritz the baking pan with cooking spray and place the thighs skin-side down on the pan. Add the sausage.
2. Slide the baking pan into Rack Position 2, select Roast, set temperature to 375ºF (190ºC), and set time to 27 minutes.
3. While the chicken and sausage cook, place the bell peppers, onion, and garlic in a large bowl. Sprinkle with the remaining kosher salt and add the olive oil. Toss to coat.
4. After 10 minutes, remove from the oven and flip the chicken thighs and sausage. Add the pepper mixture to the pan. Return the pan to the oven and continue cooking.
5. After another 10 minutes, remove from the oven and add the pickled peppers, pickling liquid, and stock. Stir the pickled peppers into the peppers and onion. Return the pan to the oven and continue cooking.
6. When cooking is complete, the peppers and onion should be soft and the chicken should read 165ºF (74ºC) on a meat thermometer. Remove from the oven. Slice the sausage into thin pieces and stir it into the pepper mixture. Spoon the peppers over four plates. Top with a chicken thigh.

Chicken Shawarma

Prep time: 10 minutes | Cook time: 18 minutes | Serves 4

1½ pounds (680 g) boneless, skinless chicken thighs
1¼ teaspoon kosher salt, divided
2 tablespoons plus 1 teaspoon olive oil, divided
⅔ cup plus 2 tablespoons plain Greek yogurt, divided
2 tablespoons freshly squeezed lemon juice (about 1 medium lemon)
4 garlic cloves, minced, divided
1 tablespoon Shawarma Seasoning
4 pita breads, cut in half
2 cups cherry tomatoes
½ small cucumber, peeled, deseeded, and chopped
1 tablespoon chopped fresh parsley

1. Sprinkle the chicken thighs on both sides with 1 teaspoon of kosher salt. Place in a resealable plastic bag and set aside while you make the marinade.
2. In a small bowl, mix 2 tablespoons of olive oil, 2 tablespoons of yogurt, the lemon juice, 3 garlic cloves, and Shawarma Seasoning until thoroughly combined. Pour the marinade over the chicken. Seal the bag, squeezing out as much air as possible. And massage the chicken to coat it with the sauce. Set aside.
3. Wrap 2 pita breads each in two pieces of aluminum foil and place in the baking pan.
4. Slide the baking pan into Rack Position 1, select Convection Bake, set temperature to 300ºF (150ºC), and set time to 6 minutes.
5. After 3 minutes, remove the pan from the oven and turn over the foil packets. Return the pan to the oven and continue cooking. When cooking is complete, remove the pan from the oven and place the foil-wrapped pitas on the top of the oven to keep warm.
6. Remove the chicken from the marinade, letting the excess drip off into the bag. Place them in the baking pan. Arrange the tomatoes around the sides of the chicken. Discard the marinade.
7. Slide the baking pan into Rack Position 2, select Convection Broil, set temperature to High, and set time to 12 minutes.
8. After 6 minutes, remove the pan from the oven and turn over the chicken. Return the pan to the oven and continue cooking.
9. Wrap the cucumber in a paper towel to remove as much moisture as possible. Place them in a small bowl. Add the remaining yogurt, kosher salt, olive oil, garlic clove, and parsley. Whisk until combined.
10. When cooking is complete, the chicken should be browned, crisp along its edges, and sizzling. Remove from the oven and place the chicken on a cutting board. Cut each thigh into several pieces. Unwrap the pitas. Spread a tablespoon of sauce into a pita half. Add some chicken and add 2 roasted tomatoes. Serve.

Fried Buffalo Chicken Taquitos

Prep time: 15 minutes | Cook time: 8 minutes | Serves 6

8 ounces (227 g) fat-free cream cheese, softened
⅛ cup Buffalo sauce
2 cups shredded
cooked chicken
12 (7-inch) low-carb flour tortillas
Olive oil spray

1. Preheat the air fryer oven to 360ºF (182ºC). Spray the air fryer basket lightly with olive oil spray.
2. In a large bowl, mix together the cream cheese and Buffalo sauce until well combined. Add the chicken and stir until combined.
3. Place the tortillas on a clean work surface. Spoon 2 to 3 tablespoons of the chicken mixture in a thin line down the center of each tortilla. Roll up the tortillas.
4. Place the tortillas in the air fryer basket, seam-side down. Spray each tortilla lightly with olive oil spray. You may need to cook the taquitos in batches.
5. Place the air fryer basket onto the baking pan and slide into Rack Position 2, select Air Fry and set time to 8 minutes, or until golden brown.
6. Serve hot.

Celery Chicken

Prep time: 10 minutes | Cook time: 15 minutes | Serves 4

½ cup soy sauce
2 tablespoons hoisin sauce
4 teaspoons minced garlic
1 teaspoon freshly ground black pepper
8 boneless, skinless chicken tenderloins
1 cup chopped celery
1 medium red bell pepper, diced
Olive oil spray

1. Preheat the air fryer oven to 375ºF (191ºC). Spray the air fryer basket lightly with olive oil spray.
2. In a large bowl, mix together the soy sauce, hoisin sauce, garlic, and black pepper to make a marinade. Add the chicken, celery, and bell pepper and toss to coat.
3. Shake the excess marinade off the chicken, place it and the vegetables in the air fryer basket, and lightly spray with olive oil spray. Reserve the remaining marinade.
4. Place the air fryer basket onto the baking pan and slide into Rack Position 2, select Air Fry and set time to 8 minutes.
5. Turn the chicken over and brush with some of the remaining marinade. Air fry for an additional 5 to 7 minutes, or until the chicken reaches an internal temperature of at least 165ºF (74ºC). Rest for 5 minutes before serving.

Fajita Chicken Strips

Prep time: 10 minutes | Cook time: 15 minutes | Serves 4

1 pound (454 g) boneless, skinless chicken tenderloins, cut into strips
3 bell peppers, any color, cut into chunks
1 onion, cut into chunks
1 tablespoon olive oil
1 tablespoon fajita seasoning mix
Cooking spray

1. Preheat the air fryer oven to 370ºF (188ºC).
2. In a large bowl, mix together the chicken, bell peppers, onion, olive oil, and fajita seasoning mix until completely coated.

3. Spray the air fryer basket lightly with cooking spray.
4. Place the chicken and vegetables in the air fryer basket and lightly spray with cooking spray.
5. Place the air fryer basket onto the baking pan and slide into Rack Position 2, select Air Fry and set time to 7 minutes.
6. Shake the basket and air fry for an additional 5 to 8 minutes, until the chicken is cooked through and the veggies are starting to char.
7. Serve warm.

Lemon Parmesan Chicken

Prep time: 10 minutes | Cook time: 20 minutes | Serves 4

1 egg
2 tablespoons lemon juice
2 teaspoons minced garlic
½ teaspoon salt
½ teaspoon freshly ground black pepper
4 boneless, skinless chicken breasts, thin cut
Olive oil spray
½ cup whole-wheat bread crumbs
¼ cup grated Parmesan cheese

1. In a medium bowl, whisk together the egg, lemon juice, garlic, salt, and pepper. Add the chicken breasts, cover, and refrigerate for up to 1 hour.
2. In a shallow bowl, combine the bread crumbs and Parmesan cheese.
3. Preheat the air fryer oven to 360ºF (182ºC). Spray the air fryer basket lightly with olive oil spray.
4. Remove the chicken breasts from the egg mixture, then dredge them in the bread crumb mixture, and place in the air fryer basket in a single layer. Lightly spray the chicken breasts with olive oil spray.
5. Place the air fryer basket onto the baking pan and slide into Rack Position 2, select Air Fry and set time to 8 minutes.
6. Flip the chicken, lightly spray with olive oil spray, and air fry until the chicken reaches an internal temperature of 165ºF (74ºC), for an additional 7 to 12 minutes.
7. Serve warm.

Cajun Turkey

Prep time: 10 minutes | Cook time: 30 minutes | Serves 4

2 pounds (907 g) turkey thighs, skinless and boneless
1 red onion, sliced
2 bell peppers, sliced
1 habanero pepper, minced
1 carrot, sliced
1 tablespoon Cajun seasoning mix
1 tablespoon fish sauce
2 cups chicken broth
Nonstick cooking spray

1. Preheat the air fryer oven to 360ºF (182ºC).
2. Spritz the bottom and sides of a baking dish with nonstick cooking spray.
3. Arrange the turkey thighs in the baking dish. Add the onion, peppers, and carrot. Sprinkle with Cajun seasoning. Add the fish sauce and chicken broth.
4. Place the baking dish into Rack Position 1, select Convection Bake and set time to 30 minutes, or until cooked through. Serve warm.

Chicken and Sweet Potato Curry

Prep time: 10 minutes | Cook time: 20 minutes | Serves 4

1 pound (454 g) boneless, skinless chicken thighs
1 teaspoon kosher salt, divided
¼ cup unsalted butter, melted
1 tablespoon curry
powder
2 medium sweet potatoes, peeled and cut in 1-inch cubes
12 ounces (340 g) Brussels sprouts, halved

1. Sprinkle the chicken thighs with ½ teaspoon of kosher salt. Place them in the single layer in the baking pan.
2. In a small bowl, stir together the butter and curry powder.
3. Place the sweet potatoes and Brussels sprouts in a large bowl. Drizzle half the curry butter over the vegetables and add the remaining kosher salt. Toss to coat. Transfer the vegetables to the baking pan and place in a single layer around the chicken. Brush half of the remaining curry butter over the chicken.

4. Slide the baking pan into Rack Position 2, select Roast, set temperature to 400ºF (205ºC), and set time to 20 minutes.
5. After 10 minutes, remove from the oven and turn over the chicken thighs. Baste them with the remaining curry butter. Return to the oven and continue cooking.
6. Cooking is complete when the sweet potatoes are tender and the chicken is cooked through and reads 165ºF (74ºC) on a meat thermometer.

Super Lemon Chicken

Prep time: 5 minutes | Cook time: 35 minutes | Serves 6

3 (8-ounce / 227-g) boneless, skinless chicken breasts, halved, rinsed
1 cup dried bread crumbs
¼ cup olive oil
¼ cup chicken broth
Zest of 1 lemon
3 medium garlic cloves, minced
½ cup fresh lemon juice
½ cup water
¼ cup minced fresh oregano
1 medium lemon, cut into wedges
¼ cup minced fresh parsley, divided
Cooking spray

1. Pour the bread crumbs in a shadow dish, then roll the chicken breasts in the bread crumbs to coat.
2. Spritz a skillet with cooking spray, and brown the coated chicken breasts over medium heat about 3 minutes on each side. Transfer the browned chicken to the baking pan.
3. In a small bowl, combine the remaining ingredients, except the lemon and parsley. Pour the sauce over the chicken.
4. Slide the baking pan into Rack Position 1, select Convection Bake, set the temperature to 325ºF (163ºC) and set the time to 30 minutes.
5. After 15 minutes, remove the pan from the oven. Flip the breasts. Return the pan to the oven and continue cooking.
6. When cooking is complete, the chicken should no longer pink.
7. Transfer to a serving platter, and spoon the sauce over the chicken. Garnish with the lemon and parsley.

Dill Chicken Strips

Prep time: 15 minutes | Cook time: 10 minutes | Serves 4

2 whole boneless, skinless chicken breasts, halved lengthwise	potato chips 1 tablespoon dried dill weed
1 cup Italian dressing	1 tablespoon garlic powder
3 cups finely crushed	1 large egg, beaten Cooking spray

1. In a large resealable bag, combine the chicken and Italian dressing. Seal the bag and refrigerate to marinate at least 1 hour.
2. In a shallow dish, stir together the potato chips, dill, and garlic powder. Place the beaten egg in a second shallow dish.
3. Remove the chicken from the marinade. Roll the chicken pieces in the egg and the potato chip mixture, coating thoroughly.
4. Preheat the air fryer oven to 325°F (163°C). Line the air fryer basket with parchment paper.
5. Place the coated chicken on the parchment and spritz with cooking spray.
6. Place the air fryer basket onto the baking pan and slide into Rack Position 2, select Air Fry and set time to 10 minutes, flipping the chicken and spritzing it with cooking spray halfway through, or until the outsides are crispy and the insides are no longer pink. Serve immediately.

Herbed Hens

Prep time: 2 hours 15 minutes | Cook time: 30 minutes | Serves 8

4 (1¼-pound / 567-g) Cornish hens, giblets removed, split lengthwise	½ teaspoon celery seeds
2 cups white wine, divided	½ teaspoon poultry seasoning
2 garlic cloves, minced	½ teaspoon paprika
1 small onion, minced	½ teaspoon dried oregano
	¼ teaspoon freshly ground black pepper

1. Place the hens, cavity side up, in the baking pan. Pour 1½ cups of the wine over the hens. Set aside.
2. In a shallow bowl, combine the garlic, onion, celery seeds, poultry seasoning, paprika, oregano, and pepper. Sprinkle half of the combined seasonings over the cavity of each split half. Cover and refrigerate. Allow the hens to marinate for 2 hours.
3. Transfer the hens to the pan. Slide the baking pan into Rack Position 1, select Convection Bake, set temperature to 350°F (180°C) and set time to 90 minutes.
4. Flip the breast halfway through and remove the skin. Pour the remaining ½ cup of wine over the top, and sprinkle with the remaining seasonings.
5. When cooking is complete, the inner temperature of the hens should be at least 165°F (74°C). Transfer the hens to a serving platter and serve hot.

Blackened Chicken Breasts

Prep time: 10 minutes | Cook time: 20 minutes | Serves 4

1 large egg, beaten	breasts (about 1 pound / 454 g each), halved
¾ cup Blackened seasoning	
2 whole boneless, skinless chicken	Cooking spray

1. Preheat the air fryer oven to 360°F (182°C). Line the air fryer basket with parchment paper.
2. Place the beaten egg in one shallow bowl and the Blackened seasoning in another shallow bowl.
3. One at a time, dip the chicken pieces in the beaten egg and the Blackened seasoning, coating thoroughly.
4. Place the chicken pieces on the parchment and spritz with cooking spray.
5. Place the air fryer basket onto the baking pan and slide into Rack Position 2, select Air Fry and set time to 20 minutes. Flip the chicken and spritz it with cooking spray halfway through, or until the internal temperature reaches 165°F (74°C) and the chicken is no longer pink inside.
6. Let sit for 5 minutes before serving.

Sweet-and-Sour Drumsticks

Prep time: 5 minutes | Cook time: 24 minutes | Serves 4

6 chicken drumsticks
3 tablespoons lemon juice, divided
3 tablespoons low-sodium soy sauce, divided
1 tablespoon peanut oil
3 tablespoons honey
3 tablespoons brown sugar
2 tablespoons ketchup
¼ cup pineapple juice

1. Preheat the air fryer oven to 350ºF (177ºC).
2. Sprinkle the chicken drumsticks with 1 tablespoon of lemon juice and 1 tablespoon of soy sauce.
3. Place them in a baking pan and drizzle with the peanut oil. Toss to coat.
4. Slide the baking pan into Rack Position 1, select Convection Bake and set time to 18 minutes, or until the chicken is almost done.
5. Meanwhile, in a large bowl, combine the remaining 2 tablespoons of lemon juice, the remaining 2 tablespoons of soy sauce, honey, brown sugar, ketchup, and pineapple juice.
6. Add the cooked chicken to the bowl and stir to coat the chicken well with the sauce.
7. Place the baking pan with the coated chicken back into Rack Position 1 and bake for 6 minutes more, or until the chicken is glazed and registers 165ºF (74ºC) on a meat thermometer.
8. Serve warm.

Crisp Paprika Chicken Drumsticks

Prep time: 5 minutes | Cook time: 25 minutes | Serves 2

2 teaspoons paprika
1 teaspoon packed brown sugar
1 teaspoon garlic powder
½ teaspoon dry mustard
½ teaspoon salt
Pinch pepper
4 (5-ounce / 142-g) chicken drumsticks, trimmed
1 teaspoon vegetable oil
1 scallion, green part only, sliced thin on bias

1. Preheat the air fryer oven to 400ºF (204ºC).
2. Combine paprika, sugar, garlic powder, mustard, salt, and pepper in a bowl. Pat drumsticks dry with paper towels. Using metal skewer, poke 10 to 15 holes in skin of each drumstick. Rub with oil and sprinkle evenly with spice mixture.
3. Arrange the drumsticks in the air fryer basket, spaced evenly apart, alternating ends.
4. Place the air fryer basket onto the baking pan and slide into Rack Position 2, select Air Fry and set time to 25 minutes, or until chicken is crisp and registers 195ºF (91ºC). Flip the chicken halfway through cooking.
5. Transfer chicken to a serving platter, tent loosely with aluminum foil, and let rest for 5 minutes. Sprinkle with scallion and serve.

Mayonnaise-Mustard Chicken

Prep time: 10 minutes | Cook time: 15 minutes | Serves 4

6 tablespoons mayonnaise
2 tablespoons coarse-ground mustard
2 teaspoons honey (optional)
2 teaspoons curry
powder
1 teaspoon kosher salt
1 teaspoon cayenne pepper
1 pound (454 g) chicken tenders

1. Preheat the air fryer oven to 350ºF (177ºC).
2. In a large bowl, whisk together the mayonnaise, mustard, honey (if using), curry powder, salt, and cayenne. Transfer half of the mixture to a serving bowl to serve as a dipping sauce. Add the chicken tenders to the large bowl and toss until well coated. Place the tenders in a baking pan.
3. Slide the baking pan into Rack Position 1, select Convection Bake and set time to 15 minutes. Use a meat thermometer to ensure the chicken has reached an internal temperature of 165ºF (74ºC).
4. Serve the chicken with the dipping sauce.

Fried Chicken Tenders with Veggies

Prep time: 10 minutes | Cook time: 20 minutes | Serves 4

1 pound (454 g) chicken tenders	bread crumbs
1 tablespoon honey	½ teaspoon dried thyme
Pinch salt	1 tablespoon olive oil
Freshly ground black pepper, to taste	2 carrots, sliced
½ cup soft fresh	12 small red potatoes

1. Preheat the air fryer oven to 380°F (193°C).
2. In a medium bowl, toss the chicken tenders with the honey, salt, and pepper.
3. In a shallow bowl, combine the bread crumbs, thyme, and olive oil, and mix.
4. Coat the tenders in the bread crumbs, pressing firmly onto the meat.
5. Place the carrots and potatoes in the air fryer basket and top with the chicken tenders.
6. Place the air fryer basket onto the baking pan and slide into Rack Position 2, select Air Fry and set time to 20 minutes, or until the chicken is cooked to 165°F (74°C) and the vegetables are tender. Shake the basket halfway during the cooking time.
7. Serve warm.

Potato Cheese Crusted Chicken

Prep time: 15 minutes | Cook time: 24 minutes | Serves 4

¼ cup buttermilk	ground black pepper
1 large egg, beaten	2 whole boneless, skinless chicken breasts (about 1 pound / 454 g each), halved
1 cup instant potato flakes	
¼ cup grated Parmesan cheese	
1 teaspoon salt	Cooking spray
½ teaspoon freshly	

1. Preheat the air fryer oven to 325°F (163°C). Line a baking pan with parchment paper.
2. In a shallow bowl, whisk the buttermilk and egg until blended. In another shallow bowl, stir together the potato flakes, cheese, salt, and pepper.
3. One at a time, dip the chicken pieces in the buttermilk mixture and the potato flake mixture, coating thoroughly.
4. Place the coated chicken on the parchment and spritz with cooking spray.
5. Slide the baking pan into Rack Position 1, select Convection Bake and set time to 24 minutes, flipping the chicken and spritzing it with cooking spray during cooking, or until the outside is crispy and the inside is no longer pink.
6. Serve immediately.

Chicken Roast

Prep time: 15 minutes | Cook time: 1 hour | Serves 6

1 teaspoon Italian seasoning	powder
½ teaspoon garlic powder	2 tablespoons olive oil
½ teaspoon paprika	1 (3-pound / 1.4-kg) whole chicken, giblets removed, pat dry
1 teaspoon salt	
½ teaspoon freshly ground black pepper	
½ teaspoon onion	Cooking spray

1. Spritz the air fryer basket with cooking spray.
2. In a small bowl, mix the Italian seasoning, garlic powder, paprika, salt, pepper, and onion powder.
3. Brush the chicken with the olive oil and rub it with the seasoning mixture.
4. Tie the chicken legs with butcher's twine. Place the chicken in the basket, breast side down.
5. Put the air fryer basket on the baking pan and slide into Rack Position 2, select Air Fry, set the temperature to 350°F (180°C) and set the time to an hour.
6. After 30 minutes, remove from the oven. Flip the chicken over and baste it with any drippings collected in the bottom drawer of the oven. Return to the oven and continue cooking.
7. When cooking is complete, a thermometer inserted into the thickest part of the thigh should reach at least 165°F (74°C).
8. Let the chicken rest for 10 minutes before carving and serving.

Chicken Satay with Peanut Sauce

Prep time: 12 minutes | Cook time: 9 minutes | Serves 4

½ cup crunchy peanut butter
⅓ cup chicken broth
3 tablespoons low-sodium soy sauce
2 tablespoons lemon juice
2 cloves garlic, minced
2 tablespoons olive oil
1 teaspoon curry powder
1 pound (454 g) chicken tenders

1. Preheat the air fryer oven to 390ºF (199ºC).
2. In a medium bowl, combine the peanut butter, chicken broth, soy sauce, lemon juice, garlic, olive oil, and curry powder, and mix well with a wire whisk until smooth. Remove 2 tablespoons of this mixture to a small bowl. Put remaining sauce into a serving bowl and set aside.
3. Add the chicken tenders to the bowl with the 2 tablespoons sauce and stir to coat. Let stand for a few minutes to marinate, then run a bamboo skewer through each chicken tender lengthwise. Put the chicken in the air fryer basket.
4. Place the air fryer basket onto the baking pan and slide into Rack Position 2, select Air Fry and set time to 9 minutes, or until the chicken reaches 165ºF (74ºC) on a meat thermometer. Serve the chicken with the reserved sauce.

Air Fried Naked Chicken Tenders

Prep time: 5 minutes | Cook time: 7 minutes | Serves 4

Seasoning:
1 teaspoon kosher salt
½ teaspoon garlic powder
½ teaspoon onion powder
½ teaspoon chili powder
¼ teaspoon sweet paprika
¼ teaspoon freshly ground black pepper

Chicken:
8 chicken breast tenders (1 pound / 454 g total)
2 tablespoons mayonnaise

1. Preheat the air fryer oven to 375ºF (191ºC).

2. For the seasoning: In a small bowl, combine the salt, garlic powder, onion powder, chili powder, paprika, and pepper.
3. For the chicken: Place the chicken in a medium bowl and add the mayonnaise. Mix well to coat all over, then sprinkle with the seasoning mix.
4. Arrange a single layer of the chicken in the air fryer basket.
5. Place the air fryer basket onto the baking pan and slide into Rack Position 2, select Air Fry and set time to 7 minutes. Flip the chicken halfway through the cooking time, or until cooked through in the center.
6. Serve immediately.

Honey Rosemary Chicken

Prep time: 10 minutes | Cook time: 20 minutes | Serves 4

¼ cup balsamic vinegar
¼ cup honey
2 tablespoons olive oil
1 tablespoon dried rosemary leaves
1 teaspoon salt
½ teaspoon freshly ground black pepper
2 whole boneless, skinless chicken breasts (about 1 pound / 454 g each), halved
Cooking spray

1. In a large resealable bag, combine the vinegar, honey, olive oil, rosemary, salt, and pepper. Add the chicken pieces, seal the bag, and refrigerate to marinate for at least 2 hours.
2. Preheat the air fryer oven to 325ºF (163ºC). Line a baking pan with parchment paper.
3. Remove the chicken from the marinade and place it on the parchment. Spritz with cooking spray.
4. Slide the baking pan into Rack Position 1, select Convection Bake and set time to 20 minutes, flipping the chicken and spraying it with cooking spray halfway through, or until the internal temperature reaches 165ºF (74ºC) and the chicken is no longer pink inside.
5. Let sit for 5 minutes before serving.

Sweet and Spicy Turkey Meatballs

Prep time: 15 minutes | Cook time: 15 minutes | Serves 6

1 pound (454 g) lean ground turkey
½ cup whole-wheat panko bread crumbs
1 egg, beaten
1 tablespoon soy sauce
¼ cup plus 1 tablespoon hoisin

sauce, divided
2 teaspoons minced garlic
⅛ teaspoon salt
⅛ teaspoon freshly ground black pepper
1 teaspoon sriracha
Olive oil spray

1. Preheat the air fryer oven to 350ºF (177ºC). Spray the air fryer basket lightly with olive oil spray.
2. In a large bowl, mix together the turkey, panko bread crumbs, egg, soy sauce, 1 tablespoon of hoisin sauce, garlic, salt, and black pepper.
3. Using a tablespoon, form the mixture into 24 meatballs.
4. In a small bowl, combine the remaining ¼ cup of hoisin sauce and sriracha to make a glaze and set aside.
5. Place the meatballs in the air fryer basket in a single layer.
6. Place the air fryer basket onto the baking pan and slide into Rack Position 2, select Air Fry and set time to 8 minutes.
7. Brush the meatballs generously with the glaze and air fry until cooked through, an additional 4 to 7 minutes. Serve warm.

Herbed Turkey Breast

Prep time: 20 minutes | Cook time: 45 minutes | Serves 6

1 tablespoon olive oil
Cooking spray
2 garlic cloves, minced
2 teaspoons Dijon mustard
1½ teaspoons rosemary

1½ teaspoons sage
1½ teaspoons thyme
1 teaspoon salt
½ teaspoon freshly ground black pepper
3 pounds (1.4 kg) turkey breast, thawed if frozen

1. Preheat the air fryer oven to 370ºF (188ºC). Spray the air fryer basket lightly with cooking spray.
2. In a small bowl, mix together the garlic, olive oil, Dijon mustard, rosemary, sage, thyme, salt, and pepper to make a paste. Smear the paste all over the turkey breast.
3. Place the turkey breast in the air fryer basket.
4. Place the air fryer basket onto the baking pan and slide into Rack Position 2, select Air Fry and set time to 20 minutes.
5. Flip turkey breast and baste it with any drippings. Air fry until the internal temperature of the meat reaches at least 170ºF (77ºC), 20 more minutes.
6. If desired, increase the temperature to 400ºF (204ºC), flip the turkey breast over one last time, and air fry for 5 minutes to get a crispy exterior.
7. Let the turkey rest for 10 minutes before slicing and serving.

Spiced Turkey Tenderloin

Prep time: 20 minutes | Cook time: 30 minutes | Serves 4

½ teaspoon paprika
½ teaspoon garlic powder
½ teaspoon salt
½ teaspoon freshly ground black pepper

Pinch cayenne pepper
1½ pounds (680 g) turkey breast tenderloin
Olive oil spray

1. Preheat the air fryer oven to 370ºF (188ºC). Spray the air fryer basket lightly with olive oil spray.
2. In a small bowl, combine the paprika, garlic powder, salt, black pepper, and cayenne pepper. Rub the mixture all over the turkey.
3. Place the turkey in the air fryer basket and lightly spray with olive oil spray.
4. Place the air fryer basket onto the baking pan and slide into Rack Position 2, select Air Fry and set time to 15 minutes.
5. Flip the turkey over and lightly spray with olive oil spray. Air fry until the internal temperature reaches at least 170ºF (77ºC) for an additional 10 to 15 minutes.
6. Let the turkey rest for 10 minutes before slicing and serving.

Apricot Glazed Turkey Tenderloin

Prep time: 20 minutes | Cook time: 30 minutes | Serves 4

¼ cup sugar-free apricot preserves
½ tablespoon spicy brown mustard
1½ pounds (680 g) turkey breast tenderloin
Salt and freshly ground black pepper, to taste
Olive oil spray

1. Preheat the air fryer oven to 370°F (188°C). Spray the air fryer basket lightly with olive oil spray.
2. In a small bowl, combine the apricot preserves and mustard to make a paste.
3. Season the turkey with salt and pepper. Spread the apricot paste all over the turkey.
4. Place the turkey in the air fryer basket and lightly spray with olive oil spray.
5. Place the air fryer basket onto the baking pan and slide into Rack Position 2, select Air Fry and set time to 15 minutes.
6. Flip the turkey and lightly spray with olive oil spray. Air fry until the internal temperature reaches at least 170°F (77°C), an additional 10 to 15 minutes.
7. Let the turkey rest for 10 minutes before slicing and serving.

Bacon-Wrapped Turkey with Carrots

Prep time: 10 minutes | Cook time: 25 minutes | Serves 4

2 (12-ounce / 340-g) turkey tenderloins
1 teaspoon kosher salt, divided
6 slices bacon
3 tablespoons balsamic vinegar
2 tablespoons honey
1 tablespoon Dijon mustard
½ teaspoon dried thyme
6 large carrots, peeled and cut into ¼-inch rounds
1 tablespoon olive oil

1. Sprinkle the turkey with ¾ teaspoon of the salt. Wrap each tenderloin with 3 strips of bacon, securing the bacon with toothpicks. Place the turkey in the baking pan.
2. In a small bowl, mix the balsamic vinegar, honey, mustard, and thyme.

3. Place the carrots in a medium bowl and drizzle with the oil. Add 1 tablespoon of the balsamic mixture and ¼ teaspoon of kosher salt and toss to coat. Place these on the pan around the turkey tenderloins. Baste the tenderloins with about one-half of the remaining balsamic mixture.
4. Slide the baking pan into Rack Position 2, select Roast, set temperature to 375°F (190°C), and set time to 25 minutes.
5. After 13 minutes, remove from the oven. Gently stir the carrots. Flip the tenderloins and baste with the remaining balsamic mixture. Return the pan to the oven and continue cooking.
6. When cooking is complete, the carrots should tender and the center of the tenderloins should register 165°F (74°C) on a meat thermometer. Remove from the oven. Slice the turkey and serve with the carrots.

Turkey, Hummus, and Cheese Wraps

Prep time: 10 minutes | Cook time: 4 minutes | Serves 4

4 large whole wheat wraps
½ cup hummus
16 thin slices deli turkey
8 slices provolone cheese
1 cup fresh baby spinach, or more to taste

1. Preheat the air fryer oven to 360°F (182°C).
2. To assemble, place 2 tablespoons of hummus on each wrap and spread to within about a half inch from edges. Top with 4 slices of turkey and 2 slices of provolone. Finish with ¼ cup of baby spinach, or pile on as much as you like.
3. Roll up each wrap. You don't need to fold or seal the ends.
4. Place the wraps in air fryer basket, seam-side down.
5. Place the air fryer basket onto the baking pan and slide into Rack Position 2, select Air Fry and set time to 4 minutes, or until the cheese is melted.
6. Serve warm.

Asian Turkey Meatballs

Prep time: 10 minutes | Cook time: 14 minutes | Serves 4

2 tablespoons peanut oil, divided
1 small onion, minced
¼ cup water chestnuts, finely chopped
½ teaspoon ground ginger
2 tablespoons low-sodium soy sauce
¼ cup panko bread crumbs
1 egg, beaten
1 pound (454 g) ground turkey

1. Preheat the air fryer oven to 400ºF (204ºC).
2. In a small bowl, combine 1 tablespoon of peanut oil and onion. Transfer the onion to the air fryer basket.
3. Place the air fryer basket onto the baking pan and slide into Rack Position 2, select Air Fry and set time to 2 minutes, or until crisp and tender. Transfer the onion to a medium bowl.
4. Add the water chestnuts, ground ginger, soy sauce, and bread crumbs to the onion and mix well. Add egg and stir well. Mix in the ground turkey until combined.
5. Form the mixture into 1-inch meatballs. Drizzle the remaining 1 tablespoon of oil over the meatballs. Put the meatballs in the air fryer basket.
6. Place the air fryer basket onto the baking pan and slide into Rack Position 2, select Air Fry and set time to 12 minutes, or until the meatballs register 165ºF (74ºC) on a meat thermometer.
7. Rest for 5 minutes before serving.

Mini Turkey Meatloaves with Carrot

Prep time: 6 minutes | Cook time: 22 minutes | Serves 4

⅓ cup minced onion
¼ cup grated carrot
2 garlic cloves, minced
2 tablespoons ground almonds
2 teaspoons olive oil
1 teaspoon dried marjoram
1 egg white
¾ pound (340 g) ground turkey breast

1. Preheat the air fryer oven to 400ºF (204ºC).

2. In a medium bowl, stir together the onion, carrot, garlic, almonds, olive oil, marjoram, and egg white.
3. Add the ground turkey. With your hands, gently but thoroughly mix until combined.
4. Double 16 foil muffin cup liners to make 8 cups. Divide the turkey mixture evenly among the liners. Place the cups in a baking pan.
5. Slide the baking pan into Rack Position 1, select Convection Bake and set time to 22 minutes, or until the meatloaves reach an internal temperature of 165ºF (74ºC) on a meat thermometer. Serve immediately.

Turkey Hoisin Burgers

Prep time: 10 minutes | Cook time: 20 minutes | Serves 4

1 pound (454 g) lean ground turkey
¼ cup whole-wheat bread crumbs
¼ cup hoisin sauce
2 tablespoons soy sauce
4 whole-wheat buns
Olive oil spray

1. In a large bowl, mix together the turkey, bread crumbs, hoisin sauce, and soy sauce.
2. Form the mixture into 4 equal patties. Cover with plastic wrap and refrigerate the patties for 30 minutes.
3. Preheat the air fryer oven to 370ºF (188ºC). Spray the air fryer basket lightly with olive oil spray.
4. Place the patties in the air fryer basket in a single layer. Spray the patties lightly with olive oil spray.
5. Place the air fryer basket onto the baking pan and slide into Rack Position 2, select Air Fry and set time to 10 minutes. Flip the patties over, lightly spray with olive oil spray, and air fry for an additional 5 to 10 minutes, until golden brown.
6. Place the patties on buns and top with your choice of low-calorie burger toppings like sliced tomatoes, onions, and cabbage slaw. Serve immediately.

Pecan-Crusted Turkey Cutlets

Prep time: 10 minutes | Cook time: 12 minutes | Serves 4

¾ cup panko bread crumbs
¼ teaspoon salt
¼ teaspoon pepper
¼ teaspoon dry mustard
¼ teaspoon poultry seasoning
½ cup pecans
¼ cup cornstarch
1 egg, beaten
1 pound (454 g) turkey cutlets, ½-inch thick
Salt and pepper, to taste
Cooking spray

1. Preheat the air fryer oven to 360ºF (182ºC).
2. Place the panko crumbs, salt, pepper, mustard, and poultry seasoning in a food processor. Process until crumbs are finely crushed. Add pecans and process just until nuts are finely chopped.
3. Place cornstarch in a shallow dish and beaten egg in another. Transfer coating mixture from food processor into a third shallow dish.
4. Sprinkle turkey cutlets with salt and pepper to taste.
5. Dip cutlets in cornstarch and shake off excess, then dip in beaten egg and finally roll in crumbs, pressing to coat well. Spray both sides with cooking spray.
6. Place the cutlets in air fryer basket in a single layer.
7. Place the air fryer basket onto the baking pan and slide into Rack Position 2, select Air Fry and set time to 12 minutes.
8. Serve warm.

Turkey and Cranberry Quesadillas

Prep time: 7 minutes | Cook time: 6 minutes | Serves 4

6 low-sodium whole-wheat tortillas
⅓ cup shredded low-sodium low-fat Swiss cheese
¾ cup shredded cooked low-sodium turkey breast
2 tablespoons cranberry sauce
2 tablespoons dried cranberries
½ teaspoon dried basil
Olive oil spray, for spraying the tortillas

1. Preheat the air fryer oven to 400ºF (204ºC).
2. Put 3 tortillas on a work surface.
3. Evenly divide the Swiss cheese, turkey, cranberry sauce, and dried cranberries among the tortillas. Sprinkle with the basil and top with the remaining tortillas.
4. Spray the outsides of the tortillas with olive oil spray, then transfer to the air fryer basket.
5. Place the air fryer basket onto the baking pan and slide into Rack Position 2, select Air Fry and set time to 6 minutes, or until crisp and the cheese is melted.
6. Cut into quarters and serve.

Tex-Mex Turkey Burgers

Prep time: 10 minutes | Cook time: 15 minutes | Serves 4

⅓ cup finely crushed corn tortilla chips
1 egg, beaten
¼ cup salsa
⅓ cup shredded pepper Jack cheese
Pinch salt
Freshly ground black pepper, to taste
1 pound (454 g) ground turkey
1 tablespoon olive oil
1 teaspoon paprika

1. Preheat the air fryer oven to 330ºF (166ºC).
2. In a medium bowl, combine the tortilla chips, egg, salsa, cheese, salt, and pepper, and mix well.
3. Add the turkey and mix gently but thoroughly with clean hands.
4. Form the meat mixture into patties about ½ inch thick. Make an indentation in the center of each patty with your thumb so the burgers don't puff up while cooking.
5. Brush the patties on both sides with the olive oil and sprinkle with paprika. Put them in the air fryer basket.
6. Place the air fryer basket onto the baking pan and slide into Rack Position 2, select Air Fry and set time to 15 minutes, or until the meat registers at least 165ºF (74ºC).
7. Let sit for 5 minutes before serving.

Piri-Piri Chicken Thighs

Prep time: 5 minutes | Cook time: 23 minutes | Serves 4

¼ cup piri-piri sauce
1 tablespoon freshly squeezed lemon juice
2 tablespoons brown sugar, divided
2 cloves garlic, minced
1 tablespoon extra-
virgin olive oil
4 bone-in, skin-on chicken thighs, each weighing approximately 7 to 8 ounces (198 to 227 g)
½ teaspoon cornstarch

1. To make the marinade, whisk together the piri-piri sauce, lemon juice, 1 tablespoon of brown sugar, and the garlic in a small bowl. While whisking, slowly pour in the oil in a steady stream and continue to whisk until emulsified. Using a skewer, poke holes in the chicken thighs and place them in a small glass dish. Pour the marinade over the chicken and turn the thighs to coat them with the sauce. Cover the dish and refrigerate for at least 15 minutes and up to 1 hour.
2. Preheat the air fryer oven to 375ºF (191ºC). Remove the chicken thighs from the dish, reserving the marinade, and place them skin-side down in the air fryer basket.
3. Place the air fryer basket onto the baking pan and slide into Rack Position 2, select Air Fry and set time to 18 minutes, or until the internal temperature reaches 165ºF (74ºC).
4. Meanwhile, whisk the remaining brown sugar and the cornstarch into the marinade and microwave it on high power for 1 minute until it is bubbling and thickened to a glaze.
5. Once the chicken is cooked, turn the thighs over and brush them with the glaze. Air fry for a few additional minutes until the glaze browns and begins to char in spots.
6. Remove the chicken to a platter and serve with additional piri-piri sauce, if desired.

Orange and Honey Glazed Duck

Prep time: 5 minutes | Cook time: 15 minutes | Serves 2 to 3

1 pound (454 g) duck breasts (2 to 3 breasts)
Kosher salt and pepper, to taste
Juice and zest of 1
orange
¼ cup honey
2 sprigs thyme, plus more for garnish
2 firm tart apples, such as Fuji

1. Preheat the air fryer oven to 400ºF (204ºC).
2. Pat the duck breasts dry and, using a sharp knife, make 3 to 4 shallow, diagonal slashes in the skin. Turn the breasts and score the skin on the diagonal in the opposite direction to create a cross-hatch pattern. Season well with salt and pepper.
3. Place the duck breasts skin-side up in the air fryer basket.
4. Place the air fryer basket onto the baking pan and slide into Rack Position 2, select Air Fry and set time to 8 minutes.
5. Flip the duck breasts and continue cooking for 4 more minutes.
6. While the duck is cooking, prepare the sauce. Combine the orange juice and zest, honey, and thyme in a small saucepan. Bring to a boil, stirring to dissolve the honey, then reduce the heat and simmer until thickened. Core the apples and cut into quarters. Cut each quarter into 3 or 4 slices depending on the size.
7. After the duck has cooked on both sides, turn it and brush the skin with the orange-honey glaze. Air fry for 1 more minute. Remove the duck breasts to a cutting board and set aside to rest.
8. Toss the apple slices with the remaining orange-honey sauce in a medium bowl.
9. Arrange the apples in a single layer in the air fryer basket.
10. Place the air fryer basket onto the baking pan and slide into Rack Position 2, select Air Fry and set time to 10 minutes.
11. Slice the duck breasts on the bias and divide them and the apples among 2 or 3 plates.
12. Serve warm, garnished with additional thyme.

Turkey Stuffed Bell Peppers

Prep time: 20 minutes | Cook time: 15 minutes | Serves 4

½ pound (227 g) lean ground turkey
4 medium bell peppers
1 (15-ounce / 425-g) can black beans, drained and rinsed
1 cup shredded reduced-fat Cheddar cheese
1 cup cooked long-grain brown rice
1 cup mild salsa
1¼ teaspoons chili powder
1 teaspoon salt
½ teaspoon ground cumin
½ teaspoon freshly ground black pepper
Olive oil spray
Chopped fresh cilantro, for garnish

1. Preheat the air fryer oven to 360ºF (182ºC).
2. In a large skillet over medium-high heat, cook the turkey, breaking it up with a spoon, until browned, about 5 minutes. Drain off any excess fat.
3. Cut about ½ inch off the tops of the peppers and then cut in half lengthwise. Remove and discard the seeds and set the peppers aside.
4. In a large bowl, combine the browned turkey, black beans, Cheddar cheese, rice, salsa, chili powder, salt, cumin, and black pepper. Spoon the mixture into the bell peppers.
5. Lightly spray the air fryer basket with olive oil spray. Place the stuffed peppers in the air fryer basket.
6. Place the air fryer basket onto the baking pan and slide into Rack Position 2, select Air Fry and set time to 15 minutes, or until heated through.
7. Garnish with cilantro and serve.

Gnocchi with Chicken and Spinach

Prep time: 10 minutes | Cook time: 13 minutes | Serves 4

1 (1-pound / 454-g) package shelf-stable gnocchi
1¼ cups chicken stock
½ teaspoon kosher salt
1 pound (454 g) chicken breast, cut into 1-inch chunks
1 cup heavy whipping cream
2 tablespoons sun-dried tomato purée
1 garlic clove, minced
1 cup frozen spinach, thawed and drained
1 cup grated Parmesan cheese

1. Place the gnocchi in an even layer in the baking pan. Pour the chicken stock over the gnocchi.
2. Slide the baking pan into Rack Position 1, select Convection Bake, set temperature to 450ºF (235ºC), and set time to 7 minutes.
3. While the gnocchi are cooking, sprinkle the salt over the chicken pieces. In a small bowl, mix the cream, tomato purée, and garlic.
4. When cooking is complete, blot off any remaining stock, or drain the gnocchi and return it to the pan. Top the gnocchi with the spinach and chicken. Pour the cream mixture over the ingredients in the pan.
5. Slide the baking pan into Rack Position 2, select Roast, set temperature to 400ºF (205ºC), and set time to 6 minutes.
6. After 4 minutes, remove from the oven and gently stir the ingredients. Return to the oven and continue cooking.
7. When cooking is complete, the gnocchi should be tender and the chicken should be cooked through. Remove from the oven. Stir in the Parmesan cheese until it's melted and serve.

Israeli Chicken Schnitzel

Prep time: 5 minutes | Cook time: 10 minutes | Serves 4

2 large boneless, skinless chicken breasts, each weighing about 1 pound (454 g)
1 cup all-purpose flour
2 teaspoons garlic powder
2 teaspoons kosher salt
1 teaspoon black pepper
1 teaspoon paprika
2 eggs beaten with 2 tablespoons water
2 cups panko bread crumbs
Vegetable oil spray
Lemon juice, for serving

1. Preheat the air fryer oven to 375°F (191°C).
2. Place 1 chicken breast between 2 pieces of plastic wrap. Use a mallet or a rolling pin to pound the chicken until it is ¼ inch thick. Set aside. Repeat with the second breast. Whisk together the flour, garlic powder, salt, pepper, and paprika on a large plate. Place the panko in a separate shallow bowl or pie plate.
3. Dredge 1 chicken breast in the flour, shaking off any excess, then dip it in the egg mixture. Dredge the chicken breast in the panko, making sure to coat it completely. Shake off any excess panko. Place the battered chicken breast on a plate. Repeat with the second chicken breast.
4. Spray the air fryer basket with oil spray. Put the battered chicken breasts in the basket and spray the top with oil spray.
5. Place the air fryer basket onto the baking pan and slide into Rack Position 2, select Air Fry and set time to 5 minutes.
6. Flip the chicken and spray with oil spray. Air fry until the second side is browned and crispy and the internal temperature reaches 165°F (74°C).
7. Serve hot with lemon juice.

Tempero Baiano Brazilian Chicken

Prep time: 5 minutes | Cook time: 25 minutes | Serves 4

1 teaspoon cumin seeds
1 teaspoon dried oregano
1 teaspoon dried parsley
1 teaspoon ground turmeric
½ teaspoon coriander seeds
1 teaspoon kosher salt
½ teaspoon black peppercorns
½ teaspoon cayenne pepper
¼ cup fresh lime juice
2 tablespoons olive oil
1½ pounds (680 g) chicken drumsticks

1. In a clean coffee grinder or spice mill, combine the cumin, oregano, parsley, turmeric, coriander seeds, salt, peppercorns, and cayenne. Process until finely ground.
2. In a small bowl, combine the ground spices with the lime juice and oil. Place the chicken in a resealable plastic bag. Add the marinade, seal, and massage until the chicken is well coated. Marinate at room temperature for 30 minutes or in the refrigerator for up to 24 hours.
3. Preheat the air fryer oven to 400°F (204°C).
4. Place the drumsticks skin-side up in the air fryer basket.
5. Place the air fryer basket onto the baking pan and slide into Rack Position 2, select Air Fry and set time to 25 minutes. Flip the drumsticks halfway through the cooking time. Use a meat thermometer to ensure that the chicken has reached an internal temperature of 165°F (74°C). Serve immediately.

Chapter 5 Meats

Char Siu

Prep time: 8 hours 10 minutes | Cook time: 15 minutes | Serves 4

¼ cup honey
1 teaspoon Chinese five-spice powder
1 tablespoon Shaoxing wine (rice cooking wine)
1 tablespoon hoisin sauce
2 teaspoons minced garlic
2 teaspoons minced fresh ginger
2 tablespoons soy sauce
1 tablespoon sugar
1 pound (454 g) fatty pork shoulder, cut into long, 1-inch-thick pieces
Cooking spray

1. Combine all the ingredients, except for the pork should, in a microwave-safe bowl. Stir to mix well. Microwave until the honey has dissolved. Stir periodically.
2. Pierce the pork pieces generously with a fork, then put the pork in a large bowl. Pour in half of the honey mixture. Set the remaining sauce aside until ready to serve.
3. Press the pork pieces into the mixture to coat and wrap the bowl in plastic and refrigerate to marinate for at least 8 hours.
4. Spritz the air fryer basket with cooking spray.
5. Discard the marinade and transfer the pork pieces in the basket.
6. Put the air fryer basket on the baking pan and slide into Rack Position 2, select Air Fry, set temperature to 400ºF (205ºC) and set time to 15 minutes.
7. Flip the pork halfway through.
8. When cooking is complete, the pork should be well browned.
9. Meanwhile, microwave the remaining marinade on high for a minute or until it has a thick consistency. Stir periodically.
10. Remove the pork from the oven and allow to cool for 10 minutes before serving with the thickened marinade.

Pork Butt with Coriander-Parsley Sauce

Prep time: 1 hour 15 minutes | Cook time: 30 minutes | Serves 4

1 teaspoon golden flaxseeds meal
1 egg white, well whisked
1 tablespoon soy sauce
1 teaspoon lemon juice, preferably freshly squeezed
1 tablespoon olive oil
1 pound (454 g) pork butt, cut into pieces 2-inches long
Salt and ground black pepper, to taste
Garlicky Coriander-Parsley Sauce:
3 garlic cloves, minced
⅓ cup fresh coriander leaves
⅓ cup fresh parsley leaves
1 teaspoon lemon juice
½ tablespoon salt
⅓ cup extra-virgin olive oil

1. Combine the flaxseeds meal, egg white, soy sauce, lemon juice, salt, black pepper, and olive oil in a large bowl. Dunk the pork strips in and press to submerge.
2. Wrap the bowl in plastic and refrigerate to marinate for at least an hour.
3. Arrange the marinated pork strips in the basket.
4. Put the air fryer basket on the baking pan and slide into Rack Position 2, select Air Fry, set temperature to 380ºF (193ºC) and set time to 30 minutes.
5. After 15 minutes, remove from the oven. Flip the pork. Return to the oven and continue cooking.
6. When cooking is complete, the pork should be well browned.
7. Meanwhile, combine the ingredients for the sauce in a small bowl. Stir to mix well. Arrange the bowl in the refrigerator to chill until ready to serve.
8. Serve the air fried pork strips with the chilled sauce.

Homemade Teriyaki Pork Ribs

Prep time: 5 minutes | Cook time: 30 minutes | Serves 4

¼ cup soy sauce
¼ cup honey
1 teaspoon garlic powder
1 teaspoon ground

dried ginger
4 (8-ounce / 227-g) boneless country-style pork ribs
Cooking spray

1. Spritz the air fryer basket with cooking spray.
2. Make the teriyaki sauce: combine the soy sauce, honey, garlic powder, and ginger in a bowl. Stir to mix well.
3. Brush the ribs with half of the teriyaki sauce, then arrange the ribs in the pan. Spritz with cooking spray.
4. Put the air fryer basket on the baking pan and slide into Rack Position 2, select Air Fry, set temperature to 350ºF (180ºC) and set time to 30 minutes.
5. After 15 minutes, remove from the oven. Flip the ribs and brush with remaining teriyaki sauce. Return to the oven and continue cooking.
6. When cooking is complete, the internal temperature of the ribs should reach at least 145ºF (63ºC).
7. Serve immediately.

Citrus Carnitas

Prep time: 1 hour 10 minutes | Cook time: 25 minutes | Serves 6

2½ pounds (1.1 kg) boneless country-style pork ribs, cut into 2-inch pieces
3 tablespoons olive brine
1 tablespoon minced fresh oregano leaves
⅓ cup orange juice

1 teaspoon ground cumin
1 tablespoon minced garlic
1 teaspoon salt
1 teaspoon ground black pepper
Cooking spray

1. Combine all the ingredients in a large bowl. Toss to coat the pork ribs well. Wrap the bowl in plastic and refrigerate for at least an hour to marinate.
2. Spritz the air fryer basket with cooking spray.

3. Arrange the marinated pork ribs in the pan and spritz with cooking spray.
4. Put the air fryer basket on the baking pan and slide into Rack Position 2, select Air Fry, set temperature to 400ºF (205ºC) and set time to 25 minutes.
5. Flip the ribs halfway through.
6. When cooking is complete, the ribs should be well browned.
7. Serve immediately.

Pork, Bell Pepper, and Pineapple Skewers

Prep time: 10 minutes | Cook time: 12 minutes | Serves 4

¼ teaspoon kosher salt or ⅛ teaspoon fine salt
1 medium pork tenderloin (about 1 pound / 454 g), cut into 1½-inch chunks
1 green bell pepper, seeded and cut into

1-inch pieces
1 red bell pepper, seeded and cut into 1-inch pieces
2 cups fresh pineapple chunks
¾ cup Teriyaki Sauce or store-bought variety, divided

Special Equipment:
12 (9- to 12-inch) wooden skewers, soaked in water for about 30 minutes

1. Sprinkle the pork cubes with the salt.
2. Thread the pork, bell peppers, and pineapple onto a skewer. Repeat until all skewers are complete. Brush the skewers generously with about half of the Teriyaki Sauce. Place them in the air fryer basket.
3. Put the air fryer basket on the baking pan and slide into Rack Position 2, select Roast, set temperature to 375ºF (190ºC), and set time to 10 minutes.
4. After about 5 minutes, remove from the oven. Turn over the skewers and brush with the remaining half of Teriyaki Sauce. Return to the oven and continue cooking until the vegetables are tender and browned in places and the pork is browned and cooked through.
5. Remove from the oven and serve.

Sirloin Steak and Pepper Fajitas

Prep time: 10 minutes | Cook time: 15 minutes | Serves 4

8 (6-inch) flour tortillas
1 pound (454 g) top sirloin steak, sliced ¼-inch thick
1 red bell pepper, deseeded and sliced ½-inch thick
1 green bell pepper, deseeded and sliced ½-inch thick
1 jalapeño, deseeded and sliced thin
1 medium onion, sliced ½-inch thick
2 tablespoons vegetable oil
2 tablespoons Mexican seasoning
1 teaspoon kosher salt
2 tablespoons salsa
1 small avocado, sliced

1. Line the baking pan with aluminum foil. Place the tortillas on the foil in two stacks and wrap in the foil.
2. Slide the baking pan into Rack Position 2, select Roast, set temperature to 325ºF (163ºC), and set time to 6 minutes.
3. After 3 minutes, remove from the oven and flip the packet of tortillas over. Return to the oven and continue cooking.
4. While the tortillas warm, place the steak, bell peppers, jalapeño, and onion in a large bowl and drizzle the oil over. Sprinkle with the Mexican seasoning and salt, and toss to coat.
5. When cooking is complete, remove from the oven and place the packet of tortillas on top of the oven to keep warm. Place the beef and peppers mixture in the baking pan, spreading out into a single layer as much as possible.
6. Select Roast, set temperature to 375ºF (190ºC), and set time to 9 minutes.
7. After about 5 minutes, remove from the oven and stir the ingredients. Return to the oven and continue cooking.
8. When cooking is complete, the vegetables will be soft and browned in places, and the beef will be browned on the outside and barely pink inside. Remove from the oven. Unwrap the tortillas and spoon the fajita mixture into the tortillas. Serve with salsa and avocado slices.

Pork with Butternut Squash and Apples

Prep time: 15 minutes | Cook time: 13 minutes | Serves 4

4 boneless pork loin chops, ¾- to 1-inch thick
1 teaspoon kosher salt, divided
2 tablespoons Dijon mustard
2 tablespoons brown sugar
1 pound (454 g) butternut squash, cut into 1-inch cubes
1 large apple, peeled and cut into 12 to 16 wedges
1 medium onion, thinly sliced
½ teaspoon dried thyme
¼ teaspoon freshly ground black pepper
1 tablespoon unsalted butter, melted
½ cup chicken stock

1. Sprinkle the pork chops on both sides with ½ teaspoon of kosher salt. In a small bowl, whisk together the mustard and brown sugar. Baste about half of the mixture on one side of the pork chops. Place the chops, basted-side up, in the baking pan.
2. Place the squash in a large bowl. Add the apple, onion, thyme, remaining kosher salt, pepper, and butter and toss to coat. Arrange the squash-fruit mixture around the chops on the pan. Pour the chicken stock over the mixture, avoiding the chops.
3. Slide the baking pan into Rack Position 2, select Roast, set temperature to 350ºF (180ºC), and set time to 13 minutes.
4. After about 7 minutes, remove from the oven. Gently toss the squash mixture and turn over the chops. Baste the chops with the remaining mustard mixture. Return the pan to the oven and continue cooking.
5. When cooking is complete, the pork chops should register at least 145ºF (63ºC) in the center on a meat thermometer, and the squash and apples should be tender. If necessary, continue cooking for up to 3 minutes more.
6. Remove from the oven. Spoon the squash and apples onto four plates, and place a pork chop on top. Serve immediately.

Lechon Kawali

Prep time: 10 minutes | Cook time: 30 minutes | Serves 4

1 pound (454 g) pork belly, cut into three thick chunks
6 garlic cloves
2 bay leaves
2 tablespoons soy sauce
1 teaspoon kosher salt
1 teaspoon ground black pepper
3 cups water
Cooking spray

1. Put all the ingredients in a pressure cooker, then put the lid on and cook on high for 15 minutes.
2. Natural release the pressure and release any remaining pressure, transfer the tender pork belly on a clean work surface. Allow to cool under room temperature until you can handle.
3. Generously Spritz the air fryer basket with cooking spray.
4. Cut each chunk into two slices, then put the pork slices in the pan.
5. Put the air fryer basket on the baking pan and slide into Rack Position 2, select Air Fry, set temperature to 400ºF (205ºC) and set time to 15 minutes.
6. After 7 minutes, remove from the oven. Flip the pork. Return to the oven and continue cooking.
7. When cooking is complete, the pork fat should be crispy.
8. Serve immediately.

Tonkatsu

Prep time: 5 minutes | Cook time: 10 minutes | Serves 4

2/3 cup all-purpose flour
2 large egg whites
1 cup panko bread crumbs
4 (4-ounce / 113-g) center-cut boneless pork loin chops (about ½ inch thick)
Cooking spray

1. Pour the flour in a bowl. Whisk the egg whites in a separate bowl. Spread the bread crumbs on a large plate.
2. Dredge the pork loin chops in the flour first, press to coat well, then shake the excess off and dunk the chops in the eggs whites, and then roll the chops over the bread crumbs. Shake the excess off.
3. Arrange the pork chops in the basket and spritz with cooking spray.
4. Put the air fryer basket on the baking pan and slide into Rack Position 2, select Air Fry, set temperature to 375ºF (190ºC) and set time to 10 minutes.
5. After 5 minutes, remove from the oven. Flip the pork chops. Return to the oven and continue cooking.
6. When cooking is complete, the pork chops should be crunchy and lightly browned.
7. Serve immediately.

Classic Walliser Schnitzel

Prep time: 5 minutes | Cook time: 14 minutes | Serves 2

½ cup pork rinds
½ tablespoon fresh parsley
½ teaspoon fennel seed
½ teaspoon mustard
1/3 tablespoon cider vinegar
1 teaspoon garlic salt
1/3 teaspoon ground black pepper
2 eggs
2 pork schnitzel, halved
Cooking spray

1. Spritz the air fryer basket with cooking spray.
2. Put the pork rinds, parsley, fennel seeds, and mustard in a food processor. Pour in the vinegar and sprinkle with salt and ground black pepper. Pulse until well combined and smooth.
3. Pour the pork rind mixture in a large bowl. Whisk the eggs in a separate bowl.
4. Dunk the pork schnitzel in the whisked eggs, then dunk in the pork rind mixture to coat well. Shake the excess off.
5. Arrange the schnitzel in the pan and spritz with cooking spray.
6. Put the air fryer basket on the baking pan and slide into Rack Position 2, select Air Fry, set temperature to 350ºF (180ºC) and set time to 14 minutes.
7. After 7 minutes, remove from the oven. Flip the schnitzel. Return to the oven and continue cooking.
8. When cooking is complete, the schnitzel should be golden and crispy.
9. Serve immediately.

Pork and Tricolor Vegetables Kebabs

Prep time: 1 hour 20 minutes | Cook time: 8 minutes | Serves 4

For the Pork:

1 pound (454 g) pork steak, cut in cubes
1 tablespoon white wine vinegar
3 tablespoons steak sauce
¼ cup soy sauce

1 teaspoon powdered chili
1 teaspoon red chili flakes
2 teaspoons smoked paprika
1 teaspoon garlic salt

For the Vegetable:

1 green squash, deseeded and cut in cubes
1 yellow squash, deseeded and cut in cubes
1 red pepper, cut in

cubes
1 green pepper, cut in cubes
Salt and ground black pepper, to taste
Cooking spray

Special Equipment:

4 bamboo skewers, soaked in water for at least 30 minutes

1. Combine the ingredients for the pork in a large bowl. Press the pork to dunk in the marinade. Wrap the bowl in plastic and refrigerate for at least an hour.
2. Spritz the air fryer basket with cooking spray.
3. Remove the pork from the marinade and run the skewers through the pork and vegetables alternatively. Sprinkle with salt and pepper to taste.
4. Arrange the skewers in the pan and spritz with cooking spray.
5. Put the air fryer basket on the baking pan and slide into Rack Position 2, select Air Fry, set temperature to 380ºF (193ºC) and set time to 8 minutes.
6. After 4 minutes, remove from the oven. Flip the skewers. Return to the oven and continue cooking.
7. When cooking is complete, the pork should be browned and the vegetables should be lightly charred and tender.
8. Serve immediately.

Lamb Meatballs

Prep time: 20 minutes | Cook time: 8 minutes | Serves 4

Meatballs:

½ small onion, finely diced
1 clove garlic, minced
1 pound (454 g) ground lamb
2 tablespoons fresh parsley, finely chopped (plus more for garnish)

2 teaspoons fresh oregano, finely chopped
2 tablespoons milk
1 egg yolk
Salt and freshly ground black pepper, to taste
½ cup crumbled feta cheese, for garnish

Tomato Sauce:

2 tablespoons butter
1 clove garlic, smashed
Pinch crushed red pepper flakes
¼ teaspoon ground

cinnamon
1 (28-ounce / 794-g) can crushed tomatoes
Salt, to taste
Olive oil, for greasing

1. Combine all ingredients for the meatballs in a large bowl and mix just until everything is combined. Shape the mixture into 1½-inch balls or shape the meat between two spoons to make quenelles.
2. Preheat the air fryer oven to 400ºF (204ºC).
3. Make the tomato sauce: Put the butter, garlic and red pepper flakes in a sauté pan and heat over medium heat on the stovetop. Let the garlic sizzle a little, but before the butter browns, add the cinnamon and tomatoes. Bring to a simmer and simmer for 15 minutes. Season with salt.
4. Grease the air fryer basket with olive oil and transfer the meatballs to the air fryer basket in a single layer.
5. Place the air fryer basket onto the baking pan and slide into Rack Position 2, select Air Fry and set time to 8 minutes, giving the basket a shake once during the cooking process.
6. To serve, spoon a pool of the tomato sauce onto plates and add the meatballs. Sprinkle the feta cheese on top and garnish with more fresh parsley.

Pork Meatballs with Red Chili

Prep time: 5 minutes | Cook time: 15 minutes | Serves 4

1 pound (454 g) ground pork	grated ginger root
2 cloves garlic, finely minced	1 teaspoon turmeric powder
1 cup scallions, finely chopped	1 tablespoon oyster sauce
1½ tablespoons Worcestershire sauce	1 small sliced red chili, for garnish
½ teaspoon freshly	Cooking spray

1. Spritz the air fryer basket with cooking spray.
2. Combine all the ingredients, except for the red chili in a large bowl. Toss to mix well.
3. Shape the mixture into equally sized balls, then arrange them in the basket and spritz with cooking spray.
4. Put the air fryer basket on the baking pan and slide into Rack Position 2, select Air Fry, set temperature to 350ºF (180ºC) and set time to 15 minutes.
5. After 7 minutes, remove from the oven. Flip the balls. Return to the oven and continue cooking.
6. When cooking is complete, the balls should be lightly browned.
7. Serve the pork meatballs with red chili on top.

Lemony Pork Loin Chop Schnitzel

Prep time: 15 minutes | Cook time: 15 minutes | Serves 4

4 thin boneless pork loin chops	1 teaspoon salt
2 tablespoons lemon juice	1 cup panko bread crumbs
½ cup flour	2 eggs
¼ teaspoon marjoram	Lemon wedges, for serving
	Cooking spray

1. On a clean work surface, drizzle the pork chops with lemon juice on both sides.
2. Combine the flour with marjoram and salt on a shallow plate. Pour the bread crumbs on a separate shallow dish. Beat the eggs in a large bowl.
3. Dredge the pork chops in the flour, then dunk in the beaten eggs to coat well. Shake the excess off and roll over the bread crumbs. Arrange the pork chops in the basket and spritz with cooking spray.
4. Put the air fryer basket on the baking pan and slide into Rack Position 2, select Air Fry, set temperature to 400ºF (205ºC) and set time to 15 minutes.
5. After 7 minutes, remove from the oven. Flip the pork. Return to the oven and continue cooking.
6. When cooking is complete, the pork should be crispy and golden.
7. Squeeze the lemon wedges over the fried chops and serve immediately.

Macadamia Nuts Crusted Pork Rack

Prep time: 5 minutes | Cook time: 35 minutes | Serves 2

1 clove garlic, minced	1 tablespoon bread crumbs
2 tablespoons olive oil	1 tablespoon rosemary, chopped
1 pound (454 g) rack of pork	1 egg
1 cup chopped macadamia nuts	Salt and ground black pepper, to taste

1. Combine the garlic and olive oil in a small bowl. Stir to mix well.
2. On a clean work surface, rub the pork rack with the garlic oil and sprinkle with salt and black pepper on both sides.
3. Combine the macadamia nuts, bread crumbs, and rosemary in a shallow dish. Whisk the egg in a large bowl.
4. Dredge the pork in the egg, then roll the pork over the macadamia nut mixture to coat well. Shake the excess off.
5. Arrange the pork in the basket.
6. Put the air fryer basket on the baking pan and slide into Rack Position 2, select Air Fry, set temperature to 350ºF (180ºC) and set time to 30 minutes.
7. After 30 minutes, remove from the oven. Flip the pork rack. Return to the oven and increase temperature to 390ºF (199ºC) and set time to 5 minutes. Keep cooking.
8. When cooking is complete, the pork should be browned.
9. Serve immediately.

Mushroom and Beef Meatloaf

Prep time: 10 minutes | Cook time: 25 minutes | Serves 4

1 pound (454 g) ground beef
1 egg, beaten
1 mushrooms, sliced
1 tablespoon thyme
1 small onion, chopped
3 tablespoons bread crumbs
Ground black pepper, to taste

1. Preheat the air fryer oven to 400ºF (204ºC).
2. Put all the ingredients into a large bowl and combine entirely. Transfer the meatloaf mixture into a loaf pan.
3. Slide the pan into Rack Position 1, select Convection Bake and set time to 25 minutes.
4. Cool for 5 minutes before slicing and serving.

Orange Pork Tenderloin

Prep time: 15 minutes | Cook time: 23 minutes | Serves 3 to 4

2 tablespoons brown sugar
2 teaspoons cornstarch
2 teaspoons Dijon mustard
½ cup orange juice
½ teaspoon soy sauce
2 teaspoons grated fresh ginger
¼ cup white wine
Zest of 1 orange
1 pound (454 g) pork tenderloin
Salt and freshly ground black pepper, to taste
Oranges, halved, for garnish
Fresh parsley, for garnish

1. Combine the brown sugar, cornstarch, Dijon mustard, orange juice, soy sauce, ginger, white wine and orange zest in a small saucepan and bring the mixture to a boil on the stovetop. Lower the heat and simmer while you air fry the pork tenderloin or until the sauce has thickened.
2. Preheat the air fryer oven to 370ºF (188ºC).
3. Season all sides of the pork tenderloin with salt and freshly ground black pepper. Transfer the tenderloin to the air fryer basket.
4. Place the air fryer basket onto the baking pan and slide into Rack Position 2, select Air Fry and set time to 23 minutes, or until the internal temperature reaches 145ºF (63ºC). Flip the tenderloin over halfway through the cooking process and baste with the sauce.
5. Transfer the tenderloin to a cutting board and let it rest for 5 minutes. Slice the pork at a slight angle and serve immediately with orange halves and fresh parsley.

Pork Leg Roast with Candy Onions

Prep time: 10 minutes | Cook time: 52 minutes | Serves 4

2 teaspoons sesame oil
1 teaspoon dried sage, crushed
1 teaspoon cayenne pepper
1 rosemary sprig, chopped
1 thyme sprig, chopped
Sea salt and ground
black pepper, to taste
2 pounds (907 g) pork leg roast, scored
½ pound (227 g) candy onions, sliced
4 cloves garlic, finely chopped
2 chili peppers, minced

1. In a mixing bowl, combine the sesame oil, sage, cayenne pepper, rosemary, thyme, salt and black pepper until well mixed. In another bowl, place the pork leg and brush with the seasoning mixture.
2. Place the seasoned pork leg in the baking pan. Put the baking pan into Rack Position 2, select Air Fry, set temperature to 400ºF (205ºC) and set time to 40 minutes.
3. After 20 minutes, remove from the oven. Flip the pork leg. Return the pan to the oven and continue cooking.
4. After another 20 minutes, add the candy onions, garlic, and chili peppers to the pan and air fry for another 12 minutes.
5. When cooking is complete, the pork leg should be browned.
6. Transfer the pork leg to a plate. Let cool for 5 minutes and slice. Spread the juices left in the pan over the pork and serve warm with the candy onions.

Pulled Pork

Prep time: 5 minutes | Cook time: 24 minutes | Serves 1

2 tablespoons barbecue dry rub
1 pound (454 g) pork tenderloin
1/3 cup heavy cream
1 teaspoon butter, melted

1. Preheat the air fryer oven to 370°F (188°C).
2. Massage the dry rub into the tenderloin, coating it well. Transfer to the air fryer basket.
3. Place the air fryer basket onto the baking pan and slide into Rack Position 2, select Air Fry and set time to 20 minutes.
4. When done, shred with two forks. Toss with the heavy cream and butter.
5. Return to the oven and air fry for a further 4 minutes.
6. Serve warm.

Potato and Prosciutto Salad

Prep time: 10 minutes | Cook time: 7 minutes | Serves 8

Salad:
4 pounds (1.8 kg) potatoes, boiled and cubed
15 slices prosciutto, diced
2 cups shredded Cheddar cheese

Dressing:
15 ounces (425 g) sour cream
2 tablespoons mayonnaise
1 teaspoon salt
1 teaspoon black pepper
1 teaspoon dried basil

1. Preheat the air fryer oven to 350°F (177°C).
2. Put the potatoes, prosciutto, and Cheddar in a baking dish.
3. Place the baking dish into Rack Position 1, select Convection Bake and set time to 7 minutes.
4. In a separate bowl, mix the sour cream, mayonnaise, salt, pepper, and basil using a whisk.
5. Coat the salad with the dressing and serve.

Pork Schnitzels with Sour Cream and Dill Sauce

Prep time: 5 minutes | Cook time: 4 minutes | Serves 4 to 6

1/2 cup flour
1½ teaspoons salt
Freshly ground black pepper, to taste
2 eggs
1/2 cup milk
1½ cups toasted bread crumbs
1 teaspoon paprika
6 boneless, center cut pork chops
(about 1½ pounds / 680 g), fat trimmed, pound to ½-inch thick
2 tablespoons olive oil
3 tablespoons melted butter
Lemon wedges, for serving

Sour Cream and Dill Sauce:
1 cup chicken stock
1½ tablespoons cornstarch
1/3 cup sour cream
1½ tablespoons
chopped fresh dill
Salt and ground black pepper, to taste

1. Combine the flour with salt and black pepper in a large bowl. Stir to mix well. Whisk the egg with milk in a second bowl. Stir the bread crumbs and paprika in a third bowl.
2. Dredge the pork chops in the flour bowl, then in the egg milk, and then into the bread crumbs bowl. Press to coat well. Shake the excess off.
3. Arrange the pork chop in the basket, then brush with olive oil and butter on all sides.
4. Put the air fryer basket on the baking pan and slide into Rack Position 2, select Air Fry, set temperature to 400°F (205°C) and set time to 4 minutes.
5. After 2 minutes, remove from the oven. Flip the pork. Return to the oven and continue cooking.
6. When cooking is complete, the pork chop should be golden brown and crispy.
7. Meanwhile, combine the chicken stock and cornstarch in a small saucepan and bring to a boil over medium-high heat. Simmer for 2 more minutes.
8. Turn off the heat, then mix in the sour cream, fresh dill, salt, and black pepper.
9. Remove the schnitzels from the oven to a plate and baste with sour cream and dill sauce. Squeeze the lemon wedges over and slice to serve.

Pork Sausage with Cauliflower Mash

Prep time: 5 minutes | Cook time: 27 minutes | Serves 6

1 pound (454 g) cauliflower, chopped	1 teaspoon cumin powder
6 pork sausages, chopped	½ teaspoon tarragon
½ onion, sliced	½ teaspoon sea salt
3 eggs, beaten	½ teaspoon ground black pepper
⅓ cup Colby cheese	Cooking spray

1. Spritz the baking pan with cooking spray.
2. In a saucepan over medium heat, boil the cauliflower until tender. Place the boiled cauliflower in a food processor and pulse until puréed. Transfer to a large bowl and combine with remaining ingredients until well blended.
3. Pour the cauliflower and sausage mixture into the pan.
4. Slide the baking pan into Rack Position 1, select Convection Bake, set temperature to 365°F (185°C) and set time to 27 minutes.
5. When cooking is complete, the sausage should be lightly browned.
6. Divide the mixture among six serving dishes and serve warm.

Pork Chops with Carrots and Mushrooms

Prep time: 10 minutes | Cook time: 15 minutes | Serves 4

2 carrots, cut into sticks	1 teaspoon dried oregano
1 cup mushrooms, sliced	1 teaspoon dried thyme
2 garlic cloves, minced	1 teaspoon cayenne pepper
2 tablespoons olive oil	Salt and ground black pepper, to taste
1 pound (454 g) boneless pork chops	Cooking spray

1. In a mixing bowl, toss together the carrots, mushrooms, garlic, olive oil and salt until well combined.
2. Add the pork chops to a different bowl and season with oregano, thyme, cayenne pepper, salt and black pepper.
3. Lower the vegetable mixture in the greased basket. Place the seasoned pork chops on top.
4. Put the air fryer basket on the baking pan and slide into Rack Position 2, select Air Fry, set temperature to 360°F (182°C) and set time to 15 minutes.
5. After 7 minutes, remove from the oven. Flip the pork and stir the vegetables. Return to the oven and continue cooking.
6. When cooking is complete, the pork chops should be browned and the vegetables should be tender.
7. Transfer the pork chops to the serving dishes and let cool for 5 minutes. Serve warm with vegetable on the side.

Spaghetti Squash Lasagna

Prep time: 5 minutes | Cook time: 1 hour 15 minutes | Serves 6

2 large spaghetti squash, cooked (about 2¾ pounds / 1.2 kg)	1.1-kg) large jar Marinara sauce
4 pounds (1.8 kg) ground beef	25 slices Mozzarella cheese
1 (2½-pound /	30 ounces whole-milk ricotta cheese

1. Preheat the air fryer oven to 375°F (191°C).
2. Slice the spaghetti squash and place it face down inside a baking dish. Fill with water until covered.
3. Place the baking dish into Rack Position 1, select Convection Bake and set time to 45 minutes, or until skin is soft.
4. Sear the ground beef in a skillet over medium-high heat for 5 minutes or until browned, then add the marinara sauce and heat until warm. Set aside.
5. Scrape the flesh off the cooked squash to resemble strands of spaghetti.
6. Layer the lasagna in a large greased pan in alternating layers of spaghetti squash, beef sauce, Mozzarella, ricotta. Repeat until all the ingredients have been used.
7. Slide the pan into Rack Position 1, select Convection Bake and set time to 30 minutes.
8. Serve warm.

Italian Sausages and Red Grapes

Prep time: 10 minutes | Cook time: 20 minutes | Serves 6

2 pounds (905 g) seedless red grapes
3 shallots, sliced
2 teaspoons fresh thyme
2 tablespoons olive oil
½ teaspoon kosher

salt
Freshly ground black pepper, to taste
6 links (about 1½ pounds / 680 g) hot Italian sausage
3 tablespoons balsamic vinegar

1. Place the grapes in a large bowl. Add the shallots, thyme, olive oil, salt, and pepper. Gently toss. Place the grapes in the baking pan. Arrange the sausage links evenly in the pan.
2. Slide the baking pan into Rack Position 2, select Roast, set temperature to 375ºF (190ºC), and set time to 20 minutes.
3. After 10 minutes, remove the pan. Turn over the sausages and sprinkle the vinegar over the sausages and grapes. Gently toss the grapes and move them to one side of the pan. Return the pan to the oven and continue cooking.
4. When cooking is complete, the grapes should be very soft and the sausages browned. Serve immediately.

Pork Fried Rice with Scrambled Egg

Prep time: 10 minutes | Cook time: 12 minutes | Serves 4

3 scallions, diced (about ½ cup)
½ red bell pepper, diced (about ½ cup)
2 teaspoons sesame oil
½ pound (227 g) pork tenderloin,

diced
½ cup frozen peas, thawed
½ cup roasted mushrooms
½ cup soy sauce
2 cups cooked rice
1 egg, beaten

1. Place the scallions and red pepper in the baking pan. Drizzle with the sesame oil and toss the vegetables to coat them in the oil.
2. Slide the baking pan into Rack Position 2, select Roast, set temperature to 375ºF (190ºC), and set time to 12 minutes.

3. While the vegetables are cooking, place the pork in a large bowl. Add the peas, mushrooms, soy sauce, and rice and toss to coat the ingredients with the sauce.
4. After about 4 minutes, remove from the oven. Place the pork mixture on the pan and stir the scallions and peppers into the pork and rice. Return the pan to the oven and continue cooking.
5. After another 6 minutes, remove from the oven. Move the rice mixture to the sides to create an empty circle in the middle of the pan. Pour the egg in the circle. Return the pan to the oven and continue cooking.
6. When cooking is complete, remove from the oven and stir the egg to scramble it. Stir the egg into the fried rice mixture. Serve immediately.

Pepperoni and Bell Pepper Pockets

Prep time: 5 minutes | Cook time: 8 minutes | Serves 4

4 bread slices, 1-inch thick
Olive oil, for misting
24 slices pepperoni
1 ounce (28 g) roasted red peppers,

drained and patted dry
1 ounce (28 g) Pepper Jack cheese, cut into 4 slices

1. Preheat the air fryer oven to 360ºF (182ºC).
2. Spray both sides of bread slices with olive oil.
3. Stand slices upright and cut a deep slit in the top to create a pocket (almost to the bottom crust, but not all the way through).
4. Stuff each bread pocket with 6 slices of pepperoni, a large strip of roasted red pepper, and a slice of cheese.
5. Put bread pockets in the air fryer basket, standing up.
6. Place the air fryer basket onto the baking pan and slide into Rack Position 2, select Air Fry and set time to 8 minutes, or until filling is heated through and bread is lightly browned.
7. Serve hot.

Air Fried London Broil

Prep time: 15 minutes | Cook time: 25 minutes | Serves 8

2 pounds (907 g) London broil
3 large garlic cloves, minced
3 tablespoons balsamic vinegar
3 tablespoons whole-grain mustard
2 tablespoons olive oil
Sea salt and ground black pepper, to taste
½ teaspoons dried hot red pepper flakes

1. Wash and dry the London broil. Score its sides with a knife.
2. Mix the remaining ingredients. Rub this mixture into the broil, coating it well. Allow to marinate for a minimum of 3 hours.
3. Preheat the air fryer oven to 400ºF (204ºC).
4. Put the broil in the air fryer basket. Place the air fryer basket onto the baking pan and slide into Rack Position 2, select Air Fry and set time to 15 minutes.
5. Turn it over and air fry for an additional 10 minutes. Serve warm.

Miso Marinated Steak

Prep time: 5 minutes | Cook time: 12 minutes | Serves 4

¾ pound (340 g) flank steak
1½ tablespoons sake
1 tablespoon brown miso paste
1 teaspoon honey
2 cloves garlic, pressed
1 tablespoon olive oil

1. Put all the ingredients in a Ziploc bag. Shake to cover the steak well with the seasonings and refrigerate for at least 1 hour.
2. Preheat the air fryer oven to 400ºF (204ºC).
3. Coat all sides of the steak with cooking spray, then put the steak in the air fryer basket.
4. Place the air fryer basket onto the baking pan and slide into Rack Position 2, select Air Fry and set time to 12 minutes, turning the steak twice during the cooking time. Serve immediately.

Spicy Pork Lettuce Wraps

Prep time: 10 minutes | Cook time: 12 minutes | Serves 4

1 (1-pound / 454-g) medium pork tenderloin, silver skin and external fat trimmed
⅔ cup soy sauce, divided
1 teaspoon cornstarch
1 medium jalapeño, deseeded and minced
1 can diced water
chestnuts
½ large red bell pepper, deseeded and chopped
2 scallions, chopped, white and green parts separated
1 head butter lettuce
½ cup roasted, chopped almonds
¼ cup coarsely chopped cilantro

1. Cut the tenderloin into ¼-inch slices and place them in the baking pan. Baste with about 3 tablespoons of soy sauce. Stir the cornstarch into the remaining sauce and set aside.
2. Slide the baking pan into Rack Position 2, select Roast, set temperature to 375ºF (190ºC), and set time to 12 minutes.
3. After 5 minutes, remove from the oven. Place the pork slices on a cutting board. Place the jalapeño, water chestnuts, red pepper, and the white parts of the scallions in the baking pan and pour the remaining sauce over. Stir to coat the vegetables with the sauce. Return the pan to the oven and continue cooking.
4. While the vegetables cook, chop the pork into small pieces. Separate the lettuce leaves, discarding any tough outer leaves and setting aside the small inner leaves for another use. You'll want 12 to 18 leaves, depending on size and your appetites.
5. After 5 minutes, remove from the oven. Add the pork to the vegetables, stirring to combine. Return the pan to the oven and continue cooking for the remaining 2 minutes until the pork is warmed back up and the sauce has reduced slightly.
6. When cooking is complete, remove from the oven. Place the pork and vegetables in a medium serving bowl and stir in half the green parts of the scallions. To serve, spoon some pork and vegetables into each of the lettuce leaves. Top with the remaining scallion greens and garnish with the nuts and cilantro.

Beef and Spinach Meatloaves

Prep time: 15 minutes | Cook time: 45 minutes | Serves 2

1 large egg, beaten
1 cup frozen spinach
⅓ cup almond meal
¼ cup chopped onion
¼ cup plain Greek milk
¼ teaspoon salt
¼ teaspoon dried sage
2 teaspoons olive oil, divided
Freshly ground black pepper, to taste
½ pound (227 g) extra-lean ground beef
¼ cup tomato paste
1 tablespoon granulated stevia
¼ teaspoon Worcestershire sauce
Cooking spray

1. Coat a shallow baking pan with cooking spray.
2. In a large bowl, combine the beaten egg, spinach, almond meal, onion, milk, salt, sage, 1 teaspoon of olive oil, and pepper.
3. Crumble the beef over the spinach mixture. Mix well to combine. Divide the meat mixture in half. Shape each half into a loaf. Place the loaves in the prepared pan.
4. In a small bowl, whisk together the tomato paste, stevia, Worcestershire sauce, and remaining 1 teaspoon of olive oil. Spoon half of the sauce over each meatloaf.
5. Slide the baking pan into Rack Position 1, select Convection Bake, set the temperature to 350ºF (180ºC) and set the time to 40 minutes.
6. When cooking is complete, an instant-read thermometer inserted in the center of the meatloaves should read at least 165ºF (74ºC).
7. Serve immediately.

Dijon Pork Tenderloin

Prep time: 15 minutes | Cook time: 15 minutes | Serves 4

3 tablespoons Dijon mustard
3 tablespoons honey
1 teaspoon dried rosemary
1 tablespoon olive oil
1 pound (454 g) pork tenderloin, rinsed and drained
Salt and freshly ground black pepper, to taste

1. In a small bowl, combine the Dijon mustard, honey, and rosemary. Stir to combine.
2. Rub the pork tenderloin with salt and pepper on all sides on a clean work surface.
3. Heat the olive oil in an oven-safe skillet over high heat. Sear the pork loin on all sides in the skillet for 6 minutes or until golden brown. Flip the pork halfway through.
4. Remove from the heat and spread honey-mustard mixture evenly to coat the pork loin.
5. Select Bake of the oven, set temperature to 425ºF (220ºC) and set time to 15 minutes.
6. When cooking is complete, an instant-read thermometer inserted in the pork should register at least 145ºF (63ºC).
7. Remove from the oven and allow to rest for 3 minutes. Slice the pork into ½-inch slices and serve.

Worcestershire Ribeye Steaks

Prep time: 35 minutes | Cook time: 10 to 12 minutes | Serves 2 to 4

2 (8-ounce / 227-g) boneless ribeye steaks
4 teaspoons Worcestershire sauce
½ teaspoon garlic powder
Salt and ground black pepper, to taste
4 teaspoons olive oil

1. Brush the steaks with Worcestershire sauce on both sides. Sprinkle with garlic powder and coarsely ground black pepper. Drizzle the steaks with olive oil. Allow steaks to marinate for 30 minutes.
2. Transfer the steaks into the basket.
3. Put the air fryer basket on the baking pan and slide into Rack Position 2, select Roast, set the temperature to 400ºF (205ºC) and set time to 4 minutes.
4. After 2 minutes, remove from the oven. Flip the steaks. Return to the oven and continue cooking.
5. When cooking is complete, the steaks should be well browned.
6. Remove the steaks from the basket and let sit for 5 minutes. Salt and serve.

Mushroom and Sausage Calzones

Prep time: 10 minutes | Cook time: 24 minutes | Serves 4

2 links Italian sausages (about ½ pound / 227 g)
1 pound (454 g) pizza dough, thawed
3 tablespoons olive oil, divided

¼ cup Marinara sauce
½ cup roasted mushrooms
1 cup shredded Mozzarella cheese

1. Place the sausages in the baking pan.
2. Slide the baking pan into Rack Position 2, select Roast, set temperature to 375ºF (190ºC), and set time to 12 minutes.
3. After 6 minutes, remove from the oven and turn over the sausages. Return to the oven and continue cooking.
4. While the sausages cook, divide the pizza dough into 4 equal pieces. One at a time, place a piece of dough onto a square of parchment paper 9 inches in diameter. Brush the dough on both sides with ¾ teaspoon of olive oil, then top the dough with another piece of parchment. Press the dough into a 7-inch circle. Remove the top piece of parchment and set aside. Repeat with the remaining pieces of dough.
5. When cooking is complete, remove from the oven. Place the sausages on a cutting board. Let them cool for several minutes, then slice into ¼-inch rounds and cut each round into 4 pieces.
6. One at a time, spread a tablespoon of marinara sauce over half of a dough circle, leaving a ½-inch border at the edges. Cover with a quarter of the sausage pieces and add a quarter of the mushrooms. Sprinkle with ¼ cup of cheese. Pull the other side of the dough over the filling and pinch the edges together to seal. Transfer from the parchment to the baking pan. Repeat with the other rounds of dough, sauce, sausage, mushrooms, and cheese.
7. Brush the tops of the calzones with 1 tablespoon of olive oil.
8. Select Roast, set temperature to 450ºF (235ºC), and set time to 12 minutes.
9. After 6 minutes, remove from the oven. The calzones should be golden brown.

Turn over the calzones and brush the tops with the remaining olive oil. Return the pan to the oven and continue cooking.
10. When cooking is complete, the crust should be a deep golden brown on both sides. Remove from the oven. The center should be molten; let cool for several minutes before serving.

Smoky Paprika Pork and Vegetable Kabobs

Prep time: 25 minutes | Cook time: 15 minutes | Serves 4

1 pound (454 g) pork tenderloin, cubed
1 teaspoon smoked paprika
Salt and ground black pepper, to taste

1 green bell pepper, cut into chunks
1 zucchini, cut into chunks
1 red onion, sliced
1 tablespoon oregano
Cooking spray

Special Equipment:
Small bamboo skewers, soaked in water for 20 minutes to keep them from burning while cooking

1. Spritz the air fryer basket with cooking spray.
2. Add the pork to a bowl and season with the smoked paprika, salt and black pepper. Thread the seasoned pork cubes and vegetables alternately onto the soaked skewers. Arrange the skewers in the pan.
3. Put the air fryer basket on the baking pan and slide into Rack Position 2, select Air Fry, set temperature to 350ºF (180ºC) and set time to 15 minutes.
4. After 7 minutes, remove from the oven. Flip the pork skewers. Return to the oven and continue cooking.
5. When cooking is complete, the pork should be browned and vegetables are tender.
6. Transfer the skewers to the serving dishes and sprinkle with oregano. Serve hot.

Chuck and Sausage Subs

Prep time: 15 minutes | Cook time: 24 minutes | Serves 4

1 large egg
¼ cup whole milk
24 saltines, crushed but not pulverized
1 pound (454 g) ground chuck
1 pound (454 g) Italian sausage, casings removed
4 tablespoons grated Parmesan cheese, divided
1 teaspoon kosher salt
4 sub rolls, split
1 cup Marinara sauce
¾ cup shredded Mozzarella cheese

1. In a large bowl, whisk the egg into the milk, then stir in the crackers. Let sit for 5 minutes to hydrate.
2. With your hands, break the ground chuck and sausage into the milk mixture, alternating beef and sausage. When you've added half of the meat, sprinkle 2 tablespoons of the grated Parmesan and the salt over it, then continue breaking up the meat until it's all in the bowl. Gently mix everything together. Try not to overwork the meat, but get it all combined.
3. Form the mixture into balls about the size of a golf ball. You should get about 24 meatballs. Flatten the balls slightly to prevent them from rolling, then place them in the baking pan, about 2 inches apart.
4. Slide the baking pan into Rack Position 2, select Roast, set temperature to 400ºF (205ºC), and set time to 20 minutes.
5. After 10 minutes, remove from the oven and turn over the meatballs. Return to the oven and continue cooking.
6. When cooking is complete, remove from the oven. Place the meatballs on a rack. Wipe off the baking pan.
7. Open the rolls, cut-side up, on the baking pan. Place 3 to 4 meatballs on the base of each roll, and top each sandwich with ¼ cup of marinara sauce. Divide the Mozzarella among the top halves of the buns and sprinkle the remaining Parmesan cheese over the Mozzarella.
8. Select Convection Broil, set temperature to High, and set time to 4 minutes.
9. Check the sandwiches after 2 minutes; the Mozzarella cheese should be melted and bubbling slightly.
10. When cooking is complete, remove from the oven. Close the sandwiches and serve.

Gold Cutlets with Aloha Salsa

Prep time: 20 minutes | Cook time: 7 minutes | Serves 4

2 eggs
2 tablespoons milk
¼ cup all-purpose flour
¼ cup panko bread crumbs
4 teaspoons sesame seeds
1 pound (454 g) boneless, thin pork cutlets (½-inch thick)
¼ cup cornstarch
Salt and ground lemon pepper, to taste
Cooking spray

Aloha Salsa:
1 cup fresh pineapple, chopped in small pieces
¼ cup red bell pepper, chopped
½ teaspoon ground cinnamon
1 teaspoon soy sauce
¼ cup red onion, finely chopped
⅛ teaspoon crushed red pepper
⅛ teaspoon ground black pepper

1. In a medium bowl, stir together all ingredients for salsa. Cover and refrigerate while cooking the pork.
2. Beat together eggs and milk in a large bowl. In another bowl, mix the flour, panko, and sesame seeds. Pour the cornstarch in a shallow dish.
3. Sprinkle pork cutlets with lemon pepper and salt. Dip pork cutlets in cornstarch, egg mixture, and then panko coating. Spritz both sides with cooking spray.
4. Put the air fryer basket on the baking pan and slide into Rack Position 2, select Air Fry, set the temperature to 400ºF (205ºC) and set the time to 7 minutes.
5. After 3 minutes, remove from the oven. Flip the cutlets with tongs. Return to the oven and continue cooking.
6. When cooking is complete, the pork should be crispy and golden brown on both sides.
7. Serve the fried cutlets with the Aloha salsa on the side.

Pork Chop Roast

Prep time: 5 minutes | Cook time: 20 minutes | Serves 2

2 (10-ounce / 284-g) bone-in, center cut pork chops, 1-inch thick
2 teaspoons

Worcestershire sauce
Salt and ground black pepper, to taste
Cooking spray

1. Rub the Worcestershire sauce on both sides of pork chops.
2. Season with salt and pepper to taste.
3. Spritz the air fryer basket with cooking spray and place the chops in the basket side by side.
4. Put the air fryer basket on the baking pan and slide into Rack Position 2, select Roast, set the temperature to 350ºF (180ºC) and set the time to 20 minutes.
5. After 10 minutes, remove from the oven. Flip the pork chops with tongs. Return to the oven and continue cooking.
6. When cooking is complete, the pork should be well browned on both sides.
7. Let rest for 5 minutes before serving.

Beef and Vegetable Cubes

Prep time: 15 minutes | Cook time: 17 minutes | Serves 4

2 tablespoons olive oil
1 tablespoon apple cider vinegar
1 teaspoon fine sea salt
½ teaspoons ground black pepper
1 teaspoon shallot powder
¾ teaspoon smoked cayenne pepper
½ teaspoons garlic powder

¼ teaspoon ground cumin
1 pound (454 g) top round steak, cut into cubes
4 ounces (113 g) broccoli, cut into florets
4 ounces (113 g) mushrooms, sliced
1 teaspoon dried basil
1 teaspoon celery seeds

1. Massage the olive oil, vinegar, salt, black pepper, shallot powder, cayenne pepper, garlic powder, and cumin into the cubed steak, ensuring to coat each piece evenly.

2. Allow to marinate for a minimum of 3 hours.
3. Preheat the air fryer oven to 365ºF (185ºC).
4. Put the beef cubes in the air fryer basket. Place the air fryer basket onto the baking pan and slide into Rack Position 2, select Air Fry and set time to 12 minutes.
5. When the steak is cooked through, place it in a bowl.
6. Wipe the grease from the basket and pour in the vegetables. Season them with basil and celery seeds.
7. Increase the temperature to 400ºF (204ºC) and air fry for 5 to 6 minutes. When the vegetables are hot, serve them with the steak.

Citrus Pork Loin Roast

Prep time: 10 minutes | Cook time: 45 minutes | Serves 8

1 tablespoon lime juice
1 tablespoon orange marmalade
1 teaspoon coarse brown mustard
1 teaspoon curry powder
1 teaspoon dried

lemongrass
2 pound (907 g) boneless pork loin roast
Salt and ground black pepper, to taste
Cooking spray

1. Preheat the air fryer oven to 360ºF (182ºC).
2. Mix the lime juice, marmalade, mustard, curry powder, and lemongrass.
3. Rub mixture all over the surface of the pork loin. Season with salt and pepper.
4. Spray the air fryer basket with cooking spray and place pork roast diagonally in the basket.
5. Place the air fryer basket onto the baking pan and slide into Rack Position 2, select Air Fry and set time to 45 minutes, or until the internal temperature reaches at least 145ºF (63ºC).
6. Wrap roast in foil and let rest for 10 minutes before slicing and serving.

Beef Steak Fingers

Prep time: 5 minutes | Cook time: 8 minutes | Serves 4

4 small beef cube steaks
Salt and ground black pepper, to
taste
½ cup flour
Cooking spray

1. Preheat the air fryer oven to 390ºF (199ºC).
2. Cut cube steaks into 1-inch-wide strips. Sprinkle lightly with salt and pepper to taste. Roll in flour to coat all sides.
3. Spritz the air fryer basket with cooking spray.
4. Put steak strips in air fryer basket in a single layer. Spritz top of steak strips with cooking spray.
5. Place the air fryer basket onto the baking pan and slide into Rack Position 2, select Air Fry and set time to 4 minutes.
6. Turn strips over and spritz with cooking spray. Air fry for 4 more minutes and test with fork for doneness. Steak fingers should be crispy outside with no red juices inside.
7. Serve immediately.

Sriracha Beef and Broccoli

Prep time: 10 minutes | Cook time: 15 minutes | Serves 4

12 ounces (340 g) broccoli, cut into florets (about 4 cups)
1 pound (454 g) flat iron steak, cut into thin strips
½ teaspoon kosher salt
¾ cup soy sauce
1 teaspoon Sriracha sauce
3 tablespoons freshly squeezed orange juice
1 teaspoon cornstarch
1 medium onion, thinly sliced

1. Line the baking pan with aluminum foil. Place the broccoli on top and sprinkle with 3 tablespoons of water. Seal the broccoli in the foil in a single layer.
2. Slide the baking pan into Rack Position 2, select Roast, set temperature to 375ºF (190ºC), and set time to 6 minutes.
3. While the broccoli steams, sprinkle the steak with the salt. In a small bowl, whisk together the soy sauce, Sriracha, orange juice, and cornstarch. Place the onion and beef in a large bowl.
4. When cooking is complete, remove from the oven. Open the packet of broccoli and use tongs to transfer the broccoli to the bowl with the beef and onion, discarding the foil and remaining water. Pour the sauce over the beef and vegetables and toss to coat. Place the mixture in the baking pan.
5. Select Roast, set temperature to 375ºF (190ºC), and set time to 9 minutes.
6. After about 4 minutes, remove from the oven and gently toss the ingredients. Return to the oven and continue cooking.
7. When cooking is complete, the sauce should be thickened, the vegetables tender, and the beef barely pink in the center. Serve warm.

Smoked Beef

Prep time: 10 minutes | Cook time: 45 minutes | Serves 8

2 pounds (907 g) roast beef, at room temperature
2 tablespoons extra-virgin olive oil
1 teaspoon sea salt flakes
1 teaspoon ground
black pepper
1 teaspoon smoked paprika
Few dashes of liquid smoke
2 jalapeño peppers, thinly sliced

1. Preheat the air fryer oven to 330ºF (166ºC).
2. With kitchen towels, pat the beef dry.
3. Massage the extra-virgin olive oil, salt, black pepper, and paprika into the meat. Cover with liquid smoke, then place in a baking pan.
4. Slide the baking pan into Rack Position 1, select Convection Bake and set time to 30 minutes.
5. Flip the roast over and allow to bake for another 15 minutes.
6. When cooked through, serve topped with sliced jalapeños.

Mongolian Flank Steak

Prep time: 20 minutes | Cook time: 15 minutes | Serves 4

1½ pounds (680 g) flank steak, thinly sliced on the bias into ¼-inch strips
Marinade:

2 tablespoons soy sauce	smashed
1 clove garlic,	Pinch crushed red pepper flakes

Sauce:

1 tablespoon vegetable oil	¾ cup chicken stock
2 cloves garlic, minced	5 to 6 tablespoons brown sugar
1 tablespoon finely grated fresh ginger	½ cup cornstarch, divided
3 dried red chili peppers	1 bunch scallions, sliced into 2-inch pieces
¾ cup soy sauce	

1. Marinate the beef in the soy sauce, garlic and red pepper flakes for one hour.
2. In the meantime, make the sauce. Heat a small saucepan over medium heat on the stovetop. Add the oil, garlic, ginger and dried chili peppers and sauté for just a minute or two. Add the soy sauce, chicken stock and brown sugar and continue to simmer for a few minutes. Dissolve 3 tablespoons of cornstarch in 3 tablespoons of water and stir this into the saucepan. Stir the sauce over medium heat until it thickens. Set this aside.
3. Preheat the air fryer oven to 400ºF (204ºC).
4. Remove the beef from the marinade and transfer it to a zipper sealable plastic bag with the remaining cornstarch. Shake it around to completely coat the beef and transfer the coated strips of beef to a baking sheet or plate, shaking off any excess cornstarch. Spray the strips with vegetable oil on all sides and transfer them to the air fryer basket.
5. Place the air fryer basket onto the baking pan and slide into Rack Position 2, select Air Fry and set time to 15 minutes, shaking the basket to toss and rotate the beef strips throughout the cooking process. Add the scallions for the last 4 minutes of the cooking.
6. Transfer the hot beef strips and scallions to a bowl and toss with the sauce, coating all the beef strips with the sauce. Serve warm.

Provolone Stuffed Beef and Pork Meatballs

Prep time: 15 minutes | Cook time: 12 minutes | Serves 4 to 6

1 tablespoon olive oil	fresh parsley
1 small onion, finely chopped	½ teaspoon dried oregano
1 to 2 cloves garlic, minced	1½ teaspoons salt
¾ pound (340 g) ground beef	Freshly ground black pepper, to taste
¾ pound (340 g) ground pork	2 eggs, lightly beaten
¾ cup bread crumbs	5 ounces (142 g) sharp or aged provolone cheese, cut into 1-inch cubes
¼ cup grated Parmesan cheese	
¼ cup finely chopped	

1. Preheat a skillet over medium-high heat. Add the oil and cook the onion and garlic until tender, but not browned.
2. Transfer the onion and garlic to a large bowl and add the beef, pork, bread crumbs, Parmesan cheese, parsley, oregano, salt, pepper and eggs. Mix well until all the ingredients are combined. Divide the mixture into 12 evenly sized balls. Make one meatball at a time, by pressing a hole in the meatball mixture with the finger and pushing a piece of provolone cheese into the hole. Mold the meat back into a ball, enclosing the cheese.
3. Preheat the air fryer oven to 380ºF (193ºC).
4. Transfer the meatballs to the air fryer basket.
5. Place the air fryer basket onto the baking pan and slide into Rack Position 2, select Air Fry and set time to 12 minutes, shaking the basket and turning the meatballs twice during the cooking process.
6. Serve warm.

Lollipop Lamb Chops

Prep time: 15 minutes | Cook time: 7 minutes | Serves 4

½ small clove garlic
¼ cup packed fresh parsley
¾ cup packed fresh mint
½ teaspoon lemon juice
¼ cup grated Parmesan cheese
1/3 cup shelled pistachios
¼ teaspoon salt

½ cup olive oil
8 lamb chops (1 rack)
2 tablespoons vegetable oil
Salt and freshly ground black pepper, to taste
1 tablespoon dried rosemary, chopped
1 tablespoon dried thyme

1. Make the pesto by combining the garlic, parsley and mint in a food processor and process until finely chopped. Add the lemon juice, Parmesan cheese, pistachios and salt. Process until all the ingredients have turned into a paste. With the processor running, slowly pour the olive oil in. Scrape the sides of the processor with a spatula and process for another 30 seconds.
2. Preheat the air fryer oven to 400ºF (204ºC).
3. Rub both sides of the lamb chops with vegetable oil and season with salt, pepper, rosemary and thyme, pressing the herbs into the meat gently with the fingers. Transfer the lamb chops to the air fryer basket.
4. Place the air fryer basket onto the baking pan and slide into Rack Position 2, select Air Fry and set time to 5 minutes.
5. Flip the chops over and air fry for an additional 2 minutes.
6. Serve the lamb chops with mint pesto drizzled on top.

Fast Lamb Satay

Prep time: 5 minutes | Cook time: 8 minutes | Serves 2

¼ teaspoon cumin
1 teaspoon ginger
½ teaspoons nutmeg
Salt and ground black pepper, to

taste
2 boneless lamb steaks
Cooking spray

1. Combine the cumin, ginger, nutmeg, salt and pepper in a bowl.
2. Cube the lamb steaks and massage the spice mixture into each one.
3. Leave to marinate for 10 minutes, then transfer onto metal skewers.
4. Preheat the air fryer oven to 400ºF (204ºC).
5. Put the skewers in the air fryer basket and spritz with cooking spray.
6. Place the air fryer basket onto the baking pan and slide into Rack Position 2, select Air Fry and set time to 8 minutes.
7. Serve hot.

Sumptuous Pizza Tortilla Rolls

Prep time: 10 minutes | Cook time: 15 minutes | Serves 4

1 teaspoon butter
½ medium onion, slivered
½ red or green bell pepper, julienned
4 ounces (113 g) fresh white mushrooms,

chopped
½ cup pizza sauce
8 flour tortillas
8 thin slices deli ham
24 pepperoni slices
1 cup shredded Mozzarella cheese
Cooking spray

1. Preheat the air fryer oven to 390ºF (199ºC).
2. Put butter, onions, bell pepper, and mushrooms in a baking pan.
3. Slide the baking pan into Rack Position 1, select Convection Bake and set time to 3 minutes.
4. Stir and bake for 3 to 4 minutes longer until just crisp and tender. Remove the pan and set aside.
5. To assemble rolls, spread about 2 teaspoons of pizza sauce on one half of each tortilla. Top with a slice of ham and 3 slices of pepperoni. Divide sautéed vegetables among tortillas and top with cheese.
6. Roll up tortillas, secure with toothpicks if needed, and spray with oil. Put the rolls in the air fryer basket.
7. Place the air fryer basket onto the baking pan and slide into Rack Position 2, select Air Fry and set time to 4 minutes.
8. Flip and air fry for 4 minutes, until heated through and lightly browned.
9. Serve immediately.

Char Siew

Prep time: 10 minutes | Cook time: 20 minutes | Serves 4 to 6

1 strip of pork shoulder butt with a good amount of fat	marbling
Marinade:	Olive oil, for brushing the pan
1 teaspoon sesame oil	1 teaspoon light soy sauce
4 tablespoons raw honey	1 tablespoon rose wine
1 teaspoon low-sodium dark soy sauce	2 tablespoons Hoisin sauce

1. Combine all the marinade ingredients together in a Ziploc bag. Put pork in bag, making sure all sections of pork strip are engulfed in the marinade. Chill for 3 to 24 hours.
2. Take out the strip 30 minutes before preheating the air fryer to 350°F (177°C).
3. Put foil on a baking pan and brush with olive oil. Put marinated pork strip onto prepared pan.
4. Slide the pan into Rack Position 1, select Convection Bake and set time to 20 minutes. Glaze with marinade every 5 to 10 minutes.
5. Remove strip and leave to cool a few minutes before slicing and serving.

Rosemary Ribeye Steaks

Prep time: 10 minutes | Cook time: 15 minutes | Serves 2

¼ cup butter	1½ tablespoons balsamic vinegar
1 clove garlic, minced	¼ cup rosemary, chopped
Salt and ground black pepper, to taste	2 ribeye steaks

1. Melt the butter in a skillet over medium heat. Add the garlic and fry until fragrant.
2. Remove the skillet from the heat and add the salt, pepper, and vinegar. Allow it to cool.
3. Add the rosemary, then pour the mixture into a Ziploc bag.
4. Put the ribeye steaks in the bag and shake well, coating the meat well. Refrigerate for an hour, then allow to sit for a further 20 minutes.
5. Preheat the air fryer oven to 400°F (204°C).
6. Put the steaks in the air fryer basket. Place the air fryer basket onto the baking pan and slide into Rack Position 2, select Air Fry and set time to 15 minutes.
7. Serve immediately.

Classic Spring Rolls

Prep time: 10 minutes | Cook time: 8 minutes | Serves 20

⅓ cup noodles	1 small onion, diced
1 cup ground beef	1 tablespoon sesame oil
1 teaspoon soy sauce	1 packet spring roll sheets
1 cup fresh mix vegetables	2 tablespoons cold water
3 garlic cloves, minced	

1. Cook the noodle in enough hot water to soften them up, drain them and snip them to make them shorter.
2. In a frying pan over medium heat, cook the beef, soy sauce, mixed vegetables, garlic, and onion in sesame oil until the beef is cooked through. Take the pan off the heat and throw in the noodles. Mix well to incorporate everything.
3. Unroll a spring roll sheet and lay it flat. Scatter the filling diagonally across it and roll it up, brushing the edges lightly with water to act as an adhesive. Repeat until you have used up all the sheets and the filling.
4. Preheat the air fryer oven to 350°F (177°C).
5. Coat each spring roll with a light brushing of oil and transfer to the air fryer basket.
6. Place the air fryer basket onto the baking pan and slide into Rack Position 2, select Air Fry and set time to 8 minutes.
7. Serve hot.

Cheesy Beef Meatballs

Prep time: 5 minutes | Cook time: 18 minutes | Serves 6

1 pound (454 g) ground beef
½ cup grated Parmesan cheese
1 tablespoon minced garlic
½ cup Mozzarella cheese
1 teaspoon freshly ground pepper

1. Preheat the air fryer oven to 400°F (204°C).
2. In a bowl, mix all the ingredients together. Roll the meat mixture into 5 generous meatballs. Arrange them in the air fryer basket.
3. Place the air fryer basket onto the baking pan and slide into Rack Position 2, select Air Fry and set time to 18 minutes.
4. Serve immediately.

Teriyaki Pork and Mushroom Rolls

Prep time: 10 minutes | Cook time: 8 minutes | Serves 6

4 tablespoons brown sugar
4 tablespoons mirin
4 tablespoons soy sauce
1 teaspoon almond flour
2-inch ginger, chopped
6 (4-ounce / 113-g) pork belly slices
6 ounces (170 g) Enoki mushrooms

1. Mix the brown sugar, mirin, soy sauce, almond flour, and ginger together until brown sugar dissolves.
2. Take pork belly slices and wrap around a bundle of mushrooms. Brush each roll with teriyaki sauce. Chill for half an hour.
3. Preheat the air fryer oven to 350°F (177°C).
4. Add the marinated pork rolls to the air fryer basket. Place the air fryer basket onto the baking pan and slide into Rack Position 2, select Air Fry and set time to 8 minutes. Flip the rolls halfway through the cooking time.
5. Serve immediately.

Barbecue Pork Ribs

Prep time: 5 minutes | Cook time: 30 minutes | Serves 4

1 tablespoon barbecue dry rub
1 teaspoon mustard
1 tablespoon apple cider vinegar
1 teaspoon sesame oil
1 pound (454 g) pork ribs, chopped

1. Combine the dry rub, mustard, apple cider vinegar, and sesame oil, then coat the ribs with this mixture. Refrigerate the ribs for 20 minutes.
2. Preheat the air fryer oven to 360°F (182°C).
3. When the ribs are ready, place them in the air fryer basket.
4. Place the air fryer basket onto the baking pan and slide into Rack Position 2, select Air Fry and set time to 15 minutes.
5. Flip them and air fry on the other side for a further 15 minutes.
6. Serve immediately.

Air Fried Lamb Ribs

Prep time: 5 minutes | Cook time: 18 minutes | Serves 4

2 tablespoons mustard
1 pound (454 g) lamb ribs
1 teaspoon rosemary, chopped
Salt and ground black pepper, to taste
¼ cup mint leaves, chopped
1 cup Greek yogurt

1. Preheat the air fryer oven to 350°F (177°C).
2. Use a brush to apply the mustard to the lamb ribs, and season with rosemary, salt, and pepper. Put them in the air fryer basket.
3. Place the air fryer basket onto the baking pan and slide into Rack Position 2, select Air Fry and set time to 18 minutes.
4. Meanwhile, combine the mint leaves and yogurt in a bowl.
5. Remove the lamb ribs from the oven when cooked and serve with the mint yogurt.

Pork and Pinto Bean Gorditas

Prep time: 20 minutes | Cook time: 21 minutes | Serves 4

1 pound (454 g) lean ground pork
2 tablespoons chili powder
2 tablespoons ground cumin
1 teaspoon dried oregano
2 teaspoons paprika
1 teaspoon garlic powder
½ cup water
1 (15-ounce / 425-g) can pinto beans, drained and rinsed
½ cup taco sauce
Salt and freshly ground black pepper,
to taste
2 cups grated Cheddar cheese
5 (12-inch) flour tortillas
4 (8-inch) crispy corn tortilla shells
4 cups shredded lettuce
1 tomato, diced
⅓ cup sliced black olives
Sour cream, for serving
Tomato salsa, for serving
Cooking spray

1. Preheat the air fryer oven to 400°F (204°C). Spritz the air fryer basket with cooking spray.
2. Put the ground pork in the air fryer basket. Place the air fryer basket onto the baking pan and slide into Rack Position 2, select Air Fry and set time to 10 minutes, stirring a few times to gently break up the meat.
3. Combine the chili powder, cumin, oregano, paprika, garlic powder and water in a small bowl. Stir the spice mixture into the browned pork. Stir in the beans and taco sauce and air fry for an additional minute. Transfer the pork mixture to a bowl. Season with salt and freshly ground black pepper.
4. Sprinkle ½ cup of the grated cheese in the center of the flour tortillas, leaving a 2-inch border around the edge free of cheese and filling. Divide the pork mixture among the four tortillas, placing it on top of the cheese. Put a crunchy corn tortilla on top of the pork and top with shredded lettuce, diced tomatoes, and black olives. Cut the remaining flour tortilla into 4 quarters. These quarters of tortilla will serve as the bottom of the gordita. Put one quarter tortilla on top of each gordita and fold the edges of the bottom flour tortilla up over the sides, enclosing the filling. While holding the seams down, brush the bottom of the gordita with olive oil and place the seam side down on the countertop while you finish the remaining three gorditas.
5. Preheat the air fryer oven to 380°F (193°C).
6. Transfer the gorditas carefully to the air fryer basket, seam-side down. Brush or spray the top tortilla with oil.
7. Place the air fryer basket onto the baking pan and slide into Rack Position 2, select Air Fry and set time to 5 minutes.
8. Carefully turn the gorditas over and air fry for an additional 4 to 5 minutes until both sides are browned.
9. Serve warm with sour cream and salsa.

Vietnamese Pork Chops

Prep time: 15 minutes | Cook time: 12 minutes | Serves 2

1 tablespoon chopped shallot
1 tablespoon chopped garlic
1 tablespoon fish sauce
3 tablespoons lemongrass
1 teaspoon soy sauce
1 tablespoon brown sugar
1 tablespoon olive oil
1 teaspoon ground black pepper
2 pork chops

1. Combine shallot, garlic, fish sauce, lemongrass, soy sauce, brown sugar, olive oil, and pepper in a bowl. Stir to mix well.
2. Put the pork chops in the bowl. Toss to coat well. Place the bowl in the refrigerator to marinate for 2 hours.
3. Preheat the air fryer oven to 400°F (204°C).
4. Remove the pork chops from the bowl and discard the marinade. Transfer the chops into the air fryer basket.
5. Place the air fryer basket onto the baking pan and slide into Rack Position 2, select Air Fry and set time to 12 minutes, or until lightly browned. Flip the pork chops halfway through the cooking time.
6. Remove the pork chops from the basket and serve hot.

Calf's Liver Golden Strips

Prep time: 15 minutes | Cook time: 4 to 5 minutes | Serves 4

1 pound (454 g) sliced calf's liver, cut into about ½-inch-wide strips
Salt and ground black pepper, to taste
2 eggs
2 tablespoons milk
½ cup whole wheat flour
1½ cups panko bread crumbs
½ cup plain bread crumbs
½ teaspoon salt
¼ teaspoon ground black pepper
Cooking spray

1. Sprinkle the liver strips with salt and pepper.
2. Beat together the egg and milk in a bowl. Place wheat flour in a shallow dish. In a second shallow dish, mix panko, plain bread crumbs, ½ teaspoon salt, and ¼ teaspoon pepper.
3. Dip liver strips in flour, egg wash, and then bread crumbs, pressing in coating slightly to make crumbs stick.
4. Spritz the air fryer basket with cooking spray. Place strips in a single layer in the basket.
5. Put the air fryer basket on the baking pan and slide into Rack Position 2, select Air Fry, set the temperature to 400ºF (205ºC) and set the time to 4 minutes.
6. After 2 minutes, remove from the oven. Flip the strips with tongs. Return to the oven and continue cooking.
7. When cooking is complete, the liver strips should be crispy and golden.
8. Serve immediately.

Ravioli with Beef-Marinara Sauce

Prep time: 10 minutes | Cook time: 10 minutes | Serves 4

1 (20-ounce / 567-g) package frozen cheese ravioli
1 teaspoon kosher salt
1¼ cups water
6 ounces (170 g) cooked ground beef
2½ cups Marinara sauce
¼ cup grated Parmesan cheese, for garnish

1. Place the ravioli in an even layer in the baking pan. Stir the salt into the water until dissolved and pour it over the ravioli.
2. Slide the baking pan into Rack Position 1, select Convection Bake, set temperature to 450ºF (235ºC), and set time to 10 minutes.
3. While the ravioli is cooking, mix the ground beef into the marinara sauce in a medium bowl.
4. After 6 minutes, remove the pan from the oven. Blot off any remaining water, or drain the ravioli and return them to the pan. Pour the meat sauce over the ravioli. Return the pan to the oven and continue cooking.
5. When cooking is complete, the ravioli should be tender and sauce heated through. Gently stir the ingredients. Serve the ravioli with the Parmesan cheese, if desired.

Beef Schnitzel

Prep time: 5 minutes | Cook time: 12 minutes | Serves 1

½ cup friendly bread crumbs
2 tablespoons olive oil
Pepper and salt, to taste
1 egg, beaten
1 thin beef schnitzel

1. Preheat the air fryer oven to 350ºF (177ºC).
2. In a shallow dish, combine the bread crumbs, oil, pepper, and salt.
3. In a second shallow dish, place the beaten egg.
4. Dredge the schnitzel in the egg before rolling it in the bread crumbs.
5. Put the coated schnitzel in the air fryer basket. Place the air fryer basket onto the baking pan and slide into Rack Position 2, select Air Fry and set time to 12 minutes. Flip the schnitzel halfway through.
6. Serve immediately.

Sweet and Sour Pork

Prep time: 20 minutes | Cook time: 14 minutes | Serves 2 to 4

⅓ cup all-purpose flour
⅓ cup cornstarch
2 teaspoons Chinese five-spice powder
1 teaspoon salt
Freshly ground black pepper, to taste
1 egg
2 tablespoons milk
¾ pound (340 g) boneless pork, cut into 1-inch cubes
Vegetable or canola oil
1½ cups large chunks of red and green peppers
½ cup ketchup
2 tablespoons rice wine vinegar or apple cider vinegar
2 tablespoons brown sugar
¼ cup orange juice
1 tablespoon soy sauce
1 clove garlic, minced
1 cup cubed pineapple
Chopped scallions, for garnish

1. Set up a dredging station with two bowls. Combine the flour, cornstarch, Chinese five-spice powder, salt and pepper in one large bowl. Whisk the egg and milk together in a second bowl. Dredge the pork cubes in the flour mixture first, then dip them into the egg and then back into the flour to coat on all sides. Spray the coated pork cubes with vegetable or canola oil.
2. Preheat the air fryer oven to 400°F (204°C).
3. Toss the pepper chunks with a little oil, then transfer to the air fryer basket.
4. Place the air fryer basket onto the baking pan and slide into Rack Position 2, select Air Fry and set time to 5 minutes, shaking the basket halfway through the cooking time.
5. While the peppers are cooking, start making the sauce. Combine the ketchup, rice wine vinegar, brown sugar, orange juice, soy sauce, and garlic in a medium saucepan and bring the mixture to a boil on the stovetop. Reduce the heat and simmer for 5 minutes. When the peppers have finished air frying, add them to the saucepan along with the pineapple chunks. Simmer the peppers and pineapple in the sauce for an additional 2 minutes. Set aside and keep warm.
6. Add the dredged pork cubes to the air fryer basket and air fry for 6 minutes, shaking the basket to turn the cubes over for the last minute of the cooking process.
7. When ready to serve, toss the cooked pork with the pineapple, peppers and sauce. Serve garnished with chopped scallions.

Pork with Aloha Salsa

Prep time: 20 minutes | Cook time: 8 minutes | Serves 4

2 eggs
2 tablespoons milk
¼ cup flour
¼ cup panko bread crumbs
4 teaspoons sesame seeds
1 pound (454 g)
Aloha Salsa:
1 cup fresh pineapple, chopped in small pieces
¼ cup red onion, finely chopped
¼ cup green or red bell pepper, chopped
½ teaspoon ground
boneless, thin pork cutlets (⅜- to ½-inch thick)
Lemon pepper and salt, to taste
¼ cup cornstarch
Cooking spray

cinnamon
1 teaspoon low-sodium soy sauce
⅛ teaspoon crushed red pepper
⅛ teaspoon ground black pepper

1. In a medium bowl, stir together all ingredients for salsa. Cover and refrigerate while cooking the pork.
2. Preheat the air fryer oven to 390°F (199°C).
3. Beat the eggs and milk in a shallow dish.
4. In another shallow dish, mix the flour, panko, and sesame seeds.
5. Sprinkle pork cutlets with lemon pepper and salt.
6. Dip pork cutlets in cornstarch, egg mixture, and then panko coating. Spray both sides with cooking spray and transfer to the air fryer basket.
7. Place the air fryer basket onto the baking pan and slide into Rack Position 2, select Air Fry and set time to 3 minutes.
8. Turn cutlets over, spraying both sides, and continue air frying for 5 minutes or until well done.
9. Serve fried cutlets with salsa on the side.

Skirt Steak Fajitas

Prep time: 15 minutes | Cook time: 30 minutes | Serves 4

2 tablespoons olive oil
¼ cup lime juice
1 clove garlic, minced
½ teaspoon ground cumin
½ teaspoon hot sauce
½ teaspoon salt
2 tablespoons chopped fresh cilantro

1 pound (454 g) skirt steak
1 onion, sliced
1 teaspoon chili powder
1 red pepper, sliced
1 green pepper, sliced
Salt and freshly ground black pepper, to taste
8 flour tortillas

Toppings:

Shredded lettuce
Crumbled Queso Fresco (or grated Cheddar cheese)

Sliced black olives
Diced tomatoes
Sour cream
Guacamole

1. Combine the olive oil, lime juice, garlic, cumin, hot sauce, salt and cilantro in a shallow dish. Add the skirt steak and turn it over several times to coat all sides. Pierce the steak with a needle-style meat tenderizer or paring knife. Marinate the steak in the refrigerator for at least 3 hours, or overnight. When you are ready to cook, remove the steak from the refrigerator and let it sit at room temperature for 30 minutes.
2. Preheat the air fryer oven to 400ºF (204ºC).
3. Toss the onion slices with the chili powder and a little olive oil and transfer them to the air fryer basket.
4. Place the air fryer basket onto the baking pan and slide into Rack Position 2, select Air Fry and set time to 5 minutes.
5. Add the red and green peppers to the air fryer basket with the onions, season with salt and pepper and air fry for 8 more minutes, until the onions and peppers are soft. Transfer the vegetables to a dish and cover with aluminum foil to keep warm.
6. Put the skirt steak in the air fryer basket and pour the marinade over the top. Air fry at 400ºF (204ºC) for 12 minutes. Flip the steak over and air fry for an additional 5 minutes. Transfer the cooked steak to a cutting board and let the steak rest for a few minutes. If the peppers and onions need to be heated, return them to the oven for just 1 to 2 minutes.
7. Thinly slice the steak at an angle, cutting against the grain of the steak. Serve the steak with the onions and peppers, the warm tortillas and the fajita toppings on the side.

Swedish Beef Meatballs

Prep time: 10 minutes | Cook time: 12 minutes | Serves 8

1 pound (454 g) ground beef
1 egg, beaten
2 carrots, shredded
2 bread slices, crumbled
1 small onion, minced

½ teaspoons garlic salt
Pepper and salt, to taste
1 cup tomato sauce
2 cups pasta sauce

1. Preheat the air fryer oven to 400ºF (204ºC).
2. In a bowl, combine the ground beef, egg, carrots, crumbled bread, onion, garlic salt, pepper and salt.
3. Divide the mixture into equal amounts and shape each one into a small meatball.
4. Put them in the air fryer basket. Place the air fryer basket onto the baking pan and slide into Rack Position 2, select Air Fry and set time to 7 minutes.
5. Transfer the meatballs to a baking dish and top with the tomato sauce and pasta sauce.
6. Reduce the temperature to 320ºF (160ºC). Place the baking dish into Rack Position 1, select Convection Bake and set time to 5 minutes.
7. Serve hot.

Chapter 6 Appetizers and Snacks

Sweet and Salty Snack Mix

Prep time: 5 minutes | Cook time: 10 minutes | Makes about 10 cups

3 tablespoons butter, melted
½ cup honey
1 teaspoon salt
2 cups granola
2 cups sesame sticks
2 cups crispy corn
puff cereal
2 cups mini pretzel crisps
1 cup cashews
1 cup pepitas
1 cup dried cherries

1. In a small mixing bowl, mix together the butter, honey, and salt until well incorporated.
2. In a large bowl, combine the granola, sesame sticks, corn puff cereal and pretzel crisps, cashews, and pepitas. Drizzle with the butter mixture and toss until evenly coated. Transfer the snack mix to the air fryer basket.
3. Put the air fryer basket on the baking pan and slide into Rack Position 2, select Air Fry, set temperature to 370ºF (188ºC), and set time to 10 minutes.
4. Stir the snack mix halfway through the cooking time.
5. When cooking is complete, they should be lightly toasted. Remove from the oven and allow to cool completely. Scatter with the dried cherries and mix well. Serve immediately.

Kale Chips with Sesame

Prep time: 15 minutes | Cook time: 8 minutes | Serves 5

8 cups deribbed kale leaves, torn into 2-inch pieces
1½ tablespoons olive oil
¾ teaspoon chili
powder
¼ teaspoon garlic powder
½ teaspoon paprika
2 teaspoons sesame seeds

1. In a large bowl, toss the kale with the olive oil, chili powder, garlic powder, paprika, and sesame seeds until well coated.
2. Transfer the kale to the air fryer basket.
3. Put the air fryer basket on the baking pan and slide into Rack Position 2, select Air Fry, set temperature to 350ºF (180ºC), and set time to 8 minutes.
4. Flip the kale twice during cooking.
5. When cooking is complete, the kale should be crispy. Remove from the oven and serve warm.

Cheese and Ham Stuffed Baby Bella

Prep time: 15 minutes | Cook time: 12 minutes | Serves 8

4 ounces (113 g) Mozzarella cheese, cut into pieces
½ cup diced ham
2 green onions, chopped
2 tablespoons bread crumbs
½ teaspoon garlic powder
¼ teaspoon ground oregano
¼ teaspoon ground black pepper
1 to 2 teaspoons olive oil
16 fresh Baby Bella mushrooms, stemmed removed

1. Process the cheese, ham, green onions, bread crumbs, garlic powder, oregano, and pepper in a food processor until finely chopped.
2. With the food processor running, slowly drizzle in 1 to 2 teaspoons olive oil until a thick paste has formed. Transfer the mixture to a bowl.
3. Evenly divide the mixture into the mushroom caps and lightly press down the mixture.
4. Lay the mushrooms in the air fryer basket in a single layer.
5. Put the air fryer basket on the baking pan and slide into Rack Position 2, select Roast, set temperature to 390ºF (199ºC), and set time to 12 minutes.
6. When cooking is complete, the mushrooms should be lightly browned and tender. Remove from the oven to a plate. Let the mushrooms cool for 5 minutes and serve warm.

Carrot Chips

Prep time: 15 minutes | Cook time: 10 minutes | Serves 4

4 to 5 medium carrots, trimmed and thinly sliced
1 tablespoon olive

oil, plus more for greasing
1 teaspoon seasoned salt

1. Toss the carrot slices with 1 tablespoon of olive oil and salt in a medium bowl until thoroughly coated.
2. Grease the air fryer basket with the olive oil. Place the carrot slices in the greased pan.
3. Put the air fryer basket on the baking pan and slide into Rack Position 2, select Air Fry, set temperature to 390ºF (199ºC), and set time to 10 minutes.
4. Stir the carrot slices halfway through the cooking time.
5. When cooking is complete, the chips should be crisp-tender. Remove from the oven and allow to cool for 5 minutes before serving.

Roasted Mixed Nuts

Prep time: 5 minutes | Cook time: 20 minutes | Serves 6

2 cups mixed nuts (walnuts, pecans, and almonds)
2 tablespoons egg white

2 tablespoons sugar
1 teaspoon paprika
1 teaspoon ground cinnamon
Cooking spray

1. Line the air fryer basket with parchment paper and spray with cooking spray.
2. Stir together the mixed nuts, egg white, sugar, paprika, and cinnamon in a small bowl until the nuts are fully coated. Place the nuts in the basket.
3. Put the air fryer basket on the baking pan and slide into Rack Position 2, select Roast, set temperature to 300ºF (150ºC), and set time to 20 minutes.
4. Stir the nuts halfway through the cooking time.
5. When cooking is complete, remove from the oven. Transfer the nuts to a bowl and serve warm.

Cinnamon Apple Wedges

Prep time: 10 minutes | Cook time: 12 minutes | Serves 4

2 medium apples, cored and sliced into ¼-inch wedges
1 teaspoon canola oil
2 teaspoons peeled and grated fresh

ginger
½ teaspoon ground cinnamon
½ cup low-fat Greek vanilla yogurt, for serving

1. In a large bowl, toss the apple wedges with the canola oil, ginger, and cinnamon until evenly coated. Put the apple wedges in the air fryer basket.
2. Put the air fryer basket on the baking pan and slide into Rack Position 2, select Air Fry, set temperature to 360ºF (182ºC), and set time to 12 minutes.
3. When cooking is complete, the apple wedges should be crisp-tender. Remove the apple wedges from the oven and serve drizzled with the yogurt.

Corn and Black Bean Salsa

Prep time: 10 minutes | Cook time: 10 minutes | Serves 4

½ (15-ounce / 425-g) can corn, drained and rinsed
½ (15-ounce / 425-g) can black beans, drained and rinsed
¼ cup chunky salsa
2 ounces (57 g) reduced-fat cream cheese, softened

¼ cup shredded reduced-fat Cheddar cheese
½ teaspoon paprika
½ teaspoon ground cumin
Salt and freshly ground black pepper, to taste

1. Combine the corn, black beans, salsa, cream cheese, Cheddar cheese, paprika, and cumin in a medium bowl. Sprinkle with salt and pepper and stir until well blended.
2. Pour the mixture into the baking pan.
3. Slide the baking pan into Rack Position 2, select Air Fry, set temperature to 325ºF (163ºC), and set time to 10 minutes.
4. When cooking is complete, the mixture should be heated through. Rest for 5 minutes and serve warm.

Spiced Apple Chips

Prep time: 10 minutes | Cook time: 10 minutes | Serves 4

4 medium apples (any type will work), cored and thinly sliced

¼ teaspoon nutmeg
¼ teaspoon cinnamon
Cooking spray

1. Place the apple slices in a large bowl and sprinkle the spices on top. Toss to coat.
2. Put the apple slices in the air fryer basket in a single layer and spray them with cooking spray.
3. Put the air fryer basket on the baking pan and slide into Rack Position 2, select Air Fry, set temperature to 360ºF (182ºC), and set time to 10 minutes.
4. Stir the apple slices halfway through.
5. When cooking is complete, the apple chips should be crispy. Transfer the apple chips to a paper towel-lined plate and rest for 5 minutes before serving.

Cheesy Crab Toasts

Prep time: 10 minutes | Cook time: 5 minutes | Makes 15 to 18 toasts

1 (6-ounce / 170-g) can flaked crab meat, well drained
3 tablespoons light mayonnaise
¼ cup shredded Parmesan cheese
¼ cup shredded Cheddar cheese

1 teaspoon Worcestershire sauce
½ teaspoon lemon juice
1 loaf artisan bread, French bread, or baguette, cut into ⅜-inch-thick slices

1. In a large bowl, stir together all the ingredients except the bread slices.
2. On a clean work surface, lay the bread slices. Spread ½ tablespoon of crab mixture onto each slice of bread.
3. Arrange the bread slices in the baking pan in a single layer.
4. Slide the baking pan into Rack Position 1, select Convection Bake, set temperature to 360ºF (182ºC), and set time to 5 minutes.
5. When cooking is complete, the tops should be lightly browned. Remove from the oven and serve warm.

Veggie Salmon Nachos

Prep time: 10 minutes | Cook time: 10 minutes | Serves 6

2 ounces (57 g) baked no-salt corn tortilla chips
1 (5-ounce / 142-g) baked salmon fillet, flaked
½ cup canned low-sodium black beans, rinsed and drained

1 red bell pepper, chopped
½ cup grated carrot
1 jalapeño pepper, minced
⅓ cup shredded low-sodium low-fat Swiss cheese
1 tomato, chopped

1. Preheat the air fryer oven to 360ºF (182ºC).
2. In a baking pan, layer the tortilla chips. Top with the salmon, black beans, red bell pepper, carrot, jalapeño, and Swiss cheese.
3. Slide the baking pan into Rack Position 1, select Convection Bake and set time to 10 minutes, or until the cheese is melted and starts to brown.
4. Top with the tomato and serve.

Honey Sriracha Chicken Wings

Prep time: 5 minutes | Cook time: 15 minutes | Serves 4

1 tablespoon Sriracha hot sauce
1 tablespoon honey
1 garlic clove, minced

½ teaspoon kosher salt
16 chicken wings and drumettes
Cooking spray

1. Preheat the air fryer oven to 360ºF (182ºC).
2. In a large bowl, whisk together the Sriracha hot sauce, honey, minced garlic, and kosher salt, then add the chicken and toss to coat.
3. Spray the air fryer basket with cooking spray, then place the wings in the basket.
4. Place the air fryer basket onto the baking pan and slide into Rack Position 2, select Air Fry and set time to 15 minutes, flipping halfway through.
5. Remove the wings and allow to cool on a wire rack for 10 minutes before serving.

Spicy Chicken Bites

Prep time: 10 minutes | Cook time: 12 minutes | Makes 30 bites

8 ounces boneless and skinless chicken thighs, cut into 30 pieces
¼ teaspoon kosher
salt
2 tablespoons hot sauce
Cooking spray

1. Preheat the air fryer oven to 390°F (199°C).
2. Spray the air fryer basket with cooking spray and season the chicken bites with the kosher salt, then place in the basket.
3. Place the air fryer basket onto the baking pan and slide into Rack Position 2, select Air Fry and set time to 12 minutes.
4. While the chicken bites cook, pour the hot sauce into a large bowl.
5. Remove the bites and add to the sauce bowl, tossing to coat. Serve warm.

Avocado Chips

Prep time: 15 minutes | Cook time: 10 minutes | Serves 4

1 egg
1 tablespoon lime juice
⅛ teaspoon hot sauce
2 tablespoons flour
¾ cup panko bread
crumbs
¼ cup cornmeal
¼ teaspoon salt
1 large avocado, pitted, peeled, and cut into ½-inch slices
Cooking spray

1. Whisk together the egg, lime juice, and hot sauce in a small bowl.
2. On a sheet of wax paper, place the flour. In a separate sheet of wax paper, combine the bread crumbs, cornmeal, and salt.
3. Dredge the avocado slices one at a time in the flour, then in the egg mixture, finally roll them in the bread crumb mixture to coat well.
4. Place the breaded avocado slices in the air fryer basket and mist them with cooking spray.
5. Put the air fryer basket on the baking pan and slide into Rack Position 2, select Air Fry, set temperature to 390°F (199°C), and set time to 10 minutes.

6. When cooking is complete, the slices should be nicely browned and crispy. Transfer the avocado slices to a plate and serve.

Italian Rice Balls

Prep time: 20 minutes | Cook time: 10 minutes | Makes 8 rice balls

1½ cups cooked sticky rice
½ teaspoon Italian seasoning blend
¾ teaspoon salt, divided
8 black olives, pitted
1 ounce (28 g) Mozzarella cheese,
cut into tiny pieces (small enough to stuff into olives)
2 eggs
⅓ cup Italian bread crumbs
¾ cup panko bread crumbs
Cooking spray

1. Stuff each black olive with a piece of Mozzarella cheese.
2. In a bowl, combine the cooked sticky rice, Italian seasoning blend, and ½ teaspoon of salt and stir to mix well. Form the rice mixture into a log with your hands and divide it into 8 equal portions. Mold each portion around a black olive and roll into a ball.
3. Transfer to the freezer to chill for 10 to 15 minutes until firm.
4. In a shallow dish, place the Italian bread crumbs. In a separate shallow dish, whisk the eggs. In a third shallow dish, combine the panko bread crumbs and remaining salt.
5. One by one, roll the rice balls in the Italian bread crumbs, then dip in the whisked eggs, finally coat them with the panko bread crumbs.
6. Arrange the rice balls in the air fryer basket and spritz both sides with cooking spray.
7. Put the air fryer basket on the baking pan and slide into Rack Position 2, select Air Fry, set temperature to 390°F (199°C), and set time to 10 minutes.
8. Flip the balls halfway through the cooking time.
9. When cooking is complete, the rice balls should be golden brown. Remove from the oven and serve warm.

Crunchy Chickpeas

Prep time: 5 minutes | Cook time: 18 minutes | Serves 4

½ teaspoon chili
powder
½ teaspoon ground
cumin
¼ teaspoon cayenne
pepper

¼ teaspoon salt
1 (19-ounce / 539-
g) can chickpeas,
drained and rinsed
Cooking spray

1. Lina the air fryer basket with parchment paper and lightly spritz with cooking spray.
2. Mix the chili powder, cumin, cayenne pepper, and salt in a small bowl.
3. Place the chickpeas in a medium bowl and lightly mist with cooking spray.
4. Add the spice mixture to the chickpeas and toss until evenly coated. Transfer the chickpeas to the parchment.
5. Put the air fryer basket on the baking pan and slide into Rack Position 2, select Air Fry, set temperature to 390°F (199°C), and set time to 18 minutes.
6. Stir the chickpeas twice during cooking.
7. When cooking is complete, the chickpeas should be crunchy. Remove from the oven and let the chickpeas cool for 5 minutes before serving.

Paprika Potato Chips

Prep time: 5 minutes | Cook time: 22 minutes | Serves 3

2 medium potatoes,
preferably Yukon
Gold, scrubbed
Cooking spray
2 teaspoons olive oil
½ teaspoon garlic
granules

¼ teaspoon paprika
¼ teaspoon plus ⅛
teaspoon sea salt
¼ teaspoon freshly
ground black pepper
Ketchup or hot
sauce, for serving

1. Spritz the air fryer basket with cooking spray.
2. On a flat work surface, cut the potatoes into ¼-inch-thick slices. Transfer the potato slices to a medium bowl, along with the olive oil, garlic granules, paprika, salt, and pepper and toss to coat well. Transfer the potato slices to the basket.

3. Put the air fryer basket on the baking pan and slide into Rack Position 2, select Air Fry, set temperature to 392°F (200°C), and set time to 22 minutes.
4. Stir the potato slices twice during the cooking process.
5. When cooking is complete, the potato chips should be tender and nicely browned. Remove from the oven and serve alongside the ketchup for dipping.

Sausage and Mushroom Empanadas

Prep time: 5 minutes | Cook time: 12 minutes | Serves 4

½ pound (227 g)
Kielbasa smoked
sausage, chopped
4 chopped canned
mushrooms
2 tablespoons
chopped onion
½ teaspoon ground
cumin

¼ teaspoon paprika
Salt and black
pepper, to taste
½ package puff
pastry dough, at
room temperature
1 egg, beaten
Cooking spray

1. Combine the sausage, mushrooms, onion, cumin, paprika, salt, and pepper in a bowl and stir to mix well.
2. Make the empanadas: Place the puff pastry dough on a lightly floured surface. Cut circles into the dough with a glass. Place 1 tablespoon of the sausage mixture into the center of each pastry circle. Fold each in half and pinch the edges to seal. Using a fork, crimp the edges. Brush them with the beaten egg and mist with cooking spray.
3. Spritz the air fryer basket with cooking spray. Place the empanadas in the basket.
4. Put the air fryer basket on the baking pan and slide into Rack Position 2, select Air Fry, set temperature to 360°F (182°C), and set time to 12 minutes.
5. Flip the empanadas halfway through the cooking time.
6. When cooking is complete, the empanadas should be golden brown. Remove from the oven. Allow them to cool for 5 minutes and serve hot.

Old Bay Chicken Wings

Prep time: 10 minutes | Cook time: 13 minutes | Serves 4

2 tablespoons Old Bay seasoning
2 teaspoons baking powder
2 teaspoons salt

2 pounds (907 g) chicken wings, patted dry
Cooking spray

1. Combine the Old Bay seasoning, baking powder, and salt in a large zip-top plastic bag. Add the chicken wings, seal, and shake until the wings are thoroughly coated in the seasoning mixture.
2. Lightly spray the air fryer basket with cooking spray. Lay the chicken wings in the basket in a single layer and lightly mist them with cooking spray.
3. Put the air fryer basket on the baking pan and slide into Rack Position 2, select Air Fry, set temperature to 400ºF (205ºC), and set time to 13 minutes.
4. Flip the wings halfway through the cooking time.
5. When cooking is complete, the wings should reach an internal temperature of 165ºF (74ºC) on a meat thermometer. Remove from the oven to a plate and serve hot.

Crispy Green Tomatoes with Horseradish

Prep time: 18 minutes | Cook time: 13 minutes | Serves 4

2 eggs
¼ cup buttermilk
½ cup bread crumbs
½ cup cornmeal
¼ teaspoon salt
Horseradish Sauce:
¼ cup sour cream
¼ cup mayonnaise
2 teaspoons prepared horseradish
½ teaspoon lemon

1½ pounds (680 g) firm green tomatoes, cut into ¼-inch slices
Cooking spray

juice
½ teaspoon Worcestershire sauce
⅛ teaspoon black pepper

1. Spritz the air fryer basket with cooking spray. Set aside.
2. In a small bowl, whisk together all the ingredients for the horseradish sauce until smooth. Set aside.

3. In a shallow dish, beat the eggs and buttermilk.
4. In a separate shallow dish, thoroughly combine the bread crumbs, cornmeal, and salt.
5. Dredge the tomato slices, one at a time, in the egg mixture, then roll in the bread crumb mixture until evenly coated.
6. Place the tomato slices in the basket in a single layer. Spray them with cooking spray.
7. Put the air fryer basket on the baking pan and slide into Rack Position 2, select Air Fry, set temperature to 390ºF (199ºC), and set time to 13 minutes.
8. Flip the tomato slices halfway through the cooking time.
9. When cooking is complete, the tomato slices should be nicely browned and crisp. Remove from the oven to a platter and serve drizzled with the prepared horseradish sauce.

Bruschetta with Tomato and Basil

Prep time: 5 minutes | Cook time: 3 minutes | Serves 6

4 tomatoes, diced
⅓ cup shredded fresh basil
¼ cup shredded Parmesan cheese
1 tablespoon balsamic vinegar
1 tablespoon minced garlic

1 teaspoon olive oil
1 teaspoon salt
1 teaspoon freshly ground black pepper
1 loaf French bread, cut into 1-inch-thick slices
Cooking spray

1. Mix together the tomatoes and basil in a medium bowl. Add the cheese, vinegar, garlic, olive oil, salt, and pepper and stir until well incorporated. Set aside.
2. Spritz the baking pan with cooking spray and lay the bread slices in the pan in a single layer. Spray the slices with cooking spray.
3. Slide the baking pan into Rack Position 1, select Convection Bake, set temperature to 250ºF (121ºC), and set time to 3 minutes.
4. When cooking is complete, remove from the oven to a plate. Top each slice with a generous spoonful of the tomato mixture and serve.

Homemade BBQ Chicken Pizza

Prep time: 5 minutes | Cook time: 8 minutes | Serves 1

1 piece naan bread
¼ cup Barbecue sauce
¼ cup shredded Monterrey Jack cheese
¼ cup shredded Mozzarella cheese
½ chicken herby sausage, sliced
2 tablespoons red onion, thinly sliced
Chopped cilantro or parsley, for garnish
Cooking spray

1. Spritz the bottom of naan bread with cooking spray, then transfer to the air fryer basket.
2. Brush with the Barbecue sauce. Top with the cheeses, sausage, and finish with the red onion.
3. Put the air fryer basket on the baking pan and slide into Rack Position 2, select Air Fry, set temperature to 400°F (205°C), and set time to 8 minutes.
4. When cooking is complete, the cheese should be melted. Remove from the oven. Garnish with the chopped cilantro or parsley before slicing to serve.

Turkey Bacon-Wrapped Dates

Prep time: 10 minutes | Cook time: 6 minutes | Makes 16 appetizers

16 whole dates, pitted
16 whole almonds
6 to 8 strips turkey bacon, cut in half

Special Equipment:
16 toothpicks, soaked in water for at least 30 minutes

1. On a flat work surface, stuff each pitted date with a whole almond.
2. Wrap half slice of bacon around each date and secure it with a toothpick.
3. Place the bacon-wrapped dates in the air fryer basket.
4. Put the air fryer basket on the baking pan and slide into Rack Position 2, select Air Fry, set temperature to 390°F (199°C), and set time to 6 minutes.
5. When cooking is complete, transfer the dates to a paper towel-lined plate to drain. Serve hot.

Mushroom and Spinach Calzones

Prep time: 15 minutes | Cook time: 26 to 27 minutes | Serves 4

2 tablespoons olive oil
1 onion, chopped
2 garlic cloves, minced
¼ cup chopped mushrooms
1 pound (454 g) spinach, chopped
1 tablespoon Italian seasoning
½ teaspoon oregano
Salt and black pepper, to taste
1½ cups marinara sauce
1 cup ricotta cheese, crumbled
1 (13-ounce / 369-g) pizza crust
Cooking spray

Make the Filling:
1. Heat the olive oil in a pan over medium heat until shimmering.
2. Add the onion, garlic, and mushrooms and sauté for 4 minutes, or until softened.
3. Stir in the spinach and sauté for 2 to 3 minutes, or until the spinach is wilted. Sprinkle with the Italian seasoning, oregano, salt, and pepper and mix well.
4. Add the marinara sauce and cook for about 5 minutes, stirring occasionally, or until the sauce is thickened.
5. Remove the pan from the heat and stir in the ricotta cheese. Set aside.

Make the Calzones:
1. Spritz the air fryer basket with cooking spray. Set aside.
2. Roll the pizza crust out with a rolling pin on a lightly floured work surface, then cut it into 4 rectangles.
3. Spoon ¼ of the filling into each rectangle and fold in half. Crimp the edges with a fork to seal. Mist them with cooking spray. Transfer the calzones to the basket.
4. Put the air fryer basket on the baking pan and slide into Rack Position 2, select Air Fry, set temperature to 375°F (190°C), and set time to 15 minutes.
5. Flip the calzones halfway through the cooking time.
6. When cooking is complete, the calzones should be golden brown and crisp. Transfer the calzones to a paper towel-lined plate and serve.

Crispy Cod Fingers

Prep time: 5 minutes | Cook time: 12 minutes | Serves 4

2 eggs
2 tablespoons milk
2 cups flour
1 cup cornmeal
1 teaspoon seafood seasoning

Salt and black pepper, to taste
1 cup bread crumbs
1 pound (454 g) cod fillets, cut into 1-inch strips

1. Beat the eggs with the milk in a shallow bowl. In another shallow bowl, combine the flour, cornmeal, seafood seasoning, salt, and pepper. On a plate, place the bread crumbs.
2. Dredge the cod strips, one at a time, in the flour mixture, then in the egg mixture, finally roll in the bread crumb to coat evenly.
3. Transfer the cod strips to the air fryer basket.
4. Put the air fryer basket on the baking pan and slide into Rack Position 2, select Air Fry, set temperature to 400°F (205°C), and set time to 12 minutes.
5. When cooking is complete, the cod strips should be crispy. Remove from the oven to a paper towel-lined plate and serve warm.

Cripsy Artichoke Bites

Prep time: 10 minutes | Cook time: 8 minutes | Serves 4

14 whole artichoke hearts packed in water
½ cup all-purpose flour
1 egg

⅓ cup panko bread crumbs
1 teaspoon Italian seasoning
Cooking spray

1. Drain the artichoke hearts and dry thoroughly with paper towels.
2. Place the flour on a plate. Beat the egg in a shallow bowl until frothy. Thoroughly combine the bread crumbs and Italian seasoning in a separate shallow bowl.
3. Dredge the artichoke hearts in the flour, then in the beaten egg, and finally roll in the bread crumb mixture until evenly coated.

4. Place the artichoke hearts in the air fryer basket and mist them with cooking spray.
5. Put the air fryer basket on the baking pan and slide into Rack Position 2, select Air Fry, set temperature to 375°F (190°C), and set time to 8 minutes.
6. Flip the artichoke hearts halfway through the cooking time.
7. When cooking is complete, the artichoke hearts should start to brown and the edges should be crispy. Remove from the oven and let the artichoke hearts sit for 5 minutes before serving.

Muffuletta Sliders with Olives

Prep time: 10 minutes | Cook time: 6 minutes | Makes 8 sliders

¼ pound (113 g) thinly sliced deli ham
¼ pound (113 g) thinly sliced pastrami
4 ounces (113 g) low-fat Mozzarella
Olive Mix:
½ cup sliced green olives with pimentos
¼ cup sliced black olives
¼ cup chopped kalamata olives

cheese, grated
8 slider buns, split in half
Cooking spray
1 tablespoon sesame seeds

1 teaspoon red wine vinegar
¼ teaspoon basil
⅛ teaspoon garlic powder

1. Combine all the ingredients for the olive mix in a small bowl and stir well.
2. Stir together the ham, pastrami, and cheese in a medium bowl and divide the mixture into 8 equal portions.
3. Assemble the sliders: Top each bottom bun with 1 portion of meat and cheese, 2 tablespoons of olive mix, finished by the remaining buns. Lightly spritz the tops with cooking spray. Scatter the sesame seeds on top.
4. Arrange the sliders in the baking pan.
5. Slide the baking pan into Rack Position 1, select Convection Bake, set temperature to 360°F (182°C), and set time to 6 minutes.
6. When cooking is complete, the cheese should be melted. Remove the pan from the oven and serve.

Crispy Spiced Chickpeas

Prep time: 5 minutes | Cook time: 12 minutes | Makes 1½ cups

1 can (15-ounce / 425-g) chickpeas, rinsed and dried with paper towels
1 tablespoon olive oil
½ teaspoon dried rosemary
½ teaspoon dried parsley
½ teaspoon dried chives
¼ teaspoon mustard powder
¼ teaspoon sweet paprika
¼ teaspoon cayenne pepper
Kosher salt and freshly ground black pepper, to taste

1. Preheat the air fryer oven to 350ºF (177ºC).
2. In a large bowl, combine all the ingredients, except for the kosher salt and black pepper, and toss until the chickpeas are evenly coated in the herbs and spices.
3. Transfer the chickpeas and seasonings to the air fryer basket.
4. Place the air fryer basket onto the baking pan and slide into Rack Position 2, select Air Fry and set time to 12 minutes, or until browned and crisp. Shake the basket halfway through the cooking time.
5. Transfer the crispy chickpeas to a bowl, sprinkle with kosher salt and black pepper, and serve warm.

Air Fried Chicken Wings

Prep time: 1 hour 20 minutes | Cook time: 18 minutes | Serves 4

2 pounds (907 g) chicken wings
Cooking spray
Marinade:
1 cup buttermilk
½ teaspoon salt
½ teaspoon black pepper
Coating:
1 cup flour
1 cup panko bread crumbs
2 tablespoons poultry seasoning
2 teaspoons salt

1. Whisk together all the ingredients for the marinade in a large bowl.
2. Add the chicken wings to the marinade and toss well. Transfer to the refrigerator to marinate for at least an hour.
3. Spritz the air fryer basket with cooking spray. Set aside.
4. Thoroughly combine all the ingredients for the coating in a shallow bowl.
5. Remove the chicken wings from the marinade and shake off any excess. Roll them in the coating mixture.
6. Place the chicken wings in the basket in a single layer. Mist the wings with cooking spray.
7. Put the air fryer basket on the baking pan and slide into Rack Position 2, select Air Fry, set temperature to 360ºF (182ºC), and set time to 18 minutes.
8. Flip the wings halfway through the cooking time.
9. When cooking is complete, the wings should be crisp and golden brown on the outside. Remove from the oven to a plate and serve hot.

Cuban Sandwiches

Prep time: 20 minutes | Cook time: 8 minutes | Makes 4 sandwiches

8 slices ciabatta bread, about ¼-inch thick
Cooking spray
1 tablespoon brown mustard
Toppings:
6 to 8 ounces (170 to 227 g) thinly sliced leftover roast pork
4 ounces (113 g) thinly sliced deli turkey
⅓ cup bread and butter pickle slices
2 to 3 ounces (57 to 85 g) Pepper Jack cheese slices

1. On a clean work surface, spray one side of each slice of bread with cooking spray. Spread the other side of each slice of bread evenly with brown mustard.
2. Top 4 of the bread slices with the roast pork, turkey, pickle slices, cheese, and finish with remaining bread slices. Transfer to the air fryer basket.
3. Put the air fryer basket on the baking pan and slide into Rack Position 2, select Air Fry, set temperature to 390ºF (199ºC), and set time to 8 minutes.
4. When cooking is complete, remove from the oven. Cool for 5 minutes and serve warm.

Deluxe Cheese Sandwiches

Prep time: 10 minutes | Cook time: 6 minutes | Serves 4 to 8

8 ounces (227 g) Brie
8 slices oat nut bread
1 large ripe pear, cored and cut into ½-inch-thick slices
2 tablespoons butter, melted

1. Make the sandwiches: Spread each of 4 slices of bread with ¼ of the Brie. Top the Brie with the pear slices and remaining 4 bread slices.
2. Brush the melted butter lightly on both sides of each sandwich.
3. Arrange the sandwiches in the baking pan.
4. Slide the baking pan into Rack Position 1, select Convection Bake, set temperature to 360°F (182°C), and set time to 6 minutes.
5. When cooking is complete, the cheese should be melted. Remove the pan from the oven and serve warm.

Tangy Fried Pickle Spears

Prep time: 5 minutes | Cook time: 15 minutes | Serves 6

2 jars sweet and sour pickle spears, patted dry
2 medium-sized eggs
⅓ cup milk
1 teaspoon garlic powder
1 teaspoon sea salt
½ teaspoon shallot powder
⅓ teaspoon chili powder
⅓ cup all-purpose flour
Cooking spray

1. Spritz the air fryer basket with cooking spray.
2. In a bowl, beat together the eggs with milk. In another bowl, combine garlic powder, sea salt, shallot powder, chili powder and all-purpose flour until well blended.
3. One by one, roll the pickle spears in the powder mixture, then dredge them in the egg mixture. Dip them in the powder mixture a second time for additional coating.

4. Place the coated pickles in the basket.
5. Put the air fryer basket on the baking pan and slide into Rack Position 2, select Air Fry, set temperature to 385°F (196°C), and set time to 15 minutes.
6. Stir the pickles halfway through the cooking time.
7. When cooking is complete, they should be golden and crispy. Transfer to a plate and let cool for 5 minutes before serving.

Spiced Sweet Potato Fries

Prep time: 10 minutes | Cook time: 15 minutes | Serves 2

2 tablespoons olive oil
1½ teaspoons smoked paprika
1½ teaspoons kosher salt, plus more as needed
1 teaspoon chili powder
½ teaspoon ground cumin
½ teaspoon ground turmeric
½ teaspoon mustard powder
¼ teaspoon cayenne pepper
2 medium sweet potatoes (about 10 ounces / 284 g each), cut into wedges, ½ inch thick and 3 inches long
Freshly ground black pepper, to taste
⅔ cup sour cream
1 garlic clove, grated

1. Preheat the air fryer oven to 400°F (204°C).
2. In a large bowl, combine the olive oil, paprika, salt, chili powder, cumin, turmeric, mustard powder, and cayenne. Add the sweet potatoes, season with black pepper, and toss to evenly coat.
3. Transfer the sweet potatoes to the air fryer basket (save the bowl with the leftover oil and spices).
4. Place the air fryer basket onto the baking pan and slide into Rack Position 2, select Air Fry and set time to 15 minutes. Shake the basket halfway through, or until golden brown and crisp.
5. Return the potato wedges to the reserved bowl and toss again while they are hot.
6. Meanwhile, in a small bowl, stir together the sour cream and garlic. Season with salt and black pepper and transfer to a serving dish.
7. Serve the potato wedges hot with the garlic sour cream.

Peppery Chicken Meatballs

Prep time: 5 minutes | Cook time: 18 minutes | Makes 16 meatballs

2 teaspoons olive oil	1 egg white
¼ cup minced onion	½ teaspoon dried thyme
¼ cup minced red bell pepper	½ pound (227 g) ground chicken breast
2 vanilla wafers, crushed	

1. Preheat the air fryer oven to 370°F (188°C).
2. In a mixing bowl, combine the olive oil, onion, and red bell pepper. Transfer to the air fryer basket.
3. Place the air fryer basket onto the baking pan and slide into Rack Position 2, select Air Fry and set time to 5 minutes, or until the vegetables are tender.
4. In a medium bowl, mix the cooked vegetables, crushed wafers, egg white, and thyme until well combined
5. Mix in the chicken, gently but thoroughly, until everything is combined.
6. Form the mixture into 16 meatballs and place them in the air fryer basket.
7. Place the air fryer basket onto the baking pan and slide into Rack Position 2, select Air Fry and set time to 13 minutes, or until the meatballs reach an internal temperature of 165°F (74°C) on a meat thermometer.
8. Serve immediately.

Shishito Peppers with Herb Dressing

Prep time: 10 minutes | Cook time: 6 minutes | Serves 2 to 4

6 ounces (170 g) shishito peppers	leaf parsley
1 tablespoon vegetable oil	1 tablespoon finely chopped fresh tarragon
Kosher salt and freshly ground black pepper, to taste	1 tablespoon finely chopped fresh chives
½ cup mayonnaise	Finely grated zest of ½ lemon
2 tablespoons finely chopped fresh basil leaves	1 tablespoon fresh lemon juice
2 tablespoons finely chopped fresh flat-	Flaky sea salt, for serving

1. Preheat the air fryer oven to 400°F (204°C).
2. In a bowl, toss together the shishitos and oil to evenly coat and season with kosher salt and black pepper. Transfer to the air fryer basket.
3. Place the air fryer basket onto the baking pan and slide into Rack Position 2, select Air Fry and set time to 6 minutes. Shake the basket halfway through, or until the shishitos are blistered and lightly charred.
4. Meanwhile, in a small bowl, whisk together the mayonnaise, basil, parsley, tarragon, chives, lemon zest, and lemon juice.
5. Pile the peppers on a plate, sprinkle with flaky sea salt, and serve hot with the dressing.

Sweet Bacon Tater Tots

Prep time: 5 minutes | Cook time: 17 minutes | Serves 4

24 frozen tater tots	syrup
6 slices cooked bacon	1 cup shredded Cheddar cheese
2 tablespoons maple	

1. Preheat the air fryer oven to 400°F (204°C).
2. Put the tater tots in the air fryer basket.
3. Place the air fryer basket onto the baking pan and slide into Rack Position 2, select Air Fry and set time to 10 minutes. Shake the basket halfway through the cooking time.
4. Meanwhile, cut the bacon into 1-inch pieces.
5. Remove the tater tots from the air fryer basket and put into a baking pan. Top with the bacon and drizzle with the maple syrup.
6. Return to the oven and air fry for an additional 5 minutes, or until the tots and bacon are crisp.
7. Top with the cheese and air fry for 2 minutes, or until the cheese is melted.
8. Serve hot.

Pigs in a Blanket

Prep time: 5 minutes | Cook time: 14 minutes | Serves 4 to 6

24 cocktail smoked sausages
6 slices deli-sliced Cheddar cheese, each cut into 8 rectangular pieces
1 (8-ounce / 227-g) tube refrigerated crescent roll dough

1. Preheat the air fryer oven to 350°F (177°C).
2. Unroll the crescent roll dough into one large sheet. If your crescent roll dough has perforated seams, pinch or roll all the perforated seams together. Cut the large sheet of dough into 4 rectangles. Then cut each rectangle into 6 pieces by making one slice lengthwise in the middle and 2 slices horizontally. You should have 24 pieces of dough.
3. Make a deep slit lengthwise down the center of the cocktail sausage. Stuff two pieces of cheese into the slit in the sausage. Roll one piece of crescent dough around the stuffed cocktail sausage, leaving the ends of the sausage exposed. Pinch the seam together. Repeat with the remaining sausages.
4. Put the sausages seam-side down in the basket. Place the air fryer basket onto the baking pan and slide into Rack Position 2, select Air Fry and set time to 7 minutes.
5. Serve hot.

Poutine with Waffle Fries

Prep time: 10 minutes | Cook time: 17 minutes | Serves 4

2 cups frozen waffle cut fries
2 teaspoons olive oil
1 red bell pepper, chopped
2 green onions, sliced
1 cup shredded Swiss cheese
½ cup bottled chicken gravy

1. Preheat the air fryer oven to 380°F (193°C).
2. Toss the waffle fries with the olive oil and place in the air fryer basket.
3. Place the air fryer basket onto the baking pan and slide into Rack Position 2, select Air Fry and set time to 12 minutes, or until the fries are crisp and light golden brown. Shake the basket halfway through the cooking time.
4. When done, transfer the fries to a baking pan and top with the pepper, green onions, and cheese.
5. Return to the oven and air fry for 3 minutes, or until the vegetables are crisp and tender.
6. Remove the pan from the oven and drizzle the gravy over the fries. Air fry for 2 minutes more, or until the gravy is hot.
7. Serve immediately.

Root Veggie Chips with Herb Salt

Prep time: 10 minutes | Cook time: 8 minutes | Serves 2

1 parsnip, washed
1 small beet, washed
1 small turnip, washed
½ small sweet potato, washed
1 teaspoon olive oil
Cooking spray
Herb Salt:
¼ teaspoon kosher salt
2 teaspoons finely chopped fresh parsley

1. Preheat the air fryer oven to 360°F (182°C).
2. Peel and thinly slice the parsnip, beet, turnip, and sweet potato, then place the vegetables in a large bowl, add the olive oil, and toss.
3. Spray the air fryer basket with cooking spray, then place the vegetables in the basket.
4. Place the air fryer basket onto the baking pan and slide into Rack Position 2, select Air Fry and set time to 8 minutes. Gently shake the basket halfway through.
5. While the chips cook, make the herb salt in a small bowl by combining the kosher salt and parsley.
6. Remove the chips and place on a serving plate, then sprinkle the herb salt on top and allow to cool for 2 to 3 minutes before serving.

Spinach and Crab Meat Cups

Prep time: 10 minutes | Cook time: 5 minutes | Makes 30 cups

1 (6-ounce / 170-g) can crab meat, drained to yield 1/3 cup meat
1/4 cup frozen spinach, thawed, drained, and chopped
1 clove garlic, minced
1/2 cup grated

Parmesan cheese
3 tablespoons plain yogurt
1/4 teaspoon lemon juice
1/2 teaspoon Worcestershire sauce
30 mini frozen phyllo shells, thawed
Cooking spray

1. Preheat the air fryer oven to 390ºF (199ºC).
2. Remove any bits of shell that might remain in the crab meat.
3. Mix the crab meat, spinach, garlic, and cheese together.
4. Stir in the yogurt, lemon juice, and Worcestershire sauce and mix well.
5. Spoon a teaspoon of filling into each phyllo shell.
6. Spray the air fryer basket with cooking spray and arrange the shells in the basket.
7. Place the air fryer basket onto the baking pan and slide into Rack Position 2, select Air Fry and set time to 5 minutes.
8. Serve immediately.

Mozzarella Arancini

Prep time: 5 minutes | Cook time: 10 minutes | Makes 16 arancini

2 cups cooked rice, cooled
2 eggs, beaten
1½ cups panko bread crumbs, divided
1/2 cup grated

Parmesan cheese
2 tablespoons minced fresh basil
16 ¾-inch cubes Mozzarella cheese
2 tablespoons olive oil

1. Preheat the air fryer oven to 400ºF (204ºC).
2. In a medium bowl, combine the rice, eggs, 1/2 cup of the bread crumbs, Parmesan cheese, and basil. Form this mixture into 16 1½-inch balls.

3. Poke a hole in each of the balls with your finger and insert a Mozzarella cube. Form the rice mixture firmly around the cheese.
4. On a shallow plate, combine the remaining 1 cup of the bread crumbs with the olive oil and mix well. Roll the rice balls in the bread crumbs to coat. Put in the air fryer basket.
5. Place the air fryer basket onto the baking pan and slide into Rack Position 2, select Air Fry and set time to 10 minutes, or until golden brown.
6. Serve hot.

Rosemary-Garlic Shoestring Fries

Prep time: 5 minutes | Cook time: 18 minutes | Serves 2

1 large russet potato (about 12 ounces / 340 g), scrubbed clean, and julienned
1 tablespoon vegetable oil
Leaves from 1 sprig fresh rosemary

Kosher salt and freshly ground black pepper, to taste
1 garlic clove, thinly sliced
Flaky sea salt, for serving

1. Preheat the air fryer oven to 400ºF (204ºC).
2. Place the julienned potatoes in a large colander and rinse under cold running water until the water runs clear. Spread the potatoes out on a double-thick layer of paper towels and pat dry.
3. In a large bowl, combine the potatoes, oil, and rosemary. Season with kosher salt and pepper and toss to coat evenly. Put the potatoes in the air fryer basket.
4. Place the air fryer basket onto the baking pan and slide into Rack Position 2, select Air Fry and set time to 18 minutes. Shake the basket every 5 minutes and adding the garlic in the last 5 minutes of cooking, or until the fries are golden brown and crisp.
5. Transfer the fries to a plate and sprinkle with flaky sea salt while they're hot. Serve immediately.

Spicy Chicken Wings

Prep time: 5 minutes | Cook time: 20 minutes | Serves 2 to 4

1¼ pounds (567 g) chicken wings, separated into flats and drumettes
1 teaspoon baking powder
1 teaspoon cayenne pepper

¼ teaspoon garlic powder
Kosher salt and freshly ground black pepper, to taste
1 tablespoon unsalted butter, melted

For serving:

Blue cheese dressing
Celery

Carrot sticks

1. Place the chicken wings on a large plate, then sprinkle evenly with the baking powder, cayenne, and garlic powder. Toss the wings with your hands, making sure the baking powder and seasonings fully coat them, until evenly incorporated. Let the wings stand in the refrigerator for 1 hour or up to overnight.
2. Preheat the air fryer oven to 400°F (204°C).
3. Season the wings with salt and black pepper, then transfer to the air fryer basket.
4. Place the air fryer basket onto the baking pan and slide into Rack Position 2, select Air Fry and set time to 20 minutes, or until the wings are crisp and golden brown.
5. Transfer the wings to a bowl and toss with the butter while they're hot.
6. Arrange the wings on a platter and serve warm with the blue cheese dressing, celery and carrot sticks.

Tortellini with Spicy Dipping Sauce

Prep time: 5 minutes | Cook time: 10 minutes | Serves 4

¾ cup mayonnaise
2 tablespoons mustard
1 egg
½ cup flour
½ teaspoon dried oregano

1½ cups bread crumbs
2 tablespoons olive oil
2 cups frozen cheese tortellini

1. Preheat the air fryer oven to 380°F (193°C).
2. In a small bowl, combine the mayonnaise and mustard and mix well. Set aside.
3. In a shallow bowl, beat the egg. In a separate bowl, combine the flour and oregano. In another bowl, combine the bread crumbs and olive oil, and mix well.
4. Drop the tortellini, a few at a time, into the egg, then into the flour, then into the egg again, and then into the bread crumbs to coat. Put them into the air fryer basket.
5. Place the air fryer basket onto the baking pan and slide into Rack Position 2, select Air Fry and set time to 10 minutes. Shake the basket halfway through the cooking time, or until the tortellini are crisp and golden brown on the outside.
6. Serve with the mayonnaise mixture.

Lemony Pear Chips

Prep time: 15 minutes | Cook time: 11 to 13 minutes | Serves 4

2 firm Bosc pears, cut crosswise into ⅛-inch-thick slices
1 tablespoon freshly squeezed lemon

juice
½ teaspoon ground cinnamon
⅛ teaspoon ground cardamom

1. Preheat the air fryer oven to 380°F (193°C).
2. Separate the smaller stem-end pear rounds from the larger rounds with seeds. Remove the core and seeds from the larger slices. Sprinkle all slices with lemon juice, cinnamon, and cardamom.
3. Put the smaller chips into the air fryer basket.
4. Place the air fryer basket onto the baking pan and slide into Rack Position 2, select Air Fry and set time to 5 minutes, or until light golden brown. Shake the basket once during cooking. Remove from the oven.
5. Repeat with the larger slices, air frying for 6 to 8 minutes, or until light golden brown, shaking the basket once during cooking.
6. Remove the chips from the oven. Cool and serve or store in an airtight container at room temperature up for to 2 days.

Herbed Pita Chips

Prep time: 5 minutes | Cook time: 5 to 6 minutes | Serves 4

¼ teaspoon dried basil
¼ teaspoon marjoram
¼ teaspoon ground oregano
¼ teaspoon garlic powder
¼ teaspoon ground thyme
¼ teaspoon salt
2 whole 6-inch pitas, whole grain or white
Cooking spray

1. Preheat the air fryer oven to 330°F (166°C).
2. Mix all the seasonings together.
3. Cut each pita half into 4 wedges. Break apart wedges at the fold.
4. Mist one side of pita wedges with oil. Sprinkle with half of seasoning mix.
5. Turn pita wedges over, mist the other side with oil, and sprinkle with remaining seasonings. Place the pita wedges in a baking pan.
6. Slide the baking pan into Rack Position 1, select Convection Bake and set time to 4 minutes. Shake the pan halfway through the cooking time.
7. If needed, bake for 1 or 2 more minutes until crisp. Serve hot.

Caramelized Peaches

Prep time: 10 minutes | Cook time: 10 to 13 minutes | Serves 4

2 tablespoons sugar
¼ teaspoon ground cinnamon
4 peaches, cut into wedges
Cooking spray

1. Toss the peaches with the sugar and cinnamon in a medium bowl until evenly coated.
2. Lightly spray the air fryer basket with cooking spray. Place the peaches in the basket in a single layer. Lightly mist the peaches with cooking spray.
3. Put the air fryer basket on the baking pan and slide into Rack Position 2, select Air Fry, set temperature to 350°F (180°C), and set time to 10 minutes.
4. After 5 minutes, remove from the oven and flip the peaches. Return to the oven and continue cooking for 5 minutes.

5. When cooking is complete, the peaches should be caramelized. If necessary, continue cooking for 3 minutes. Remove from the oven. Let the peaches cool for 5 minutes and serve warm.

Tortilla Chips

Prep time: 5 minutes | Cook time: 3 minutes | Serves 2

8 corn tortillas
1 tablespoon olive oil
Salt, to taste

1. Preheat the air fryer oven to 390°F (199°C).
2. Slice the corn tortillas into triangles. Coat with a light brushing of olive oil.
3. Put the tortilla pieces in the air fryer basket. Place the air fryer basket onto the baking pan and slide into Rack Position 2, select Air Fry and set time to 3 minutes.
4. Season with salt before serving.

Lemony Endive in Curried Yogurt

Prep time: 5 minutes | Cook time: 10 minutes | Serves 6

6 heads endive
½ cup plain and fat-free yogurt
3 tablespoons lemon juice
1 teaspoon garlic powder
½ teaspoon curry powder
Salt and ground black pepper, to taste

1. Wash the endives, and slice them in half lengthwise.
2. In a bowl, mix together the yogurt, lemon juice, garlic powder, curry powder, salt and pepper.
3. Brush the endive halves with the marinade, coating them completely. Allow to sit for at least 30 minutes or up to 24 hours.
4. Preheat the air fryer oven to 320°F (160°C).
5. Put the endives in the air fryer basket.
6. Place the air fryer basket onto the baking pan and slide into Rack Position 2, select Air Fry and set time to 10 minutes.
7. Serve hot.

Lemony Chicken Drumsticks

Prep time: 5 minutes | Cook time: 30 minutes | Serves 2

2 teaspoons freshly ground coarse black pepper
1 teaspoon baking powder
½ teaspoon garlic powder

4 chicken drumsticks (4 ounces / 113 g each)
Kosher salt, to taste
1 lemon

1. In a small bowl, stir together the pepper, baking powder, and garlic powder. Place the drumsticks on a plate and sprinkle evenly with the baking powder mixture, turning the drumsticks so they're well coated. Let the drumsticks stand in the refrigerator for at least 1 hour or up to overnight.
2. Preheat the air fryer oven to 375ºF (191ºC).
3. Sprinkle the drumsticks with salt, then transfer them to the air fryer basket.
4. Place the air fryer basket onto the baking pan and slide into Rack Position 2, select Air Fry and set time to 30 minutes, or until cooked through and crisp on the outside.
5. Transfer the drumsticks to a serving platter and finely grate the zest of the lemon over them while they're hot. Cut the lemon into wedges and serve with the warm drumsticks.

Rosemary Baked Cashews

Prep time: 5 minutes | Cook time: 3 minutes | Makes 2 cups

2 sprigs of fresh rosemary (1 chopped and 1 whole)
1 teaspoon olive oil
1 teaspoon kosher salt

½ teaspoon honey
2 cups roasted and unsalted whole cashews
Cooking spray

1. Preheat the air fryer oven to 300ºF (149ºC).
2. In a medium bowl, whisk together the chopped rosemary, olive oil, kosher salt, and honey. Set aside.
3. Spray a baking pan with cooking spray, then place the cashews and the whole rosemary sprig in the pan.
4. Slide the baking pan into Rack Position 1, select Convection Bake and set time to 3 minutes.
5. Remove the cashews and rosemary from the oven, then discard the rosemary and add the cashews to the olive oil mixture, tossing to coat.
6. Allow to cool for 15 minutes before serving.

Spiced Mixed Nuts

Prep time: 5 minutes | Cook time: 6 minutes | Makes 2 cups

½ cup raw cashews
½ cup raw pecan halves
½ cup raw walnut halves
½ cup raw whole almonds
2 tablespoons olive oil
1 tablespoon light brown sugar
1 teaspoon chopped fresh rosemary leaves

1 teaspoon chopped fresh thyme leaves
1 teaspoon kosher salt
½ teaspoon ground coriander
¼ teaspoon onion powder
¼ teaspoon freshly ground black pepper
⅛ teaspoon garlic powder

1. Preheat the air fryer oven to 350ºF (177ºC).
2. In a large bowl, combine all the ingredients and toss until the nuts are evenly coated in the herbs, spices, and sugar. Transfer to the air fryer basket.
3. Place the air fryer basket onto the baking pan and slide into Rack Position 2, select Air Fry and set time to 6 minutes, or until golden brown and fragrant. Shake the basket halfway through the cooking time.
4. Transfer the nuts to a bowl and serve warm.

Spicy Kale Chips

Prep time: 5 minutes | Cook time: 6 minutes | Serves 4

5 cups kale, large stems removed and chopped
2 teaspoons canola oil

¼ teaspoon smoked paprika
¼ teaspoon kosher salt
Cooking spray

1. Preheat the air fryer oven to 390ºF (199ºC).
2. In a large bowl, toss the kale, canola oil, smoked paprika, and kosher salt.
3. Spray the air fryer basket with cooking spray, then place the kale in the basket.
4. Place the air fryer basket onto the baking pan and slide into Rack Position 2, select Air Fry and set time to 6 minutes. Shake the basket halfway through the cooking time, or until crispy.
5. Remove the kale and allow to cool on a wire rack for 3 to 5 minutes before serving.

Veggie Shrimp Toast

Prep time: 15 minutes | Cook time: 6 minutes | Serves 4

8 large raw shrimp, peeled and finely chopped
1 egg white
2 garlic cloves, minced
3 tablespoons minced red bell pepper

1 medium celery stalk, minced
2 tablespoons cornstarch
¼ teaspoon Chinese five-spice powder
3 slices firm thin-sliced no-sodium whole-wheat bread

1. Preheat the air fryer oven to 350ºF (177ºC).
2. In a small bowl, stir together the shrimp, egg white, garlic, red bell pepper, celery, cornstarch, and five-spice powder. Top each slice of bread with one-third of the shrimp mixture, spreading it evenly to the edges. With a sharp knife, cut each slice of bread into 4 strips.
3. Place the shrimp toasts in the air fryer basket in a single layer.
4. Place the air fryer basket onto the baking pan and slide into Rack Position 2, select Air Fry and set time to 6 minutes, or until crisp and golden brown.
5. Serve hot.

Chapter 7 Desserts

Crispy Pineapple Rings

Prep time: 5 minutes | Cook time: 7 minutes | Serves 6

1 cup rice milk
2/3 cup flour
½ cup water
¼ cup unsweetened flaked coconut
4 tablespoons sugar
½ teaspoon baking soda
½ teaspoon baking powder
½ teaspoon vanilla essence
½ teaspoon ground cinnamon
¼ teaspoon ground anise star
Pinch of kosher salt
1 medium pineapple, peeled and sliced

1. In a large bowl, stir together all the ingredients except the pineapple.
2. Dip each pineapple slice into the batter until evenly coated.
3. Arrange the pineapple slices in the air fryer basket.
4. Put the air fryer basket on the baking pan and slide into Rack Position 2, select Air Fry, set temperature to 380ºF (193ºC), and set time to 7 minutes.
5. When cooking is complete, the pineapple rings should be golden brown.
6. Remove from the oven to a plate and cool for 5 minutes before serving.

Pineapple Sticks

Prep time: 5 minutes | Cook time: 10 minutes | Serves 4

½ fresh pineapple, cut into sticks
¼ cup desiccated coconut

1. Preheat the air fryer oven to 400ºF (204ºC).
2. Coat the pineapple sticks in the desiccated coconut and put each one in the air fryer basket.
3. Place the air fryer basket onto the baking pan and slide into Rack Position 2, select Air Fry and set time to 10 minutes.
4. Serve immediately

Coconut Pineapple Sticks

Prep time: 10 minutes | Cook time: 10 minutes | Serves 4

½ fresh pineapple, cut into sticks
¼ cup desiccated coconut

1. Place the desiccated coconut on a plate and roll the pineapple sticks in the coconut until well coated.
2. Lay the pineapple sticks in the air fryer basket.
3. Put the air fryer basket on the baking pan and slide into Rack Position 2, select Air Fry, set temperature to 400ºF (205ºC), and set time to 10 minutes.
4. When cooking is complete, the pineapple sticks should be crisp-tender.
5. Serve warm.

Cinnamon S'mores

Prep time: 5 minutes | Cook time: 3 minutes | Makes 12 s'mores

12 whole cinnamon graham crackers, halved
2 (1.55-ounce / 44-g) chocolate bars, cut into 12 pieces
12 marshmallows

1. Arrange 12 graham cracker squares in the baking pan in a single layer.
2. Top each square with a piece of chocolate.
3. Slide the baking pan into Rack Position 1, select Convection Bake, set temperature to 350ºF (180ºC), and set time to 3 minutes.
4. Bake for 2 minutes. Remove the pan and place a marshmallow on each piece of melted chocolate. Bake for another 1 minute.
5. Remove from the oven to a serving plate.
6. Serve topped with the remaining graham cracker squares

Black and White Brownies

Prep time: 10 minutes | Cook time: 20 minutes | Makes 1 dozen brownies

1 egg
¼ cup brown sugar
2 tablespoons white sugar
2 tablespoons safflower oil
1 teaspoon vanilla
⅓ cup all-purpose flour
¼ cup cocoa powder
¼ cup white chocolate chips
Nonstick cooking spray

1. Spritz the baking pan with nonstick cooking spray.
2. Whisk together the egg, brown sugar, and white sugar in a medium bowl. Mix in the safflower oil and vanilla and stir to combine.
3. Add the flour and cocoa powder and stir just until incorporated. Fold in the white chocolate chips.
4. Scrape the batter into the prepared baking pan.
5. Slide the baking pan into Rack Position 1, select Convection Bake, set temperature to 340ºF (171ºC), and set time to 20 minutes.
6. When done, the brownie should spring back when touched lightly with your fingers.
7. Transfer to a wire rack and let cool for 30 minutes before slicing to serve.

Peanut Butter-Chocolate Bread Pudding

Prep time: 10 minutes | Cook time: 10 minutes | Serves 8

1 egg
1 egg yolk
¾ cup chocolate milk
3 tablespoons brown sugar
3 tablespoons peanut butter
2 tablespoons cocoa powder
1 teaspoon vanilla
5 slices firm white bread, cubed
Nonstick cooking spray

1. Spritz the baking pan with nonstick cooking spray.
2. Whisk together the egg, egg yolk, chocolate milk, brown sugar, peanut butter, cocoa powder, and vanilla until well combined.
3. Fold in the bread cubes and stir to mix well. Allow the bread soak for 10 minutes.
4. When ready, transfer the egg mixture to the prepared baking pan.
5. Slide the baking pan into Rack Position 1, select Convection Bake, set temperature to 330ºF (166ºC), and set time to 10 minutes.
6. When done, the pudding should be just firm to the touch.
7. Serve at room temperature.

Chocolate Cheesecake

Prep time: 5 minutes | Cook time: 18 minutes | Serves 6

Crust:
½ cup butter, melted
½ cup coconut flour
2 tablespoons stevia
Cooking spray
Topping:
4 ounces (113 g) unsweetened baker's chocolate
1 cup mascarpone cheese, at room temperature
1 teaspoon vanilla extract
2 drops peppermint extract

1. Lightly coat the baking pan with cooking spray.
2. In a mixing bowl, whisk together the butter, flour, and stevia until well combined. Transfer the mixture to the prepared baking pan.
3. Slide the baking pan into Rack Position 1, select Convection Bake, set temperature to 350ºF (180ºC), and set time to 18 minutes.
4. When done, a toothpick inserted in the center should come out clean.
5. Remove the crust from the oven to a wire rack to cool.
6. Once cooled completely, place it in the freezer for 20 minutes.
7. When ready, combine all the ingredients for the topping in a small bowl and stir to incorporate.
8. Spread this topping over the crust and let it sit for another 15 minutes in the freezer.
9. Serve chilled.

Summer Berry Crisp

Prep time: 10 minutes | Cook time: 12 minutes | Serves 4

½ cup fresh blueberries
½ cup chopped fresh strawberries
⅓ cup frozen raspberries, thawed
1 tablespoon honey
1 tablespoon freshly squeezed lemon juice
⅔ cup whole-wheat pastry flour
3 tablespoons packed brown sugar
2 tablespoons unsalted butter, melted

1. Place the blueberries, strawberries, and raspberries in the baking pan and drizzle the honey and lemon juice over the top.
2. Combine the pastry flour and brown sugar in a small mixing bowl.
3. Add the butter and whisk until the mixture is crumbly. Scatter the flour mixture on top of the fruit.
4. Slide the baking pan into Rack Position 1, select Convection Bake, set temperature to 380ºF (193ºC), and set time to 12 minutes.
5. When cooking is complete, the fruit should be bubbly and the topping should be golden brown.
6. Remove from the oven and serve on a plate.

Apple Fritters

Prep time: 30 minutes | Cook time: 7 minutes | Serves 6

1 cup chopped, peeled Granny Smith apple
½ cup granulated sugar
1 teaspoon ground cinnamon
1 cup all-purpose flour
1 teaspoon baking powder
1 teaspoon salt
2 tablespoons milk
2 tablespoons butter, melted
1 large egg, beaten
Cooking spray
¼ cup confectioners' sugar (optional)

1. Mix together the apple, granulated sugar, and cinnamon in a small bowl. Allow to sit for 30 minutes.
2. Combine the flour, baking powder, and salt in a medium bowl. Add the milk, butter, and egg and stir to incorporate.
3. Pour the apple mixture into the bowl of flour mixture and stir with a spatula until a dough forms.
4. Make the fritters: On a clean work surface, divide the dough into 12 equal portions and shape into 1-inch balls. Flatten them into patties with your hands.
5. Line the baking pan with parchment paper and spray it with cooking spray.
6. Transfer the apple fritters onto the parchment paper, evenly spaced but not too close together. Spray the fritters with cooking spray.
7. Slide the baking pan into Rack Position 1, select Convection Bake, set temperature to 350ºF (180ºC), and set time to 7 minutes.
8. Flip the fritters halfway through the cooking time.
9. When cooking is complete, the fritters should be lightly browned.
10. Remove from the oven to a plate and serve with the confectioners' sugar sprinkled on top, if desired.

Apple Wedges with Apricots

Prep time: 5 minutes | Cook time: 15 to 18 minutes | Serves 4

4 large apples, peeled and sliced into 8 wedges
2 tablespoons olive oil
½ cup dried apricots, chopped
1 to 2 tablespoons sugar
½ teaspoon ground cinnamon

1. Toss the apple wedges with the olive oil in a mixing bowl until well coated.
2. Place the apple wedges in the air fryer basket.
3. Put the air fryer basket on the baking pan and slide into Rack Position 2, select Air Fry, set temperature to 350ºF (180ºC), and set time to 15 minutes.
4. After about 12 minutes, remove from the oven. Sprinkle with the dried apricots and air fry for another 3 minutes.
5. Meanwhile, thoroughly combine the sugar and cinnamon in a small bowl.
6. Remove the apple wedges from the oven to a plate. Serve sprinkled with the sugar mixture.

Pumpkin Pudding

Prep time: 10 minutes | Cook time: 15 minutes | Serves 4

3 cups pumpkin purée
3 tablespoons honey
1 tablespoon ginger
1 tablespoon cinnamon

1 teaspoon clove
1 teaspoon nutmeg
1 cup full-fat cream
2 eggs
1 cup sugar

1. Preheat the air fryer oven to 390ºF (199ºC).
2. In a bowl, stir all the ingredients together to combine. Scrape the mixture into a greased baking dish.
3. Place the baking dish into Rack Position 1, select Convection Bake and set time to 15 minutes.
4. Serve warm.

Pumpkin Pudding and Vanilla Wafers

Prep time: 10 minutes | Cook time: 15 minutes | Serves 4

1 cup canned no-salt-added pumpkin purée (not pumpkin pie filling)
¼ cup packed brown sugar
3 tablespoons all-purpose flour
1 egg, whisked

2 tablespoons milk
1 tablespoon unsalted butter, melted
1 teaspoon pure vanilla extract
4 low-fat vanilla wafers, crumbled
Cooking spray

1. Coat the baking pan with cooking spray. Set aside.
2. Mix the pumpkin purée, brown sugar, flour, whisked egg, milk, melted butter, and vanilla in a medium bowl and whisk to combine. Transfer the mixture to the baking pan.
3. Slide the baking pan into Rack Position 1, select Convection Bake, set temperature to 350ºF (180ºC), and set time to 15 minutes.
4. When cooking is complete, the pudding should be set.
5. Remove the pudding from the oven to a wire rack to cool.
6. Divide the pudding into four bowls and serve with the vanilla wafers sprinkled on top.

Baked Peaches and Blueberries

Prep time: 10 minutes | Cook time: 10 minutes | Serves 6

3 peaches, peeled, halved, and pitted
2 tablespoons packed brown sugar
1 cup plain Greek yogurt

¼ teaspoon ground cinnamon
1 teaspoon pure vanilla extract
1 cup fresh blueberries

1. Place the peaches in the baking pan, cut-side up. Top with a generous sprinkle of brown sugar.
2. Slide the baking pan into Rack Position 1, select Convection Bake, set temperature to 380ºF (193ºC), and set time to 10 minutes.
3. Meanwhile, whisk together the yogurt, cinnamon, and vanilla in a small bowl until smooth.
4. When cooking is complete, the peaches should be lightly browned and caramelized.
5. Remove the peaches from the oven to a plate. Serve topped with the yogurt mixture and fresh blueberries.

Chia Pudding

Prep time: 5 minutes | Cook time: 4 minutes | Serves 2

1 cup chia seeds
1 cup unsweetened coconut milk
1 teaspoon liquid stevia

1 tablespoon coconut oil
1 teaspoon butter, melted

1. Mix together the chia seeds, coconut milk, and stevia in a large bowl. Add the coconut oil and melted butter and stir until well blended.
2. Divide the mixture evenly between the ramekins, filling only about ⅔ of the way.
3. Put the ramekins into Rack Position 1, select Convection Bake, set temperature to 360ºF (182ºC), and set time to 4 minutes.
4. When cooking is complete, allow to cool for 5 minutes and serve warm.

Oatmeal Raisin Bars

Prep time: 15 minutes | Cook time: 15 minutes | Serves 8

$1/3$ cup all-purpose flour
¼ teaspoon kosher salt
¼ teaspoon baking powder
¼ teaspoon ground cinnamon
¼ cup light brown sugar, lightly packed
¼ cup granulated sugar
½ cup canola oil
1 large egg
1 teaspoon vanilla extract
$1 1/3$ cups quick-cooking oats
$1/3$ cup raisins

1. Preheat the air fryer oven to 360°F (182°C).
2. In a large bowl, combine the all-purpose flour, kosher salt, baking powder, ground cinnamon, light brown sugar, granulated sugar, canola oil, egg, vanilla extract, quick-cooking oats, and raisins.
3. Spray a baking pan with nonstick cooking spray, then pour the oat mixture into the pan and press down to evenly distribute.
4. Slide the baking pan into Rack Position 1, select Convection Bake and set time to 15 minutes, or until golden brown.
5. Remove from the oven and allow to cool in the pan on a wire rack for 20 minutes before slicing and serving.

Pear and Apple Crisp

Prep time: 10 minutes | Cook time: 20 minutes | Serves 6

½ pound (227 g) apples, cored and chopped
½ pound (227 g) pears, cored and chopped
1 cup flour
1 cup sugar
1 tablespoon butter
1 teaspoon ground cinnamon
¼ teaspoon ground cloves
1 teaspoon vanilla extract
¼ cup chopped walnuts
Whipped cream, for serving

1. Preheat the air fryer oven to 340°F (171°C).
2. Lightly grease a baking dish and place the apples and pears inside.

3. Combine the rest of the ingredients, except the walnuts and whipped cream, until a coarse, crumbly texture is achieved.
4. Pour the mixture over the fruits and spread it evenly. Top with the chopped walnuts.
5. Place the baking dish into Rack Position 1, select Convection Bake and set time to 20 minutes, or until the top turns golden brown.
6. Serve at room temperature with whipped cream.

Orange Cake

Prep time: 10 minutes | Cook time: 23 minutes | Serves 8

Nonstick baking spray with flour
1¼ cups all-purpose flour
$1/3$ cup yellow cornmeal
¾ cup white sugar
1 teaspoon baking soda
¼ cup safflower oil
1¼ cups orange juice, divided
1 teaspoon vanilla
¼ cup powdered sugar

1. Preheat the air fryer oven to 350°F (177°C).
2. Spray a baking pan with nonstick spray and set aside.
3. In a medium bowl, combine the flour, cornmeal, sugar, baking soda, safflower oil, 1 cup of the orange juice, and vanilla, and mix well.
4. Pour the batter into the baking pan. Slide the baking pan into Rack Position 1, select Convection Bake and set time to 23 minutes, or until a toothpick inserted in the center of the cake comes out clean.
5. Remove the cake from the oven and place on a cooling rack. Using a toothpick, make about 20 holes in the cake.
6. In a small bowl, combine remaining ¼ cup of orange juice and the powdered sugar and stir well. Drizzle this mixture over the hot cake slowly so the cake absorbs it.
7. When cooled completely, cut into wedges and serve.

Chocolate Pecan Pie

Prep time: 20 minutes | Cook time: 25 minutes | Serves 8

1 (9-inch) unbaked pie crust
Filling:

2 large eggs
⅓ cup butter, melted
1 cup sugar
½ cup all-purpose flour
1 cup milk chocolate

chips
1½ cups coarsely chopped pecans
2 tablespoons bourbon

1. Whisk the eggs and melted butter in a large bowl until creamy.
2. Add the sugar and flour and stir to incorporate. Mix in the milk chocolate chips, pecans, and bourbon and stir until well combined.
3. Use a fork to prick holes in the bottom and sides of the pie crust. Pour the prepared filling into the pie crust. Place the pie crust in the baking pan.
4. Slide the baking pan into Rack Position 1, select Convection Bake, set temperature to 350ºF (180ºC), and set time to 25 minutes.
5. When cooking is complete, a toothpick inserted in the center should come out clean.
6. Allow the pie cool for 10 minutes in the pan before serving.

Almond Flour Blackberry Muffins

Prep time: 5 minutes | Cook time: 12 minutes | Serves 8

½ cup fresh blackberries
Dry Ingredients:

1½ cups almond flour
1 teaspoon baking powder
½ teaspoon baking

soda
½ cup Swerve
¼ teaspoon kosher salt

Wet Ingredients:

2 eggs
¼ cup coconut oil, melted

½ cup milk
½ teaspoon vanilla paste

1. Line an 8-cup muffin tin with paper liners.
2. Thoroughly combine the almond flour, baking powder, baking soda, Swerve, and salt in a mixing bowl.
3. Whisk together the eggs, coconut oil, milk, and vanilla in a separate mixing bowl until smooth.
4. Add the wet mixture to the dry and fold in the blackberries. Stir with a spatula just until well incorporated.
5. Spoon the batter into the prepared muffin cups, filling each about three-quarters full.
6. Put the muffin tin into Rack Position 1, select Convection Bake, set temperature to 350ºF (180ºC), and set time to 12 minutes.
7. When done, the tops should be golden and a toothpick inserted in the middle should come out clean.
8. Allow the muffins to cool in the muffin tin for 10 minutes before removing and serving

Glazed Apples

Prep time: 5 minutes | Cook time: 10 minutes | Serves 4

4 small apples, cored and cut in half
2 tablespoons salted butter or coconut oil, melted
2 tablespoons sugar

1 teaspoon apple pie spice
Ice cream, heavy cream, or whipped cream, for serving

1. Preheat the air fryer oven to 350ºF (177ºC).
2. Put the apples in a large bowl. Drizzle with the melted butter and sprinkle with the sugar and apple pie spice. Use the hands to toss, ensuring the apples are evenly coated. Put the apples in the air fryer basket.
3. Place the air fryer basket onto the baking pan and slide into Rack Position 2, select Air Fry and set time to 10 minutes. Pierce the apples with a fork to ensure they are tender.
4. Serve with ice cream, or top with a splash of heavy cream or a spoonful of whipped cream.

Caramelized Fruit Kebabs

Prep time: 10 minutes | Cook time: 4 minutes | Serves 4

2 peaches, peeled, pitted, and thickly sliced
3 plums, halved and pitted
3 nectarines, halved and pitted

1 tablespoon honey
½ teaspoon ground cinnamon
¼ teaspoon ground allspice
Pinch cayenne pepper

Special Equipment:
8 metal skewers

1. Thread, alternating peaches, plums, and nectarines onto the metal skewers.
2. Thoroughly combine the honey, cinnamon, allspice, and cayenne in a small bowl. Brush generously the glaze over the fruit skewers.
3. Transfer the fruit skewers to the air fryer basket.
4. Put the air fryer basket on the baking pan and slide into Rack Position 2, select Air Fry, set temperature to 400°F (205°C), and set time to 4 minutes.
5. When cooking is complete, the fruit should be caramelized.
6. Remove the fruit skewers from the oven and let rest for 5 minutes before serving.

Apple-Peach Crumble with Honey

Prep time: 10 minutes | Cook time: 11 minutes | Serves 4

1 apple, peeled and chopped
2 peaches, peeled, pitted, and chopped
2 tablespoons honey
½ cup quick-cooking oatmeal
1/3 cup whole-wheat

pastry flour
2 tablespoons unsalted butter, at room temperature
3 tablespoons packed brown sugar
½ teaspoon ground cinnamon

1. Mix together the apple, peaches, and honey in the baking pan until well incorporated.
2. In a bowl, combine the oatmeal, pastry flour, butter, brown sugar, and cinnamon and stir to mix well. Spread this mixture evenly over the fruit.

3. Slide the baking pan into Rack Position 1, select Convection Bake, set temperature to 380°F (193°C), and set time to 11 minutes.
4. When cooking is complete, the fruit should be bubbling around the edges and the topping should be golden brown.
5. Remove from the oven and serve warm.

Pineapple Galette

Prep time: 10 minutes | Cook time: 40 minutes | Serves 2

¼ medium-size pineapple, peeled, cored, and cut crosswise into ¼-inch-thick slices
2 tablespoons dark rum
1 teaspoon vanilla extract
½ teaspoon kosher salt
Finely grated zest of

½ lime
1 store-bought sheet puff pastry, cut into an 8-inch round
3 tablespoons granulated sugar
2 tablespoons unsalted butter, cubed and chilled
Coconut ice cream, for serving

1. Preheat the air fryer oven to 310°F (154°C).
2. In a small bowl, combine the pineapple slices, rum, vanilla, salt, and lime zest and let stand for at least 10 minutes to allow the pineapple to soak in the rum.
3. Meanwhile, press the puff pastry round into the bottom and up the sides of a round metal cake pan and use the tines of a fork to dock the bottom and sides.
4. Arrange the pineapple slices on the bottom of the pastry in more or less a single layer, then sprinkle with the sugar and dot with the butter. Drizzle with the leftover juices from the bowl.
5. Slide the pan into Rack Position 1, select Convection Bake and set time to 40 minutes, or until the pastry is puffed and golden brown and the pineapple is lightly caramelized on top.
6. Transfer the pan to a wire rack to cool for 15 minutes. Unmold the galette from the pan and serve warm with coconut ice cream.

Graham Cracker Cheesecake

Prep time: 10 minutes | Cook time: 20 minutes | Serves 8

1 cup graham cracker crumbs
3 tablespoons softened butter
1½ (8-ounce / 227-g) packages cream cheese, softened
⅓ cup sugar
2 eggs
1 tablespoon flour
1 teaspoon vanilla
¼ cup chocolate syrup

1. For the crust, combine the graham cracker crumbs and butter in a small bowl and mix well. Press into the bottom of a baking pan and put in the freezer to set.
2. For the filling, combine the cream cheese and sugar in a medium bowl and mix well. Beat in the eggs, one at a time. Add the flour and vanilla.
3. Preheat the air fryer oven to 450ºF (232ºC).
4. Remove ⅔ cup of the filling to a small bowl and stir in the chocolate syrup until combined.
5. Pour the vanilla filling into the pan with the crust. Drop the chocolate filling over the vanilla filling by the spoonful. With a clean butter knife, stir the fillings in a zigzag pattern to marbleize them.
6. Slide the baking pan into Rack Position 1, select Convection Bake and set time to 20 minutes, or until the cheesecake is just set.
7. Cool on a wire rack for 1 hour, then chill in the refrigerator until the cheesecake is firm.
8. Serve immediately.

Coconut Chip Mixed Berry Crisp

Prep time: 5 minutes | Cook time: 20 minutes | Serves 6

1 tablespoon butter, melted
12 ounces (340 g) mixed berries
⅓ cup granulated Swerve
1 teaspoon pure vanilla extract
½ teaspoon ground cinnamon
¼ teaspoon ground cloves
¼ teaspoon grated nutmeg
½ cup coconut chips, for garnish

1. Coat the baking pan with melted butter.
2. Put the remaining ingredients except the coconut chips in the prepared baking pan.
3. Slide the baking pan into Rack Position 1, select Convection Bake, set temperature to 330ºF (166ºC), and set time to 20 minutes.
4. When cooking is complete, remove from the oven. Serve garnished with the coconut chips.

Blackberry and Peach Cobbler

Prep time: 10 minutes | Cook time: 20 minutes | Serves 4

Filling:
1 (6-ounce / 170-g) package blackberries
1½ cups chopped peaches, cut into ½-inch thick slices
2 teaspoons arrowroot or cornstarch
2 tablespoons coconut sugar
1 teaspoon lemon juice
Topping:
2 tablespoons sunflower oil
1 tablespoon maple syrup
1 teaspoon vanilla
3 tablespoons coconut sugar
½ cup rolled oats
⅓ cup whole-wheat pastry flour
1 teaspoon cinnamon
¼ teaspoon nutmeg
⅛ teaspoon sea salt

Make the Filling:
1. Combine the blackberries, peaches, arrowroot, coconut sugar, and lemon juice in the baking pan.
2. Using a rubber spatula, stir until well incorporated. Set aside.
Make the Topping:
1. Combine the oil, maple syrup, and vanilla in a mixing bowl and stir well. Whisk in the remaining ingredients. Spread this mixture evenly over the filling.
2. Slide the baking pan into Rack Position 1, select Convection Bake, set temperature to 320ºF (160ºC), and set time to 20 minutes.
3. When cooked, the topping should be crispy and golden brown. Serve warm

Breaded Bananas with Chocolate Sauce

Prep time: 10 minutes | Cook time: 7 minutes | Serves 6

¼ cup cornstarch
¼ cup plain bread crumbs
1 large egg, beaten
3 bananas, halved

crosswise
Cooking spray
Chocolate sauce, for serving

1. Place the cornstarch, bread crumbs, and egg in three separate bowls.
2. Roll the bananas in the cornstarch, then in the beaten egg, and finally in the bread crumbs to coat well.
3. Spritz the air fryer basket with cooking spray.
4. Arrange the banana halves in the basket and mist them with cooking spray.
5. Put the air fryer basket on the baking pan and slide into Rack Position 2, select Air Fry, set temperature to 350ºF (180ºC), and set time to 7 minutes.
6. After about 5 minutes, flip the bananas and continue to air fry for another 2 minutes.
7. When cooking is complete, remove the bananas from the oven to a serving plate. Serve with the chocolate sauce drizzled over the top.

Berry Crumble

Prep time: 5 minutes | Cook time: 35 minutes | Serves 6

2 ounces (57 g) unsweetened mixed berries
½ cup granulated Swerve
2 tablespoons golden flaxseed meal
Topping:
½ stick butter, cut into small pieces
1 cup powdered Swerve
²⁄₃ cup almond flour
¹⁄₃ cup unsweetened

1 teaspoon xanthan gum
½ teaspoon ground cinnamon
¼ teaspoon ground star anise

coconut, finely shredded
½ teaspoon baking powder
Cooking spray

1. Coat 6 ramekins with cooking spray.
2. In a mixing dish, stir together the mixed berries, granulated Swerve, flaxseed meal, xanthan gum, cinnamon, star anise. Divide the berry mixture evenly among the prepared ramekins.
3. Combine the remaining ingredients in a separate mixing dish and stir well. Scatter the topping over the berry mixture.
4. Put the ramekins into Rack Position 1, select Convection Bake, set temperature to 330ºF (166ºC), and set time to 35 minutes.
5. When done, the topping should be golden brown.
6. Serve warm.

Fudgy Chocolate Brownies

Prep time: 5 minutes | Cook time: 21 minutes | Serves 8

1 stick butter, melted
1 cup Swerve
2 eggs
1 cup coconut flour
½ cup unsweetened cocoa powder
2 tablespoons flaxseed meal

1 teaspoon baking powder
1 teaspoon vanilla essence
A pinch of salt
A pinch of ground cardamom
Cooking spray

1. Spray the baking pan with cooking spray.
2. Beat together the melted butter and Swerve in a large mixing dish until fluffy. Whisk in the eggs.
3. Add the coconut flour, cocoa powder, flaxseed meal, baking powder, vanilla essence, salt, and cardamom and stir with a spatula until well incorporated. Spread the mixture evenly into the prepared baking pan.
4. Slide the baking pan into Rack Position 1, select Convection Bake, set temperature to 350ºF (180ºC), and set time to 21 minutes.
5. When cooking is complete, a toothpick inserted in the center should come out clean.
6. Remove from the oven and place on a wire rack to cool completely. Cut into squares and serve immediately.

Honey-Baked Pears

Prep time: 5 minutes | Cook time: 20 minutes | Serves 4

2 large Bosc pears, halved and deseeded
3 tablespoons honey
1 tablespoon unsalted butter
½ teaspoon ground

cinnamon
¼ cup walnuts, chopped
¼ cup part skim low-fat ricotta cheese, divided

1. Preheat the air fryer oven to 350°F (177°C).
2. In a baking pan, place the pears, cut side up.
3. In a small microwave-safe bowl, melt the honey, butter, and cinnamon. Brush this mixture over the cut sides of the pears.
4. Pour 3 tablespoons of water around the pears in the pan.
5. Slide the baking pan into Rack Position 1, select Convection Bake and set time to 20 minutes, or until tender when pierced with a fork and slightly crisp on the edges, basting once with the liquid in the pan.
6. Carefully remove the pears from the pan and place on a serving plate. Drizzle each with some liquid from the pan, sprinkle the walnuts on top, and serve with a spoonful of ricotta cheese.

Jelly Doughnuts

Prep time: 5 minutes | Cook time: 5 minutes | Serves 8

1 (16.3-ounce / 462-g) package large refrigerator biscuits
Cooking spray
1¼ cups good-

quality raspberry jam
Confectioners' sugar, for dusting

1. Preheat the air fryer oven to 350°F (177°C).
2. Separate biscuits into 8 rounds. Spray both sides of rounds lightly with oil.
3. Spray the air fryer basket with oil and place the rounds in the basket.
4. Place the air fryer basket onto the baking pan and slide into Rack Position 2, select Air Fry and set time to 5 minutes, or until golden brown.

5. Transfer to a wire rack and let cool.
6. Fill a pastry bag, fitted with small plain tip, with raspberry jam; use tip to poke a small hole in the side of each doughnut, then fill the centers with the jam. Dust doughnuts with confectioners' sugar. Serve immediately.

Ricotta Lemon Poppy Seed Cake

Prep time: 15 minutes | Cook time: 55 minutes | Serves 4

Unsalted butter, at room temperature
1 cup almond flour
½ cup sugar
3 large eggs
¼ cup heavy cream
¼ cup full-fat ricotta cheese
¼ cup coconut oil, melted

2 tablespoons poppy seeds
1 teaspoon baking powder
1 teaspoon pure lemon extract
Grated zest and juice of 1 lemon, plus more zest for garnish

1. Preheat the air fryer oven to 325°F (163°C).
2. Generously butter a round baking pan. Line the bottom of the pan with parchment paper cut to fit.
3. In a large bowl, combine the almond flour, sugar, eggs, cream, ricotta, coconut oil, poppy seeds, baking powder, lemon extract, lemon zest, and lemon juice. Beat with a hand mixer on medium speed until well blended and fluffy.
4. Pour the batter into the prepared pan. Cover the pan tightly with aluminum foil.
5. Slide the baking pan into Rack Position 1, select Convection Bake and set time to 45 minutes.
6. Remove the foil and bake for 10 to 15 minutes more until a knife (do not use a toothpick) inserted into the center of the cake comes out clean.
7. Let the cake cool in the pan on a wire rack for 10 minutes. Remove the cake from pan and let it cool on the rack for 15 minutes before slicing.
8. Top with additional lemon zest, slice and serve.

Lemony Apple Butter

Prep time: 10 minutes | Cook time: 1 hour | Makes 1¼ cups

Cooking spray
2 cups unsweetened applesauce
⅔ cup packed light brown sugar
3 tablespoons fresh lemon juice
½ teaspoon kosher salt
¼ teaspoon ground cinnamon
⅛ teaspoon ground allspice

1. Preheat the air fryer oven to 340°F (171°C).
2. Spray a metal cake pan with cooking spray. Whisk together all the ingredients in a bowl until smooth, then pour into the greased pan.
3. Slide the pan into Rack Position 1, select Convection Bake and set time to 60 minutes, or until the apple mixture is caramelized, reduced to a thick purée, and fragrant.
4. Remove the pan from the oven, stir to combine the caramelized bits at the edge with the rest, then let cool completely to thicken.
5. Serve immediately.

Spice Cookies

Prep time: 15 minutes | Cook time: 12 minutes | Serves 4

4 tablespoons (½ stick) unsalted butter, at room temperature
2 tablespoons agave nectar
1 large egg
2 tablespoons water
2½ cups almond flour
½ cup sugar
2 teaspoons ground ginger
1 teaspoon ground cinnamon
½ teaspoon freshly grated nutmeg
1 teaspoon baking soda
¼ teaspoon kosher salt

1. Preheat the air fryer oven to 325°F (163°C).
2. Line the bottom of a baking pan with parchment paper.
3. In a large bowl using a hand mixer, beat together the butter, agave, egg, and water on medium speed until fluffy.

4. Add the almond flour, sugar, ginger, cinnamon, nutmeg, baking soda, and salt. Beat on low speed until well combined.
5. Roll the dough into 2-tablespoon balls and arrange them on the parchment paper in the pan. (They don't really spread too much, but try to leave a little room between them).
6. Slide the baking pan into Rack Position 1, select Convection Bake and set time to 12 minutes, or until the tops of cookies are lightly browned.
7. Transfer to a wire rack and let cool completely. Serve immediately

Pineapple and Chocolate Cake

Prep time: 10 minutes | Cook time: 38 minutes | Serves 4

2 cups flour
4 ounces (113 g) butter, melted
¼ cup sugar
½ pound (227 g) pineapple, chopped
½ cup pineapple
juice
1 ounce (28 g) dark chocolate, grated
1 large egg
2 tablespoons skimmed milk

1. Preheat the air fryer oven to 370°F (188°C).
2. Grease a cake tin with a little oil or butter.
3. In a bowl, combine the butter and flour to create a crumbly consistency.
4. Add the sugar, chopped pineapple, juice, and grated dark chocolate and mix well.
5. In a separate bowl, combine the egg and milk. Add this mixture to the flour mixture and stir well until a soft dough forms. Pour the mixture into the cake tin.
6. Place the cake tin into Rack Position 1, select Convection Bake and set time to 38 minutes.
7. Cool for 5 minutes before serving.

Apple Turnovers

Prep time: 10 minutes | Cook time: 10 minutes | Serves 4

1 apple, peeled, quartered, and thinly sliced
½ teaspoons pumpkin pie spice
Juice of ½ lemon
1 tablespoon granulated sugar
Pinch of kosher salt
6 sheets phyllo dough
Nonstick cooking spray

1. Preheat the air fryer oven to 330°F (166°C).
2. In a medium bowl, combine the apple, pumpkin pie spice, lemon juice, granulated sugar, and kosher salt.
3. Cut the phyllo dough sheets into 4 equal pieces and place individual tablespoons of apple filling in the center of each piece, then fold in both sides and roll from front to back.
4. Spray the air fryer basket with nonstick cooking spray, then place the turnovers in the basket.
5. Place the air fryer basket onto the baking pan and slide into Rack Position 2, select Air Fry and set time to 10 minutes, or until golden brown.
6. Remove the turnovers and allow to cool on a wire rack for 10 minutes before serving.

Lemony Blackberry Crisp

Prep time: 5 minutes | Cook time: 15 minutes | Serves 1

2 tablespoons lemon juice
1/3 cup powdered erythritol
¼ teaspoon xantham gum
2 cup blackberries
1 cup crunchy granola

1. Preheat the air fryer oven to 350°F (177°C).
2. In a bowl, combine the lemon juice, erythritol, xantham gum, and blackberries. Transfer to a round baking dish and cover with aluminum foil.
3. Place the baking dish into Rack Position 1, select Convection Bake and set time to 12 minutes.

4. Remove the dish from the oven, give the blackberries a stir, and top with the granola.
5. Return the dish to the oven and bake at 320°F (160°C) for an additional 3 minutes.
6. Let rest for 5 to 10 minutes before serving.

Oatmeal and Carrot Cookie Cups

Prep time: 10 minutes | Cook time: 8 minutes | Makes 16 cups

3 tablespoons unsalted butter, at room temperature
¼ cup packed brown sugar
1 tablespoon honey
1 egg white
½ teaspoon vanilla extract
1/3 cup finely grated carrot
½ cup quick-cooking oatmeal
1/3 cup whole-wheat pastry flour
½ teaspoon baking soda
¼ cup dried cherries

1. Preheat the air fryer oven to 350°F (177°C)
2. In a medium bowl, beat the butter, brown sugar, and honey until well combined.
3. Add the egg white, vanilla, and carrot. Beat to combine.
4. Stir in the oatmeal, pastry flour, and baking soda.
5. Stir in the dried cherries.
6. Double up 32 mini muffin foil cups to make 16 cups. Fill each with about 4 teaspoons of dough. Put the cups in a baking pan.
7. Slide the baking pan into Rack Position 1, select Convection Bake and set time to 8 minutes, or until light golden brown and just set.
8. Serve warm.

Pecan and Cherry Stuffed Apples

Prep time: 10 minutes | Cook time: 22 minutes | Serves 4

4 apples (about 1¼ pounds / 567 g)
¼ cup chopped pecans
⅓ cup dried tart cherries
1 tablespoon melted butter

3 tablespoons brown sugar
¼ teaspoon allspice
Pinch salt
Ice cream, for serving

1. Cut off top ½ inch from each apple; reserve tops. With a melon baller, core through stem ends without breaking through the bottom. (Do not trim bases.)
2. Preheat the air fryer oven to 350°F (177°C).
3. Combine pecans, cherries, butter, brown sugar, allspice, and a pinch of salt. Stuff mixture into the hollow centers of the apples. Cover with apple tops. Arrange the stuffed apples in the air fryer basket.
4. Place the air fryer basket onto the baking pan and slide into Rack Position 2, select Air Fry and set time to 22 minutes, or just until tender.
5. Serve warm with ice cream.

Rich Chocolate Cookie

Prep time: 10 minutes | Cook time: 9 minutes | Serves 4

Nonstick baking spray with flour
3 tablespoons softened butter
⅓ cup plus 1 tablespoon brown sugar
1 egg yolk
½ cup flour

2 tablespoons ground white chocolate
¼ teaspoon baking soda
½ teaspoon vanilla
¾ cup chocolate chips

1. Preheat the air fryer oven to 350°F (177°C).
2. In a medium bowl, beat the butter and brown sugar together until fluffy. Stir in the egg yolk.
3. Add the flour, white chocolate, baking soda, and vanilla, and mix well. Stir in the chocolate chips.
4. Line a baking pan with parchment paper. Spray the parchment paper with nonstick baking spray with flour.
5. Spread the batter into the prepared pan, leaving a ½-inch border on all sides.
6. Slide the baking pan into Rack Position 1, select Convection Bake and set time to 9 minutes, or until the cookie is light brown and just barely set.
7. Remove the pan from the oven and let cool for 10 minutes. Remove the cookie from the pan, remove the parchment paper, and let cool on a wire rack.
8. Serve immediately.

Chapter 8 Casseroles, Frittatas, and Quiches

Sumptuous Beef and Bean Chili Casserole

Prep time: 15 minutes | Cook time: 31 minutes | Serves 4

1 tablespoon olive oil
½ cup finely chopped bell pepper
½ cup chopped celery
1 onion, chopped
2 garlic cloves, minced
1 pound (454 g) ground beef
1 can diced tomatoes
½ teaspoon parsley
½ tablespoon chili powder
1 teaspoon chopped cilantro
1½ cups vegetable broth
1 (8-ounce / 227-g) can cannellini beans
Salt and ground black pepper, to taste

1. Heat the olive oil in a nonstick skillet over medium heat until shimmering.
2. Add the bell pepper, celery, onion, and garlic to the skillet and sauté for 5 minutes or until the onion is translucent.
3. Add the ground beef and sauté for an additional 6 minutes or until lightly browned.
4. Mix in the tomatoes, parsley, chili powder, cilantro and vegetable broth, then cook for 10 more minutes. Stir constantly.
5. Pour them in the baking pan, then mix in the beans and sprinkle with salt and ground black pepper.
6. Slide the baking pan into Rack Position 1, select Convection Bake, set temperature to 350ºF (180ºC) and set time to 10 minutes.
7. When cooking is complete, the vegetables should be tender and the beef should be well browned.
8. Remove from the oven and serve immediately.

Chicken Divan

Prep time: 5 minutes | Cook time: 24 minutes | Serves 4

4 chicken breasts
Salt and ground black pepper, to taste
1 head broccoli, cut into florets
½ cup cream of mushroom soup
1 cup shredded Cheddar cheese
½ cup croutons
Cooking spray

1. Spritz the air fryer basket with cooking spray.
2. Put the chicken breasts in the basket and sprinkle with salt and ground black pepper.
3. Put the air fryer basket on the baking pan and slide into Rack Position 2, select Air Fry, set temperature to 390ºF (199ºC) and set time to 14 minutes.
4. Flip the breasts halfway through the cooking time.
5. When cooking is complete, the breasts should be well browned and tender.
6. Remove the breasts from the oven and allow to cool for a few minutes on a plate, then cut the breasts into bite-size pieces.
7. Combine the chicken, broccoli, mushroom soup, and Cheddar cheese in a large bowl. Stir to mix well.
8. Spritz the baking pan with cooking spray. Pour the chicken mixture into the pan. Spread the croutons over the mixture.
9. Slide the baking pan into Rack Position 1, select Convection Bake, set time to 10 minutes.
10. When cooking is complete, the croutons should be lightly browned and the mixture should be set.
11. Remove from the oven and serve immediately.

Spinach and Chickpea Casserole

Prep time: 10 minutes | Cook time: 21 to 22 minutes | Serves 4

2 tablespoons olive oil
2 garlic cloves, minced
1 tablespoon ginger, minced
1 onion, chopped
1 chili pepper, minced
Salt and ground
black pepper, to taste
1 pound (454 g) spinach
1 can coconut milk
½ cup dried tomatoes, chopped
1 (14-ounce / 397-g) can chickpeas, drained

1. Heat the olive oil in a saucepan over medium heat. Sauté the garlic and ginger in the olive oil for 1 minute, or until fragrant.
2. Add the onion, chili pepper, salt and pepper to the saucepan. Sauté for 3 minutes.
3. Mix in the spinach and sauté for 3 to 4 minutes or until the vegetables become soft. Remove from heat.
4. Pour the vegetable mixture into the baking pan. Stir in coconut milk, dried tomatoes and chickpeas until well blended.
5. Slide the baking pan into Rack Position 1, select Convection Bake, set temperature to 370ºF (188ºC) and set time to 15 minutes.
6. When cooking is complete, transfer the casserole to a serving dish. Let cool for 5 minutes before serving.

Creamy Pork Gratin

Prep time: 15 minutes | Cook time: 21 minutes | Serves 4

2 tablespoons olive oil
2 pounds (907 g) pork tenderloin, cut into serving-size pieces
1 teaspoon dried marjoram
¼ teaspoon chili powder
1 teaspoon coarse sea salt
½ teaspoon freshly ground black pepper
1 cup Ricotta cheese
1½ cups chicken broth
1 tablespoon mustard
Cooking spray

1. Spritz the baking pan with cooking spray.
2. Heat the olive oil in a nonstick skillet over medium-high heat until shimmering.
3. Add the pork and sauté for 6 minutes or until lightly browned.
4. Transfer the pork to the prepared baking pan and sprinkle with marjoram, chili powder, salt, and ground black pepper.
5. Combine the remaining ingredients in a large bowl. Stir to mix well. Pour the mixture over the pork in the pan.
6. Slide the baking pan into Rack Position 1, select Convection Bake, set temperature to 350ºF (180ºC) and set time to 15 minutes.
7. Stir the mixture halfway through.
8. When cooking is complete, the mixture should be frothy and the cheese should be melted.
9. Serve immediately.

Chorizo, Corn, and Potato Frittata

Prep time: 8 minutes | Cook time: 12 minutes | Serves 4

2 tablespoons olive oil
1 chorizo, sliced
4 eggs
½ cup corn
1 large potato, boiled and cubed
1 tablespoon chopped parsley
½ cup feta cheese, crumbled
Salt and ground black pepper, to taste

1. Heat the olive oil in a nonstick skillet over medium heat until shimmering.
2. Add the chorizo and cook for 4 minutes or until golden brown.
3. Whisk the eggs in a bowl, then sprinkle with salt and ground black pepper.
4. Mix the remaining ingredients in the egg mixture, then pour the chorizo and its fat into the baking pan. Pour in the egg mixture.
5. Slide the baking pan into Rack Position 1, select Convection Bake, set temperature to 330ºF (166ºC) and set time to 8 minutes.
6. Stir the mixture halfway through.
7. When cooking is complete, the eggs should be set.
8. Serve immediately.

Herbed Cheddar Frittata

Prep time: 10 minutes | Cook time: 20 minutes | Serves 4

½ cup shredded Cheddar cheese
½ cup half-and-half
4 large eggs
2 tablespoons chopped scallion greens
2 tablespoons

chopped fresh parsley
½ teaspoon kosher salt
½ teaspoon ground black pepper
Cooking spray

1. Spritz the baking pan with cooking spray.
2. Whisk together all the ingredients in a large bowl, then pour the mixture into the prepared baking pan.
3. Slide the baking pan into Rack Position 1, select Convection Bake, set temperature to 300ºF (150ºC) and set time to 20 minutes.
4. Stir the mixture halfway through.
5. When cooking is complete, the eggs should be set.
6. Serve immediately.

Goat Cheese and Asparagus Frittata

Prep time: 5 minutes | Cook time: 25 minutes | Serves 2 to 4

1 cup asparagus spears, cut into 1-inch pieces
1 teaspoon vegetable oil
1 tablespoon milk
6 eggs, beaten

2 ounces (57 g) goat cheese, crumbled
1 tablespoon minced chives, optional
Kosher salt and pepper, to taste

1. Add the asparagus spears to a small bowl and drizzle with the vegetable oil. Toss until well coated and transfer to the air fryer basket.
2. Put the air fryer basket on the baking pan and slide into Rack Position 2, select Air Fry, set temperature to 400ºF (205ºC) and set time to 5 minutes.
3. Flip the asparagus halfway through.
4. When cooking is complete, the asparagus should be tender and slightly wilted.
5. Remove from the oven to the baking pan.

6. Stir together the milk and eggs in a medium bowl. Pour the mixture over the asparagus in the pan. Sprinkle with the goat cheese and the chives (if using) over the eggs. Season with salt and pepper.
7. Slide the baking pan into Rack Position 1, select Convection Bake, set temperature to 320ºF (160ºC) and set time to 20 minutes.
8. When cooking is complete, the top should be golden and the eggs should be set.
9. Transfer to a serving dish. Slice and serve.

Kale Frittata

Prep time: 5 minutes | Cook time: 11 minutes | Serves 2

1 cup kale, chopped
1 teaspoon olive oil
4 large eggs, beaten
Kosher salt, to taste

2 tablespoons water
3 tablespoons crumbled feta
Cooking spray

1. Spritz the baking pan with cooking spray.
2. Add the kale to the baking pan and drizzle with olive oil.
3. Slide the baking pan into Rack Position 2, select Convection Broil, set temperature to 360ºF (182ºC) and set time to 3 minutes.
4. Stir the kale halfway through.
5. When cooking is complete, the kale should be wilted.
6. Meanwhile, combine the eggs with salt and water in a large bowl. Stir to mix well.
7. Make the frittata: When broiling is complete, pour the eggs into the baking pan and spread with feta cheese.
8. Slide the baking pan into Rack Position 1, select Convection Bake, set temperature to 300ºF (150ºC) and set time to 8 minutes.
9. When cooking is complete, the eggs should be set and the cheese should be melted.
10. Remove from the oven and serve the frittata immediately.

Greek Frittata

Prep time: 7 minutes | Cook time: 8 minutes | Serves 2

1 cup chopped mushrooms	2 tablespoons heavy cream
2 cups spinach, chopped	A handful of fresh parsley, chopped
4 eggs, lightly beaten	Salt and ground black pepper, to taste
3 ounces (85 g) feta cheese, crumbled	Cooking spray

1. Spritz the baking pan with cooking spray.
2. Whisk together all the ingredients in a large bowl. Stir to mix well.
3. Pour the mixture in the prepared baking pan.
4. Slide the baking pan into Rack Position 1, select Convection Bake, set temperature to 350ºF (180ºC) and set time to 8 minutes.
5. Stir the mixture halfway through.
6. When cooking is complete, the eggs should be set.
7. Serve immediately.

Broccoli, Carrot, and Tomato Quiche

Prep time: 6 minutes | Cook time: 14 minutes | Serves 4

4 eggs	¼ cup crumbled feta cheese
1 teaspoon dried thyme	1 cup grated Cheddar cheese
1 cup whole milk	1 teaspoon chopped parsley
1 steamed carrots, diced	
2 cups steamed broccoli florets	Salt and ground black pepper, to taste
2 medium tomatoes, diced	Cooking spray

1. Spritz the baking pan with cooking spray.
2. Whisk together the eggs, thyme, salt, and ground black pepper in a bowl and fold in the milk while mixing.
3. Put the carrots, broccoli, and tomatoes in the prepared baking pan, then spread with feta cheese and ½ cup Cheddar cheese. Pour the egg mixture over, then scatter with remaining Cheddar on top.

4. Slide the baking pan into Rack Position 1, select Convection Bake, set temperature to 350ºF (180ºC) and set time to 14 minutes.
5. When cooking is complete, the egg should be set and the quiche should be puffed.
6. Remove the quiche from the oven and top with chopped parsley, then slice to serve.

Sumptuous Vegetable Frittata

Prep time: 15 minutes | Cook time: 20 minutes | Serves 2

4 eggs	sliced
⅓ cup milk	⅓ cup crumbled feta cheese
2 teaspoons olive oil	
1 large zucchini, sliced	⅓ cup grated Cheddar cheese
2 asparagus, sliced thinly	¼ cup chopped chives
⅓ cup sliced mushrooms	Salt and ground black pepper, to taste
1 cup baby spinach	
1 small red onion,	

1. Line the baking pan with parchment paper.
2. Whisk together the eggs, milk, salt, and ground black pepper in a large bowl. Set aside.
3. Heat the olive oil in a nonstick skillet over medium heat until shimmering.
4. Add the zucchini, asparagus, mushrooms, spinach, and onion to the skillet and sauté for 5 minutes or until tender.
5. Pour the sautéed vegetables into the prepared baking pan, then spread the egg mixture over and scatter with cheeses.
6. Slide the baking pan into Rack Position 1, select Convection Bake, set temperature to 380ºF (193ºC) and set time to 15 minutes.
7. Stir the mixture halfway through.
8. When cooking is complete, the egg should be set and the edges should be lightly browned.
9. Remove the frittata from the oven and sprinkle with chives before serving.

Keto Cheese Quiche

Prep time: 20 minutes | Cook time: 1 hour | Serves 8

Crust:

1¼ cups blanched almond flour
1 large egg, beaten
1¼ cups grated

Parmesan cheese
¼ teaspoon fine sea salt

Filling:

4 ounces (113 g) cream cheese
1 cup shredded Swiss cheese
⅓ cup minced leeks
4 large eggs, beaten
½ cup chicken broth
⅛ teaspoon cayenne pepper

¾ teaspoon fine sea salt
1 tablespoon unsalted butter, melted
Chopped green onions, for garnish
Cooking spray

1. Spritz the baking pan with cooking spray.
2. Combine the flour, egg, Parmesan, and salt in a large bowl. Stir to mix until a satiny and firm dough forms.
3. Arrange the dough between two grease parchment papers, then roll the dough into a ¹⁄₁₆-inch thick circle.
4. Make the crust: Transfer the dough into the prepared pan and press to coat the bottom.
5. Slide the baking pan into Rack Position 1, select Convection Bake, set temperature to 325°F (163°C) and set time to 12 minutes.
6. When cooking is complete, the edges of the crust should be lightly browned.
7. Meanwhile, combine the ingredient for the filling, except for the green onions in a large bowl.
8. Pour the filling over the cooked crust and cover the edges of the crust with aluminum foil.
9. Slide the baking pan into Rack Position 1, select Convection Bake, set time to 15 minutes.
10. When cooking is complete, reduce the heat to 300°F (150°C) and set time to 30 minutes.
11. When cooking is complete, a toothpick inserted in the center should come out clean.
12. Remove from the oven and allow to cool for 10 minutes before serving.

Mac and Cheese

Prep time: 10 minutes | Cook time: 10 minutes | Serves 2

1 cup cooked macaroni
1 cup grated Cheddar cheese
½ cup warm milk

Salt and ground black pepper, to taste
1 tablespoon grated Parmesan cheese

1. Preheat the air fryer oven to 350°F (177°C).
2. In a baking dish, mix all the ingredients, except for Parmesan.
3. Place the baking dish into Rack Position 1, select Convection Bake and set time to 10 minutes.
4. Add the Parmesan cheese on top and serve.

Mediterranean Quiche

Prep time: 10 minutes | Cook time: 30 minutes | Serves 4

4 eggs
¼ cup chopped Kalamata olives
½ cup chopped tomatoes
¼ cup chopped onion
½ cup milk
1 cup crumbled feta cheese

½ tablespoon chopped oregano
½ tablespoon chopped basil
Salt and ground black pepper, to taste
Cooking spray

1. Spritz the baking pan with cooking spray.
2. Whisk the eggs with remaining ingredients in a large bowl. Stir to mix well.
3. Pour the mixture into the prepared baking pan.
4. Slide the baking pan into Rack Position 1, select Convection Bake, set temperature to 340°F (171°C) and set time to 30 minutes.
5. When cooking is complete, the eggs should be set and a toothpick inserted in the center should come out clean.
6. Serve immediately.

Cheesy Bacon Quiche

Prep time: 15 minutes | Cook time: 20 minutes | Serves 4

1 tablespoon olive oil
1 shortcrust pastry
3 tablespoons Greek yogurt
½ cup grated Cheddar cheese
3 ounces (85 g) chopped bacon
4 eggs, beaten
¼ teaspoon garlic powder
Pinch of black pepper
¼ teaspoon onion powder
¼ teaspoon sea salt
Flour, for sprinkling

1. Preheat the air fryer oven to 330°F (166°C).
2. Take 8 ramekins and grease with olive oil. Coat with a sprinkling of flour, tapping to remove any excess.
3. Cut the shortcrust pastry in 8 and place each piece at the bottom of each ramekin.
4. Put all the other ingredients in a bowl and combine well. Spoon equal amounts of the filling into each piece of pastry.
5. Place the ramekins into Rack Position 1, select Convection Bake and set time to 20 minutes.
6. Serve warm.

Vegetable Frittata

Prep time: 15 minutes | Cook time: 21 minutes | Serves 2

4 eggs
¼ cup milk
Sea salt and ground black pepper, to taste
1 zucchini, sliced
½ bunch asparagus, sliced
½ cup mushrooms, sliced
½ cup spinach, shredded
½ cup red onion, sliced
½ tablespoon olive oil
5 tablespoons feta cheese, crumbled
4 tablespoons Cheddar cheese, grated
¼ bunch chives, minced

1. In a bowl, mix the eggs, milk, salt and pepper.
2. Over a medium heat, sauté the vegetables for 6 minutes with the olive oil in a nonstick pan.

3. Put some parchment paper in the bottom of a baking tin. Pour in the vegetables, followed by the egg mixture. Top with the feta and grated Cheddar.
4. Preheat the air fryer oven to 320°F (160°C).
5. Place the baking tin into Rack Position 1, select Convection Bake and set time to 15 minutes.
6. Remove the frittata and leave to cool for 5 minutes.
7. Top with the minced chives and serve.

Shrimp Quiche

Prep time: 15 minutes | Cook time: 20 minutes | Serves 2

2 teaspoons vegetable oil
4 large eggs
½ cup half-and-half
4 ounces (113 g) raw shrimp, chopped
1 cup shredded Parmesan or Swiss cheese
¼ cup chopped
scallions
1 teaspoon sweet smoked paprika
1 teaspoon herbes de Provence
1 teaspoon black pepper
½ to 1 teaspoon kosher salt

1. Preheat the air fryer oven to 300°F (149°C). Generously grease a baking pan with vegetable oil.
2. In a large bowl, beat together the eggs and half-and-half. Add the shrimp, ¾ cup of the cheese, the scallions, paprika, herbes de Provence, pepper, and salt. Stir with a fork to thoroughly combine. Pour the egg mixture into the prepared pan.
3. Slide the baking pan into Rack Position 1, select Convection Bake and set time to 20 minutes.
4. After 17 minutes, sprinkle the remaining ¼ cup cheese on top and bake for the remaining 3 minutes, or until the cheese has melted, the eggs are set, and a toothpick inserted into the center comes out clean.
5. Serve the quiche warm.

Shrimp Spinach Frittata

Prep time: 6 minutes | Cook time: 14 minutes | Serves 4

4 whole eggs
1 teaspoon dried basil
½ cup shrimp, cooked and chopped
½ cup baby spinach

½ cup rice, cooked
½ cup Monterey Jack cheese, grated
Salt, to taste
Cooking spray

1. Spritz the baking pan with cooking spray.
2. Whisk the eggs with basil and salt in a large bowl until bubbly, then mix in the shrimp, spinach, rice, and cheese.
3. Pour the mixture into the baking pan.
4. Slide the baking pan into Rack Position 1, select Convection Bake, set temperature to 360ºF (182ºC) and set time to 14 minutes.
5. Stir the mixture halfway through.
6. When cooking is complete, the eggs should be set and the frittata should be golden brown.
7. Slice to serve.

Smoked Trout and Crème Fraiche Frittata

Prep time: 8 minutes | Cook time: 17 minutes | Serves 4

2 tablespoons olive oil
1 onion, sliced
1 egg, beaten
½ tablespoon horseradish sauce
6 tablespoons crème

fraiche
1 cup diced smoked trout
2 tablespoons chopped fresh dill
Cooking spray

1. Spritz the baking pan with cooking spray.
2. Heat the olive oil in a nonstick skillet over medium heat until shimmering.
3. Add the onion and sauté for 3 minutes or until translucent.
4. Combine the egg, horseradish sauce, and crème fraiche in a large bowl. Stir to mix well, then mix in the sautéed onion, smoked trout, and dill.
5. Pour the mixture in the prepared baking pan.
6. Slide the baking pan into Rack Position 1, select Convection Bake, set temperature to 350ºF (180ºC) and set time to 14 minutes.

7. Stir the mixture halfway through.
8. When cooking is complete, the egg should be set and the edges should be lightly browned.
9. Serve immediately.

Mini Quiche Cups

Prep time: 15 minutes | Cook time: 14 minutes | Makes 10 quiche cups

4 ounces (113 g) ground pork sausage
3 eggs
¾ cup milk

Cooking spray
4 ounces (113 g) sharp Cheddar cheese, grated

Special Equipment:
1. 20 foil muffin cups
2.
3. Preheat the air fryer oven to 390ºF (199ºC). Spritz the air fryer basket with cooking spray.
4. Divide sausage into 3 portions and shape each into a thin patty.
5. Put the patties in the air fryer basket. Place the air fryer basket onto the baking pan and slide into Rack Position 2, select Air Fry and set time to 6 minutes.
6. While sausage is cooking, prepare the egg mixture. Combine the eggs and milk in a large bowl and whisk until well blended. Set aside.
7. When sausage has cooked fully, remove patties from the basket, drain well, and use a fork to crumble the meat into small pieces.
8. Double the foil cups into 10 sets. Remove paper liners from the top muffin cups and spray the foil cups lightly with cooking spray.
9. Divide crumbled sausage among the 10 muffin cup sets.
10. Top each with grated cheese, divided evenly among the cups. Put the cups in a baking pan.
11. Pour egg mixture into each cup, filling until each cup is at least ²/₃ full.
12. Slide the baking pan into Rack Position 1, select Convection Bake and set time to 8 minutes. A knife inserted into the center shouldn't have any raw egg on it when removed.
13. Serve warm.

Chapter 9 Wraps and Sandwiches

Bulgogi Burgers

Prep time: 15 minutes | Cook time: 10 minutes | Serves 4

Burgers:

1 pound (454 g) 85% lean ground beef
2 tablespoons gochujang
¼ cup chopped scallions
2 teaspoons minced garlic
2 teaspoons minced

fresh ginger
1 tablespoon soy sauce
1 tablespoon toasted sesame oil
2 teaspoons sugar
½ teaspoon kosher salt
4 hamburger buns
Cooking spray

Korean Mayo:

1 tablespoon gochujang
¼ cup mayonnaise
2 teaspoons sesame seeds

¼ cup chopped scallions
1 tablespoon toasted sesame oil

1. Combine the ingredients for the burgers, except for the buns, in a large bowl. Stir to mix well, then wrap the bowl in plastic and refrigerate to marinate for at least an hour.
2. Spritz the air fryer basket with cooking spray.
3. Divide the meat mixture into four portions and form into four balls. Bash the balls into patties.
4. Arrange the patties in the pan and spritz with cooking spray.
5. Put the air fryer basket on the baking pan and slide into Rack Position 2, select Air Fry, set temperature to 350°F (180°C) and set time to 10 minutes.
6. Flip the patties halfway through the cooking time.
7. Meanwhile, combine the ingredients for the Korean mayo in a small bowl. Stir to mix well.
8. When cooking is complete, the patties should be golden brown.
9. Remove the patties from the oven and assemble with the buns, then spread the Korean mayo over the patties to make the burgers. Serve immediately.

Sweet Potato and Black Bean Burritos

Prep time: 15 minutes | Cook time: 30 minutes | Makes 6 burritos

2 sweet potatoes, peeled and cut into a small dice
1 tablespoon vegetable oil
Kosher salt and ground black pepper, to taste
6 large flour tortillas
1 (16-ounce / 454-g) can refried black

beans, divided
1½ cups baby spinach, divided
6 eggs, scrambled
¾ cup grated Cheddar cheese, divided
¼ cup salsa
¼ cup sour cream
Cooking spray

1. Put the sweet potatoes in a large bowl, then drizzle with vegetable oil and sprinkle with salt and black pepper. Toss to coat well.
2. Place the potatoes in the air fryer basket.
3. Put the air fryer basket on the baking pan and slide into Rack Position 2, select Air Fry, set temperature to 400°F (205°C) and set time to 10 minutes.
4. Flip the potatoes halfway through the cooking time.
5. When done, the potatoes should be lightly browned. Remove the potatoes from the oven.
6. Unfold the tortillas on a clean work surface. Divide the black beans, spinach, air fried sweet potatoes, scrambled eggs, and cheese on top of the tortillas.
7. Fold the long side of the tortillas over the filling, then fold in the shorter side to wrap the filling to make the burritos.
8. Wrap the burritos in the aluminum foil and put in the pan.
9. Put the air fryer basket on the baking pan and slide into Rack Position 2, select Air Fry, set temperature to 350°F (180°C) and set time to 20 minutes.
10. Flip the burritos halfway through the cooking time.
11. Remove the burritos from the oven and spread with sour cream and salsa. Serve immediately.

Air Fried Cream Cheese Wontons

Prep time: 5 minutes | Cook time: 6 minutes | Serves 4

2 ounces (57 g) cream cheese, softened
1 tablespoon sugar
16 square wonton wrappers
Cooking spray

1. Spritz the air fryer basket with cooking spray.
2. In a mixing bowl, stir together the cream cheese and sugar until well mixed. Prepare a small bowl of water alongside.
3. On a clean work surface, lay the wonton wrappers. Scoop ¼ teaspoon of cream cheese in the center of each wonton wrapper. Dab the water over the wrapper edges. Fold each wonton wrapper diagonally in half over the filling to form a triangle.
4. Arrange the wontons in the pan. Spritz the wontons with cooking spray.
5. Put the air fryer basket on the baking pan and slide into Rack Position 2, select Air Fry, set temperature to 350ºF (180ºC) and set time to 6 minutes.
6. Flip the wontons halfway through the cooking time.
7. When cooking is complete, the wontons will be golden brown and crispy.
8. Divide the wontons among four plates. Let rest for 5 minutes before serving.

Bacon and Bell Pepper Sandwich

Prep time: 10 minutes | Cook time: 6 minutes | Serves 4

¹/₃ cup spicy barbecue sauce
2 tablespoons honey
8 slices cooked bacon, cut into thirds
1 red bell pepper, sliced
1 yellow bell pepper, sliced
3 pita pockets, cut in half
1¼ cups torn butter lettuce leaves
2 tomatoes, sliced

1. Preheat the air fryer oven to 350ºF (177ºC).
2. In a small bowl, combine the barbecue sauce and the honey. Brush this mixture lightly onto the bacon slices and the red and yellow pepper slices.
3. Put the peppers into the air fryer basket. Place the air fryer basket onto the baking pan and slide into Rack Position 2, select Air Fry and set time to 4 minutes. Shake the basket, add the bacon, and air fry for 2 minutes, or until the bacon is browned and the peppers are tender.
4. Fill the pita halves with the bacon, peppers, any remaining barbecue sauce, lettuce, and tomatoes, and serve immediately.

Cabbage and Pork Gyoza

Prep time: 10 minutes | Cook time: 10 minutes | Makes 48 gyozas

1 pound (454 g) ground pork
1 head Napa cabbage (about 1 pound / 454 g), sliced thinly and minced
½ cup minced scallions
1 teaspoon minced fresh chives
1 teaspoon soy sauce
1 teaspoon minced fresh ginger
1 tablespoon minced garlic
1 teaspoon granulated sugar
2 teaspoons kosher salt
48 to 50 wonton or dumpling wrappers
Cooking spray

1. Spritz the air fryer basket with cooking spray. Set aside.
2. Make the filling: Combine all the ingredients, except for the wrappers in a large bowl. Stir to mix well.
3. Unfold a wrapper on a clean work surface, then dab the edges with a little water. Scoop up 2 teaspoons of the filling mixture in the center.
4. Make the gyoza: Fold the wrapper over to filling and press the edges to seal. Pleat the edges if desired. Repeat with remaining wrappers and fillings.
5. Arrange the gyozas in the pan and spritz with cooking spray.
6. Put the air fryer basket on the baking pan and slide into Rack Position 2, select Air Fry, set temperature to 360ºF (182ºC) and set time to 10 minutes.
7. Flip the gyozas halfway through the cooking time.
8. When cooked, the gyozas will be golden brown.
9. Serve immediately.

Crispy Chicken Egg Rolls

Prep time: 10 minutes | Cook time: 23 to 24 minutes | Serves 4

1 pound (454 g) ground chicken
2 teaspoons olive oil
2 garlic cloves, minced
1 teaspoon grated fresh ginger
2 cups white cabbage, shredded
1 onion, chopped
¼ cup soy sauce
8 egg roll wrappers
1 egg, beaten
Cooking spray

1. Spritz the air fryer basket with cooking spray.
2. Heat olive oil in a saucepan over medium heat. Sauté the garlic and ginger in the olive oil for 1 minute, or until fragrant. Add the ground chicken to the saucepan. Sauté for 5 minutes, or until the chicken is cooked through. Add the cabbage, onion and soy sauce and sauté for 5 to 6 minutes, or until the vegetables become soft. Remove the saucepan from the heat.
3. Unfold the egg roll wrappers on a clean work surface. Divide the chicken mixture among the wrappers and brush the edges of the wrappers with the beaten egg. Tightly roll up the egg rolls, enclosing the filling. Arrange the rolls in the pan.
4. Put the air fryer basket on the baking pan and slide into Rack Position 2, select Air Fry, set temperature to 370ºF (188ºC) and set time to 12 minutes.
5. Flip the rolls halfway through the cooking time.
6. When cooked, the rolls will be crispy and golden brown.
7. Transfer to a platter and let cool for 5 minutes before serving.

Pork Momos

Prep time: 20 minutes | Cook time: 20 minutes | Serves 4

2 tablespoons olive oil
1 pound (454 g) ground pork
1 shredded carrot
1 onion, chopped
1 teaspoon soy
sauce
16 wonton wrappers
Salt and ground black pepper, to taste
Cooking spray

1. Heat the olive oil in a nonstick skillet over medium heat until shimmering.
2. Add the ground pork, carrot, onion, soy sauce, salt, and ground black pepper and sauté for 10 minutes or until the pork is well browned and carrots are tender.
3. Unfold the wrappers on a clean work surface, then divide the cooked pork and vegetables on the wrappers. Fold the edges around the filling to form momos. Nip the top to seal the momos.
4. Arrange the momos in the air fryer basket and spritz with cooking spray.
5. Put the air fryer basket on the baking pan and slide into Rack Position 2, select Air Fry, set temperature to 320ºF (160ºC) and set time to 10 minutes.
6. When cooking is complete, the wrappers will be lightly browned.
7. Serve immediately.

Cheesy Shrimp Sandwich

Prep time: 10 minutes | Cook time: 6 minutes | Serves 4

1¼ cups shredded Colby, Cheddar, or Havarti cheese
1 (6-ounce / 170-g) can tiny shrimp, drained
3 tablespoons mayonnaise
2 tablespoons minced green onion
4 slices whole grain or whole-wheat bread
2 tablespoons softened butter

1. Preheat the air fryer oven to 400ºF (204ºC).
2. In a medium bowl, combine the cheese, shrimp, mayonnaise, and green onion, and mix well.
3. Spread this mixture on two of the slices of bread. Top with the other slices of bread to make two sandwiches. Spread the sandwiches lightly with butter.
4. Lay the sandwiches in the air fryer basket. Place the air fryer basket onto the baking pan and slide into Rack Position 2, select Air Fry and set time to 6 minutes, or until the bread is browned and crisp and the cheese is melted.
5. Cut in half and serve warm.

Salsa Verde Golden Chicken Empanadas

Prep time: 25 minutes | Cook time: 12 minutes | Makes 12 empanadas

1 cup boneless, skinless rotisserie chicken breast meat, chopped finely
¼ cup salsa verde
⅔ cup shredded Cheddar cheese
1 teaspoon ground cumin
1 teaspoon ground

black pepper
2 purchased refrigerated pie crusts, from a minimum 14.1-ounce (400 g) box
1 large egg
2 tablespoons water
Cooking spray

1. Spritz the air fryer basket with cooking spray. Set aside.
2. Combine the chicken meat, salsa verde, Cheddar, cumin, and black pepper in a large bowl. Stir to mix well. Set aside.
3. Unfold the pie crusts on a clean work surface, then use a large cookie cutter to cut out 3½-inch circles as much as possible.
4. Roll the remaining crusts to a ball and flatten into a circle which has the same thickness of the original crust. Cut out more 3½-inch circles until you have 12 circles in total.
5. Make the empanadas: Divide the chicken mixture in the middle of each circle, about 1½ tablespoons each. Dab the edges of the circle with water. Fold the circle in half over the filling to shape like a half-moon and press to seal, or you can press with a fork.
6. Whisk the egg with water in a small bowl.
7. Arrange the empanadas in the pan and spritz with cooking spray. Brush with whisked egg.
8. Put the air fryer basket on the baking pan and slide into Rack Position 2, select Air Fry, set temperature to 350ºF (180ºC) and set time to 12 minutes.
9. Flip the empanadas halfway through the cooking time.
10. When cooking is complete, the empanadas will be golden and crispy.
11. Serve immediately.

Smoky Chicken Sandwich

Prep time: 10 minutes | Cook time: 11 minutes | Serves 2

2 boneless, skinless chicken breasts (8 ounces / 227 g each), sliced horizontally in half and separated into 4 thinner cutlets
Kosher salt and freshly ground black pepper, to taste
½ cup all-purpose flour
3 large eggs, lightly beaten

½ cup dried bread crumbs
1 tablespoon smoked paprika
Cooking spray
½ cup marinara sauce
6 ounces (170 g) smoked Mozzarella cheese, grated
2 store-bought soft, sesame-seed hamburger or Italian buns, split

1. Preheat the air fryer oven to 350ºF (177ºC).
2. Season the chicken cutlets all over with salt and pepper. Set up three shallow bowls: Place the flour in the first bowl, the eggs in the second, and stir together the bread crumbs and smoked paprika in the third. Coat the chicken pieces in the flour, then dip fully in the egg. Dredge in the paprika bread crumbs, then transfer to a wire rack set over a baking sheet and spray both sides liberally with cooking spray.
3. Transfer the chicken cutlets to the air fryer basket.
4. Place the air fryer basket onto the baking pan and slide into Rack Position 2, select Air Fry and set time to 6 minutes, or until the chicken begins to brown.
5. Spread each cutlet with 2 tablespoons of the marinara sauce and sprinkle with one-quarter of the smoked Mozzarella.
6. Increase the temperature to 400ºF (204ºC) and air fry for 5 minutes more, or until the chicken is cooked through and crisp and the cheese is melted and golden brown.
7. Transfer the cutlets to a plate and place two cutlets inside each of two buns. Serve the sandwiches warm.

Eggplant Hoagies

Prep time: 15 minutes | Cook time: 12 minutes | Makes 3 hoagies

6 peeled eggplant slices (about ½ inch thick and 3 inches in diameter)
¼ cup jarred pizza sauce

6 tablespoons grated Parmesan cheese
3 Italian sub rolls, split open lengthwise, warmed
Cooking spray

1. Spritz the air fryer basket with cooking spray.
2. Arrange the eggplant slices in the pan and spritz with cooking spray.
3. Put the air fryer basket on the baking pan and slide into Rack Position 2, select Air Fry, set temperature to 350ºF (180ºC) and set time to 10 minutes.
4. Flip the slices halfway through the cooking time.
5. When cooked, the eggplant slices should be lightly wilted and tender.
6. Divide and spread the pizza sauce and cheese on top of the eggplant slice
7. Put the air fryer basket on the baking pan and slide into Rack Position 2, select Air Fry, set temperature to 375ºF (190ºC) and set time to 2 minutes.
8. When cooked, the cheese will be melted.
9. Assemble each sub roll with two slices of eggplant and serve immediately.

Lamb and Feta Hamburgers

Prep time: 15 minutes | Cook time: 16 minutes | Makes 4 burgers

1½ pounds (680 g) ground lamb
¼ cup crumbled feta
1½ teaspoons tomato paste
1½ teaspoons minced garlic
1 teaspoon ground dried ginger
1 teaspoon ground

coriander
¼ teaspoon salt
¼ teaspoon cayenne pepper
4 kaiser rolls or hamburger buns, split open lengthwise, warmed
Cooking spray

1. Spritz the air fryer basket with cooking spray.
2. Combine all the ingredients, except for the buns, in a large bowl. Coarsely stir to mix well.

3. Shape the mixture into four balls, then pound the balls into four 5-inch diameter patties.
4. Arrange the patties in the pan and spritz with cooking spray.
5. Put the air fryer basket on the baking pan and slide into Rack Position 2, select Air Fry, set temperature to 375ºF (190ºC) and set time to 16 minutes.
6. Flip the patties halfway through the cooking time.
7. When cooking is complete, the patties should be well browned.
8. Assemble the buns with patties to make the burgers and serve immediately.

Chicken and Yogurt Taquitos

Prep time: 15 minutes | Cook time: 12 minutes | Serves 4

1 cup cooked chicken, shredded
¼ cup Greek yogurt
¼ cup salsa
1 cup shredded Mozzarella cheese

Salt and ground black pepper, to taste
4 flour tortillas
Cooking spray

1. Spritz the air fryer basket with cooking spray.
2. Combine all the ingredients, except for the tortillas, in a large bowl. Stir to mix well.
3. Make the taquitos: Unfold the tortillas on a clean work surface, then scoop up 2 tablespoons of the chicken mixture in the middle of each tortilla. Roll the tortillas up to wrap the filling.
4. Arrange the taquitos in the pan and spritz with cooking spray.
5. Put the air fryer basket on the baking pan and slide into Rack Position 2, select Air Fry, set temperature to 380ºF (193ºC) and set time to 12 minutes.
6. Flip the taquitos halfway through the cooking time.
7. When cooked, the taquitos should be golden brown and the cheese should be melted.
8. Serve immediately.

Turkey, Leek, and Pepper Hamburger

Prep time: 10 minutes | Cook time: 20 minutes | Serves 4

1 cup leftover turkey, cut into bite-sized chunks
1 leek, sliced
1 Serrano pepper, deveined and chopped
2 bell peppers, deveined and chopped
2 tablespoons Tabasco sauce
½ cup sour cream
1 heaping tablespoon fresh cilantro, chopped
1 teaspoon hot paprika
¾ teaspoon kosher salt
½ teaspoon ground black pepper
4 hamburger buns
Cooking spray

1. Spritz the baking pan with cooking spray.
2. Mix all the ingredients, except for the buns, in a large bowl. Toss to combine well.
3. Pour the mixture in the baking pan.
4. Slide the baking pan into Rack Position 1, select Convection Bake, set temperature to 385ºF (196ºC) and set time to 20 minutes.
5. When done, the turkey will be well browned and the leek will be tender.
6. Assemble the hamburger buns with the turkey mixture and serve immediately.

Thai Pork Sliders

Prep time: 10 minutes | Cook time: 14 minutes | Makes 6 sliders

1 pound (454 g) ground pork
1 tablespoon Thai curry paste
1½ tablespoons fish sauce
¼ cup thinly sliced scallions, white and green parts
2 tablespoons
minced peeled fresh ginger
1 tablespoon light brown sugar
1 teaspoon ground black pepper
6 slider buns, split open lengthwise, warmed
Cooking spray

1. Spritz the air fryer basket with cooking spray.
2. Combine all the ingredients, except for the buns in a large bowl. Stir to mix well.
3. Divide and shape the mixture into six balls, then bash the balls into six 3-inch-diameter patties.
4. Arrange the patties in the basket and spritz with cooking spray.
5. Put the air fryer basket on the baking pan and slide into Rack Position 2, select Air Fry, set temperature to 375ºF (190ºC) and set time to 14 minutes.
6. Flip the patties halfway through the cooking time.
7. When cooked, the patties should be well browned.
8. Assemble the buns with patties to make the sliders and serve immediately.

Crispy Crab and Cream Cheese Wontons

Prep time: 10 minutes | Cook time: 10 minutes | Serves 6 to 8

24 wonton wrappers, thawed if frozen
Filling:
5 ounces (142 g) lump crabmeat, drained and patted dry
4 ounces (113 g) cream cheese, at room temperature
2 scallions, sliced
Cooking spray

1½ teaspoons toasted sesame oil
1 teaspoon Worcestershire sauce
Kosher salt and ground black pepper, to taste

1. Spritz the air fryer basket with cooking spray.
2. In a medium-size bowl, place all the ingredients for the filling and stir until well mixed. Prepare a small bowl of water alongside.
3. On a clean work surface, lay the wonton wrappers. Scoop 1 teaspoon of the filling in the center of each wrapper. Wet the edges with a touch of water. Fold each wonton wrapper diagonally in half over the filling to form a triangle.
4. Arrange the wontons in the pan. Spritz the wontons with cooking spray.
5. Put the air fryer basket on the baking pan and slide into Rack Position 2, select Air Fry, set temperature to 350ºF (180ºC) and set time to 10 minutes.
6. Flip the wontons halfway through the cooking time.
7. When cooking is complete, the wontons will be crispy and golden brown.
8. Serve immediately.

Veggie Pita Sandwich

Prep time: 10 minutes | Cook time: 12 minutes | Serves 4

1 baby eggplant, peeled and chopped	1 teaspoon olive oil
1 red bell pepper, sliced	1/3 cup low-fat Greek yogurt
1/2 cup diced red onion	1/2 teaspoon dried tarragon
1/2 cup shredded carrot	2 low-sodium whole-wheat pita breads, halved crosswise

1. Preheat the air fryer oven to 390°F (199°C).
2. In a baking pan, stir together the eggplant, red bell pepper, red onion, carrot, and olive oil.
3. Slide the baking pan into Rack Position 1, select Convection Bake and set time to 9 minutes, stirring once, or until the vegetables are tender. Drain if necessary.
4. In a small bowl, thoroughly mix the yogurt and tarragon until well combined. Stir the yogurt mixture into the vegetables. Stuff one-fourth of this mixture into each pita pocket.
5. Place the baking pan with the pita sandwiches back into Rack Position 1 and bake for an additional 3 minutes, or until the bread is toasted.
6. Serve immediately.

Chicken Pita Sandwich

Prep time: 10 minutes | Cook time: 10 minutes | Serves 4

2 boneless, skinless chicken breasts, cut into 1-inch cubes	dressing, divided
	1/2 teaspoon dried thyme
1 small red onion, sliced	4 pita pockets, split
1 red bell pepper, sliced	2 cups torn butter lettuce
1/3 cup Italian salad	1 cup chopped cherry tomatoes

1. Preheat the air fryer oven to 380°F (193°C).
2. Place the chicken, onion, and bell pepper in the air fryer basket. Drizzle with 1 tablespoon of the Italian salad dressing, add the thyme, and toss.

3. Place the air fryer basket onto the baking pan and slide into Rack Position 2, select Air Fry and set time to 10 minutes, or until the chicken is 165°F (74°C) on a meat thermometer, stirring once during cooking time.
4. Transfer the chicken and vegetables to a bowl and toss with the remaining salad dressing.
5. Assemble sandwiches with the pita pockets, butter lettuce, and cherry tomatoes. Serve immediately.

Cheesy Chicken Sandwich

Prep time: 10 minutes | Cook time: 7 minutes | Serves 1

1/3 cup chicken, cooked and shredded	1 teaspoon olive oil
2 Mozzarella slices	1/2 teaspoon balsamic vinegar
1 hamburger bun	1/4 teaspoon smoked paprika
1/4 cup shredded cabbage	1/4 teaspoon black pepper
1 teaspoon mayonnaise	1/4 teaspoon garlic powder
2 teaspoons butter, melted	Pinch of salt

1. Preheat the air fryer oven to 370°F (188°C).
2. Brush some butter onto the outside of the hamburger bun.
3. In a bowl, coat the chicken with the garlic powder, salt, pepper, and paprika.
4. In a separate bowl, stir together the mayonnaise, olive oil, cabbage, and balsamic vinegar to make coleslaw.
5. Slice the bun in two. Start building the sandwich, starting with the chicken, followed by the Mozzarella, the coleslaw, and finally the top bun. Transfer the sandwich to a baking pan.
6. Slide the baking pan into Rack Position 1, select Convection Bake and set time to 7 minutes.
7. Serve immediately.

Mexican Flavor Chicken Burgers

Prep time: 15 minutes | Cook time: 20 minutes | Serves 6 to 8

4 skinless and boneless chicken breasts
1 small head of cauliflower, sliced into florets
1 jalapeño pepper
3 tablespoons smoked paprika
1 tablespoon thyme
1 tablespoon oregano
1 tablespoon mustard powder
1 teaspoon cayenne pepper
1 egg
Salt and ground black pepper, to taste
2 tomatoes, sliced
2 lettuce leaves, chopped
6 to 8 brioche buns, sliced lengthwise
¾ cup taco sauce
Cooking spray

1. Spritz the air fryer basket with cooking spray. Set aside.
2. In a blender, add the cauliflower florets, jalapeño pepper, paprika, thyme, oregano, mustard powder and cayenne pepper and blend until the mixture has a texture similar to bread crumbs.
3. Transfer ¾ of the cauliflower mixture to a medium bowl and set aside. Beat the egg in a different bowl and set aside.
4. Add the chicken breasts to the blender with remaining cauliflower mixture. Sprinkle with salt and pepper. Blend until finely chopped and well mixed.
5. Remove the mixture from the blender and form into 6 to 8 patties. One by one, dredge each patty in the reserved cauliflower mixture, then into the egg. Dip them in the cauliflower mixture again for additional coating.
6. Place the coated patties into the pan and spritz with cooking spray.
7. Put the air fryer basket on the baking pan and slide into Rack Position 2, select Air Fry, set temperature to 350°F (180°C) and set time to 20 minutes.
8. Flip the patties halfway through the cooking time.
9. When cooking is complete, the patties should be golden and crispy.
10. Transfer the patties to a clean work surface and assemble with the buns, tomato slices, chopped lettuce leaves and taco sauce to make burgers. Serve and enjoy.

Classic Sloppy Joes

Prep time: 10 minutes | Cook time: 19 minutes | Makes 4 large sandwiches or 8 sliders

1 pound (454 g) very lean ground beef
1 teaspoon onion powder
$^1/_3$ cup ketchup
¼ cup water
½ teaspoon celery seed
1 tablespoon lemon juice
1½ teaspoons brown sugar
1¼ teaspoons low-sodium Worcestershire sauce
½ teaspoon salt (optional)
½ teaspoon vinegar
⅛ teaspoon dry mustard
Hamburger or slider buns, for serving
Cooking spray

1. Preheat the air fryer oven to 390°F (199°C). Spray the air fryer basket with cooking spray.
2. Break raw ground beef into small chunks and pile into the basket.
3. Place the air fryer basket onto the baking pan and slide into Rack Position 2, select Air Fry and set time to 12 minutes. Stir the meat twice during cooking, or until meat is well done.
4. Remove the meat from the oven, drain, and use a knife and fork to crumble into small pieces.
5. Place all the remaining ingredients, except for the buns, in a baking pan and mix together. Add the meat and stir well.
6. Slide the baking pan into Rack Position 1, select Convection Bake, set temperature to 330°F (166°C) and set time to 7 minutes.
7. After 5 minutes, remove from the oven. Stir and return to the oven to continue cooking.
8. Scoop onto buns and serve hot.

Turkey Sliders with Chive Mayo

Prep time: 10 minutes | Cook time: 15 minutes | Serves 6

12 burger buns
Turkey Sliders:
¾ pound (340 g) turkey, minced
1 tablespoon oyster sauce
¼ cup pickled jalapeno, chopped
2 tablespoons chopped scallions
1 tablespoon chopped fresh cilantro
1 to 2 cloves garlic, minced
Sea salt and ground black pepper, to taste
Chive Mayo:
1 tablespoon chives
1 cup mayonnaise

Cooking spray

Zest of 1 lime
1 teaspoon salt

1. Spritz the air fryer basket with cooking spray.
2. Combine the ingredients for the turkey sliders in a large bowl. Stir to mix well. Shape the mixture into 6 balls, then bash the balls into patties.
3. Arrange the patties in the pan and spritz with cooking spray.
4. Put the air fryer basket on the baking pan and slide into Rack Position 2, select Air Fry, set temperature to 365ºF (185ºC) and set time to 15 minutes.
5. Flip the patties halfway through the cooking time.
6. Meanwhile, combine the ingredients for the chive mayo in a small bowl. Stir to mix well.
7. When cooked, the patties will be well browned.
8. Smear the patties with chive mayo, then assemble the patties between two buns to make the sliders. Serve immediately.

Montreal Steak and Seeds Burgers

Prep time: 15 minutes | Cook time: 10 minutes | Serves 4

1 teaspoon cumin seeds
1 teaspoon mustard seeds
1 teaspoon coriander seeds
1 teaspoon dried minced garlic
1 teaspoon dried red pepper flakes
1 teaspoon kosher salt

2 teaspoons ground black pepper
1 pound (454 g) 85% lean ground beef
2 tablespoons Worcestershire sauce
4 hamburger buns
Mayonnaise, for serving
Cooking spray

1. Spritz the air fryer basket with cooking spray.
2. Put the seeds, garlic, red pepper flakes, salt, and ground black pepper in a food processor. Pulse to coarsely ground the mixture.
3. Put the ground beef in a large bowl. Pour in the seed mixture and drizzle with Worcestershire sauce. Stir to mix well.
4. Divide the mixture into four parts and shape each part into a ball, then bash each ball into a patty. Arrange the patties in the pan.
5. Put the air fryer basket on the baking pan and slide into Rack Position 2, select Air Fry, set temperature to 350ºF (180ºC) and set time to 10 minutes.
6. Flip the patties with tongs halfway through the cooking time.
7. When cooked, the patties will be well browned.
8. Assemble the buns with the patties, then drizzle the mayo over the patties to make the burgers. Serve immediately.

Pea and Potato Samosas with Chutney

Prep time: 30 minutes | Cook time: 22 minutes | Makes 16 samosas

Dough:
4 cups all-purpose flour, plus more for flouring the work surface
¼ cup plain yogurt
½ cup cold unsalted butter, cut into cubes
2 teaspoons kosher salt
1 cup ice water

Filling:
2 tablespoons vegetable oil
1 onion, diced
1½ teaspoons coriander
1½ teaspoons cumin
1 clove garlic, minced
1 teaspoon turmeric
1 teaspoon kosher salt
½ cup peas, thawed if frozen
2 cups mashed potatoes
2 tablespoons yogurt
Cooking spray

Chutney:
1 cup mint leaves, lightly packed
2 cups cilantro leaves, lightly packed
1 green chile pepper, deseeded and minced
½ cup minced onion
Juice of 1 lime
1 teaspoon granulated sugar
1 teaspoon kosher salt
2 tablespoons vegetable oil

1. Put the flour, yogurt, butter, and salt in a food processor. Pulse to combine until grainy. Pour in the water and pulse until a smooth and firm dough forms.
2. Transfer the dough on a clean and lightly floured working surface. Knead the dough and shape it into a ball. Cut in half and flatten the halves into 2 discs. Wrap them in plastic and let sit in refrigerator until ready to use.
3. Meanwhile, make the filling: Heat the vegetable oil in a saucepan over medium heat.
4. Add the onion and sauté for 5 minutes or until lightly browned.
5. Add the coriander, cumin, garlic, turmeric, and salt and sauté for 2 minutes or until fragrant.
6. Add the peas, potatoes, and yogurt and stir to combine well. Turn off the heat and allow to cool.
7. Meanwhile, combine the ingredients for the chutney in a food processor. Pulse to mix well until glossy. Pour the chutney in a bowl and refrigerate until ready to use.
8. Make the samosas: Remove the dough discs from the refrigerator and cut each disc into 8 parts. Shape each part into a ball, then roll the ball into a 6-inch circle. Cut the circle in half and roll each half into a cone.
9. Scoop up 2 tablespoons of the filling into the cone, press the edges of the cone to seal and form into a triangle. Repeat with remaining dough and filling.
10. Spritz the air fryer basket with cooking spray. Arrange the samosas in the pan and spritz with cooking spray.
11. Put the air fryer basket on the baking pan and slide into Rack Position 2, select Air Fry, set temperature to 360ºF (182ºC) and set time to 15 minutes.
12. Flip the samosas halfway through the cooking time.
13. When cooked, the samosas will be golden brown and crispy.
14. Serve the samosas with the chutney.

Chapter 10 Fast and Easy Everyday Favorites

Air Fried Okra Chips

Prep time: 5 minutes | Cook time: 16 minutes | Serves 6

2 pounds (907 g) fresh okra pods, cut into 1-inch pieces
2 tablespoons canola

oil
1 teaspoon coarse sea salt

1. Stir the oil and salt in a bowl to mix well. Add the okra and toss to coat well. Place the okra in the air fryer basket.
2. Put the air fryer basket on the baking pan and slide into Rack Position 2, select Air Fry, set temperature to 400°F (205°C) and set time to 16 minutes.
3. Flip the okra at least three times during cooking.
4. When cooked, the okra should be lightly browned. Remove from the oven and serve immediately.

Sweet and Sour Peanuts

Prep time: 5 minutes | Cook time: 5 minutes | Serves 9

3 cups shelled raw peanuts
1 tablespoon hot red pepper sauce

3 tablespoons granulated white sugar

1. Put the peanuts in a large bowl, then drizzle with hot red pepper sauce and sprinkle with sugar. Toss to coat well.
2. Pour the peanuts in the air fryer basket.
3. Put the air fryer basket on the baking pan and slide into Rack Position 2, select Air Fry, set temperature to 400°F (205°C) and set time to 5 minutes.
4. Stir the peanuts halfway through the cooking time.
5. When cooking is complete, the peanuts will be crispy and browned. Remove from the oven and serve immediately.

Hot Wings

Prep time: 5 minutes | Cook time: 15 minutes | Makes 16 wings

16 chicken wings
3 tablespoons hot

sauce
Cooking spray

1. Spritz the air fryer basket with cooking spray.
2. Arrange the chicken wings in the basket.
3. Put the air fryer basket on the baking pan and slide into Rack Position 2, select Air Fry, set temperature to 360°F (182°C) and set time to 15 minutes.
4. Flip the wings at lease three times during cooking.
5. When cooking is complete, the chicken wings will be well browned. Remove from the oven.
6. Transfer the air fried wings to a plate and serve with hot sauce.

Pea Delight

Prep time: 5 minutes | Cook time: 15 minutes | Serves 2 to 4

1 cup flour
1 teaspoon baking powder
3 eggs
1 cup coconut milk
1 cup cream cheese
3 tablespoons pea

protein
½ cup chicken or turkey strips
Pinch of sea salt
1 cup Mozzarella cheese

1. Preheat the air fryer oven to 390°F (199°C).
2. In a large bowl, mix all ingredients together using a large wooden spoon.
3. Spoon equal amounts of the mixture into muffin cups. Place the muffin cups in a baking pan.
4. Slide the baking pan into Rack Position 1, select Convection Bake and set time to 15 minutes.
5. Serve immediately.

Chicken Wings

Prep time: 5 minutes | Cook time: 15 minutes | Serves 6

2 pounds (907 g) chicken wings, tips removed
⅛ teaspoon salt

1. Preheat the air fryer oven to 400ºF (204ºC).
2. Season the wings with salt. Put the chicken wings in the air fryer basket.
3. Place the air fryer basket onto the baking pan and slide into Rack Position 2, select Air Fry and set time to 15 minutes, or until the skin is browned and cooked through, turning the wings with tongs halfway through cooking.
4. Transfer to a large bowl and serve immediately.

Spanakopita

Prep time: 10 minutes | Cook time: 8 minutes | Serves 6

½ (10-ounce / 284-g) package frozen spinach, thawed and squeezed dry
1 egg, lightly beaten
¼ cup pine nuts, toasted
¼ cup grated Parmesan cheese
¾ cup crumbled feta cheese
⅛ teaspoon ground nutmeg
½ teaspoon salt
Freshly ground black pepper, to taste
6 sheets phyllo dough
½ cup butter, melted

1. Combine all the ingredients, except for the phyllo dough and butter, in a large bowl. Whisk to combine well. Set aside.
2. Place a sheet of phyllo dough on a clean work surface. Brush with butter then top with another layer sheet of phyllo. Brush with butter, then cut the layered sheets into six 3-inch-wide strips.
3. Top each strip with 1 tablespoon of the spinach mixture, then fold the bottom left corner over the mixture towards the right strip edge to make a triangle. Keep folding triangles until each strip is folded over.
4. Brush the triangles with butter and repeat with remaining strips and phyllo dough.
5. Place the triangles in the baking pan.
6. Put the air fryer basket on the baking pan and slide into Rack Position 2, select Air Fry, set temperature to 350ºF (180ºC) and set time to 8 minutes.
7. Flip the triangles halfway through the cooking time.
8. When cooking is complete, the triangles should be golden brown. Remove from the oven and serve immediately.

Garlicky Spiralized Zucchini and Squash

Prep time: 10 minutes | Cook time: 10 minutes | Serves 4

2 large zucchini, peeled and spiralized
2 large yellow summer squash, peeled and spiralized
1 tablespoon olive oil, divided
½ teaspoon kosher salt
1 garlic clove, whole
2 tablespoons fresh basil, chopped
Cooking spray

1. Spritz the air fryer basket with cooking spray.
2. Combine the zucchini and summer squash with 1 teaspoon of the olive oil and salt in a large bowl. Toss to coat well.
3. Transfer the zucchini and summer squash to the basket and add the garlic.
4. Put the air fryer basket on the baking pan and slide into Rack Position 2, select Air Fry, set temperature to 360ºF (182ºC) and set time to 10 minutes.
5. Stir the zucchini and summer squash halfway through the cooking time.
6. When cooked, the zucchini and summer squash will be tender and fragrant. Transfer the cooked zucchini and summer squash onto a plate and set aside.
7. Remove the garlic from the oven and allow to cool for 5 minutes. Mince the garlic and combine with remaining olive oil in a small bowl. Stir to mix well.
8. Drizzle the spiralized zucchini and summer squash with garlic oil and sprinkle with basil. Toss to serve.

Southwest Corn and Bell Pepper Roast

Prep time: 10 minutes | Cook time: 10 minutes | Serves 4

Corn:

1½ cups thawed frozen corn kernels
1 cup mixed diced bell peppers
1 jalapeño, diced
1 cup diced yellow onion
½ teaspoon ancho

chile powder
1 tablespoon fresh lemon juice
1 teaspoon ground cumin
½ teaspoon kosher salt
Cooking spray

For Serving:

¼ cup feta cheese
¼ cup chopped fresh cilantro

1 tablespoon fresh lemon juice

1. Spritz the air fryer basket with cooking spray.
2. Combine the ingredients for the corn in a large bowl. Stir to mix well.
3. Pour the mixture into the basket.
4. Put the air fryer basket on the baking pan and slide into Rack Position 2, select Air Fry, set temperature to 375°F (190°C) and set time to 10 minutes.
5. Stir the mixture halfway through the cooking time.
6. When done, the corn and bell peppers should be soft.
7. Transfer them onto a large plate, then spread with feta cheese and cilantro. Drizzle with lemon juice and serve.

Lemony and Garlicky Asparagus

Prep time: 5 minutes | Cook time: 10 minutes | Makes 10 spears

10 spears asparagus (about ½ pound / 227 g in total), snap the ends off
1 tablespoon lemon juice

2 teaspoons minced garlic
½ teaspoon salt
¼ teaspoon ground black pepper
Cooking spray

1. Line the air fryer basket with parchment paper.
2. Put the asparagus spears in a large bowl. Drizzle with lemon juice and sprinkle with minced garlic, salt, and ground black pepper. Toss to coat well.
3. Transfer the asparagus to the basket and spritz with cooking spray.
4. Put the air fryer basket on the baking pan and slide into Rack Position 2, select Air Fry, set temperature to 400°F (205°C) and set time to 10 minutes.
5. Flip the asparagus halfway through cooking.
6. When cooked, the asparagus should be wilted and soft. Remove from the oven and serve immediately.

Golden Salmon and Carrot Croquettes

Prep time: 15 minutes | Cook time: 10 minutes | Serves 6

2 egg whites
1 cup almond flour
1 cup panko bread crumbs
1 pound (454 g) chopped salmon fillet
²/₃ cup grated carrots

2 tablespoons minced garlic cloves
½ cup chopped onion
2 tablespoons chopped chives
Cooking spray

1. Spritz the air fryer basket with cooking spray.
2. Whisk the egg whites in a bowl. Put the flour in a second bowl. Pour the bread crumbs in a third bowl. Set aside.
3. Combine the salmon, carrots, garlic, onion, and chives in a large bowl. Stir to mix well.
4. Form the mixture into balls with your hands. Dredge the balls into the flour, then egg, and then bread crumbs to coat well.
5. Arrange the salmon balls on the basket and spritz with cooking spray.
6. Put the air fryer basket on the baking pan and slide into Rack Position 2, select Air Fry, set temperature to 350°F (180°C) and set time to 10 minutes.
7. Flip the salmon balls halfway through cooking.
8. When cooking is complete, the salmon balls will be crispy and browned. Remove from the oven and serve immediately.

Spicy Air Fried Old Bay Shrimp

Prep time: 10 minutes | Cook time: 10 minutes | Makes 2 cups

½ teaspoon Old Bay Seasoning
1 teaspoon ground cayenne pepper
½ teaspoon paprika
1 tablespoon olive oil

⅛ teaspoon salt
½ pound (227 g) shrimps, peeled and deveined
Juice of half a lemon

1. Combine the Old Bay Seasoning, cayenne pepper, paprika, olive oil, and salt in a large bowl, then add the shrimps and toss to coat well.
2. Put the shrimps in the air fryer basket.
3. Put the air fryer basket on the baking pan and slide into Rack Position 2, select Air Fry, set temperature to 390ºF (199ºC) and set time to 10 minutes.
4. Flip the shrimps halfway through the cooking time.
5. When cooking is complete, the shrimps should be opaque. Serve the shrimps with lemon juice on top.

South Carolina Shrimp and Corn Bake

Prep time: 10 minutes | Cook time: 18 minutes | Serves 2

1 ear corn, husk and silk removed, cut into 2-inch rounds
8 ounces (227 g) red potatoes, unpeeled, cut into 1-inch pieces
2 teaspoons Old Bay Seasoning, divided
2 teaspoons vegetable oil, divided
¼ teaspoon ground black pepper
8 ounces (227

g) large shrimps (about 12 shrimps), deveined
6 ounces (170 g) andouille or chorizo sausage, cut into 1-inch pieces
2 garlic cloves, minced
1 tablespoon chopped fresh parsley

1. Put the corn rounds and potatoes in a large bowl. Sprinkle with 1 teaspoon of Old Bay seasoning and drizzle with vegetable oil. Toss to coat well.
2. Transfer the corn rounds and potatoes into the baking pan.
3. Slide the baking pan into Rack Position 1, select Convection Bake, set temperature to 400ºF (205ºC) and set time to 18 minutes.
4. After 6 minutes, remove from the oven. Stir the corn rounds and potatoes. Return the pan to the oven and continue cooking.
5. Meanwhile, cut slits into the shrimps but be careful not to cut them through. Combine the shrimps, sausage, remaining Old Bay seasoning, and remaining vegetable oil in the large bowl. Toss to coat well.
6. After 6 minutes, remove the pan from the oven. Add the shrimps and sausage to the pan. Return the pan to the oven and continue cooking for 6 minutes. Stir the shrimp mixture halfway through the cooking time.
7. When done, the shrimps should be opaque. Transfer the dish to a plate and spread with parsley before serving.

Herb-Fried Veggies

Prep time: 10 minutes | Cook time: 16 minutes | Serves 4

1 red bell pepper, sliced
1 (8-ounce / 227-g) package sliced mushrooms
1 cup green beans, cut into 2-inch pieces
⅓ cup diced red

onion
3 garlic cloves, sliced
1 teaspoon olive oil
½ teaspoon dried basil
½ teaspoon dried tarragon

1. Preheat the air fryer oven to 350ºF (177ºC).
2. In a medium bowl, mix the red bell pepper, mushrooms, green beans, red onion, and garlic. Drizzle with the olive oil. Toss to coat.
3. Add the herbs and toss again. Place the vegetables in the air fryer basket.
4. Place the air fryer basket onto the baking pan and slide into Rack Position 2, select Air Fry and set time to 16 minutes, or until tender.
5. Serve immediately.

Cheesy Shrimps

Prep time: 10 minutes | Cook time: 8 minutes | Serves 4 to 6

⅔ cup grated Parmesan cheese
4 minced garlic cloves
1 teaspoon onion powder
½ teaspoon oregano
1 teaspoon basil
1 teaspoon ground black pepper

2 tablespoons olive oil
2 pounds (907 g) cooked large shrimps, peeled and deveined
Lemon wedges, for topping
Cooking spray

1. Spritz the air fryer basket with cooking spray.
2. Combine all the ingredients, except for the shrimps, in a large bowl. Stir to mix well.
3. Dunk the shrimps in the mixture and toss to coat well. Shake the excess off. Arrange the shrimps in the basket.
4. Put the air fryer basket on the baking pan and slide into Rack Position 2, select Air Fry, set temperature to 350ºF (180ºC) and set time to 8 minutes.
5. Flip the shrimps halfway through the cooking time.
6. When cooking is complete, the shrimps should be opaque. Transfer the cooked shrimps onto a large plate and squeeze the lemon wedges over before serving.

Baked Cherry Tomatoes with Basil

Prep time: 5 minutes | Cook time: 5 minutes | Serves 2

2 cups cherry tomatoes
1 clove garlic, thinly sliced
1 teaspoon olive oil
⅛ teaspoon kosher

salt
1 tablespoon freshly chopped basil, for topping
Cooking spray

1. Spritz the baking pan with cooking spray and set aside.
2. In a large bowl, toss together the cherry tomatoes, sliced garlic, olive oil, and kosher salt. Spread the mixture in an even layer in the prepared pan.

3. Slide the baking pan into Rack Position 1, select Convection Bake, set temperature to 360ºF (182ºC) and set time to 5 minutes.
4. When cooking is complete, the tomatoes should be the soft and wilted.
5. Transfer to a bowl and rest for 5 minutes. Top with the chopped basil and serve warm.

Parsnip Fries with Garlic-Yogurt Dip

Prep time: 10 minutes | Cook time: 10 minutes | Serves 4

3 medium parsnips, peeled, cut into sticks
¼ teaspoon kosher salt
Dip:
¼ cup plain Greek yogurt
⅛ teaspoon garlic powder
1 tablespoon sour

1 teaspoon olive oil
1 garlic clove, unpeeled
Cooking spray

cream
¼ teaspoon kosher salt
Freshly ground black pepper, to taste

1. Spritz the air fryer basket with cooking spray.
2. Put the parsnip sticks in a large bowl, then sprinkle with salt and drizzle with olive oil.
3. Transfer the parsnip into the basket and add the garlic.
4. Put the air fryer basket on the baking pan and slide into Rack Position 2, select Air Fry, set temperature to 360ºF (182ºC) and set time to 10 minutes.
5. Stir the parsnip halfway through the cooking time.
6. Meanwhile, peel the garlic and crush it. Combine the crushed garlic with the ingredients for the dip. Stir to mix well.
7. When cooked, the parsnip sticks should be crisp. Remove the parsnip fries from the oven and serve with the dipping sauce.

Croutons

Prep time: 5 minutes | Cook time: 8 minutes | Serves 4

2 slices friendly bread	1 tablespoon olive oil
	Hot soup, for serving

1. Preheat the air fryer oven to 390ºF (199ºC).
2. Cut the slices of bread into medium-size chunks.
3. Brush the air fryer basket with the oil. Place the chunks in the air fryer basket.
4. Place the air fryer basket onto the baking pan and slide into Rack Position 2, select Air Fry and set time to 8 minutes.
5. Serve with hot soup.

Indian-Style Sweet Potato Fries

Prep time: 5 minutes | Cook time: 8 minutes | Makes 20 fries

Seasoning Mixture:

¾ teaspoon ground coriander	powder
½ teaspoon garam masala	½ teaspoon ground cumin
½ teaspoon garlic	¼ teaspoon ground cayenne pepper

Fries:
2 large sweet potatoes, peeled
2 teaspoons olive oil

1. Preheat the air fryer oven to 400ºF (204ºC).
2. In a small bowl, combine the coriander, garam masala, garlic powder, cumin, and cayenne pepper.
3. Slice the sweet potatoes into ¼-inch-thick fries.
4. In a large bowl, toss the sliced sweet potatoes with the olive oil and the seasoning mixture.
5. Transfer the seasoned sweet potatoes to the air fryer basket.
6. Place the air fryer basket onto the baking pan and slide into Rack Position 2, select Air Fry and set time to 8 minutes, until crispy.
7. Serve warm.

Apple Fritters with Sugary Glaze

Prep time: 10 minutes | Cook time: 8 minutes | Makes 15 fritters

Apple Fritters:

2 firm apples, peeled, cored, and diced	½ teaspoon kosher salt
½ teaspoon cinnamon	2 eggs
Juice of 1 lemon	¼ cup milk
1 cup all-purpose flour	2 tablespoons unsalted butter, melted
1½ teaspoons baking powder	2 tablespoons granulated sugar
	Cooking spray

Glaze:

½ teaspoon vanilla extract	sugar, sifted
1¼ cups powdered	¼ cup water

1. Line the air fryer basket with parchment paper.
2. Combine the apples with cinnamon and lemon juice in a small bowl. Toss to coat well.
3. Combine the flour, baking powder, and salt in a large bowl. Stir to mix well.
4. Whisk the egg, milk, butter, and sugar in a medium bowl. Stir to mix well.
5. Make a well in the center of the flour mixture, then pour the egg mixture into the well and stir to mix well. Mix in the apple until a dough forms.
6. Use an ice cream scoop to scoop 15 balls from the dough onto the pan. Spritz with cooking spray.
7. Put the air fryer basket on the baking pan and slide into Rack Position 2, select Air Fry, set temperature to 360ºF (182ºC) and set time to 8 minutes.
8. Flip the apple fritters halfway through the cooking time.
9. Meanwhile, combine the ingredients for the glaze in a separate small bowl. Stir to mix well.
10. When cooking is complete, the apple fritters will be golden brown. Serve the fritters with the glaze on top or use the glaze for dipping.

Pomegranate Avocado Fries

Prep time: 5 minutes | Cook time: 8 minutes | Serves 4

1 cup panko bread crumbs
1 teaspoon kosher salt, plus more for sprinkling
1 teaspoon garlic powder
½ teaspoon cayenne pepper
2 ripe but firm avocados
1 egg, beaten with 1 tablespoon water
Cooking spray
Pomegranate molasses, for serving

1. Preheat the air fryer oven to 375ºF (191ºC).
2. Whisk together the panko, salt, and spices on a plate. Cut each avocado in half and remove the pit. Cut each avocado half into 4 slices and scoop the slices out with a large spoon, taking care to keep the slices intact.
3. Dip each avocado slice in the egg wash and then dredge it in the panko. Place the breaded avocado slices on a plate.
4. Arrange the avocado slices in a single layer in the air fryer basket. Spray lightly with oil.
5. Place the air fryer basket onto the baking pan and slide into Rack Position 2, select Air Fry and set time to 8 minutes, turning once halfway through.
6. Remove the cooked slices to a platter. Sprinkle the warm avocado slices with salt and drizzle with pomegranate molasses. Serve immediately.

Air Fried Crispy Brussels Sprouts

Prep time: 5 minutes | Cook time: 20 minutes | Serves 4

¼ teaspoon salt
⅛ teaspoon ground black pepper
1 tablespoon extra-virgin olive oil
1 pound (454 g) Brussels sprouts, trimmed and halved
Lemon wedges, for garnish

1. Combine the salt, black pepper, and olive oil in a large bowl. Stir to mix well.
2. Add the Brussels sprouts to the bowl of mixture and toss to coat well. Arrange the Brussels sprouts in the air fryer basket.
3. Put the air fryer basket on the baking pan and slide into Rack Position 2, select Air Fry, set temperature to 350ºF (180ºC) and set time to 20 minutes.
4. Stir the Brussels sprouts two times during cooking.
5. When cooked, the Brussels sprouts will be lightly browned and wilted. Transfer the cooked Brussels sprouts to a large plate and squeeze the lemon wedges on top to serve.

Purple Potato Chips with Rosemary

Prep time: 10 minutes | Cook time: 12 minutes | Serves 6

1 cup Greek yogurt
2 chipotle chiles, minced
2 tablespoons adobo sauce
1 teaspoon paprika
1 tablespoon lemon juice
10 purple fingerling potatoes
1 teaspoon olive oil
2 teaspoons minced fresh rosemary leaves
⅛ teaspoon cayenne pepper
¼ teaspoon coarse sea salt

1. Preheat the air fryer oven to 400ºF (204ºC).
2. In a medium bowl, combine the yogurt, minced chiles, adobo sauce, paprika, and lemon juice. Mix well and refrigerate.
3. Wash the potatoes and dry them with paper towels. Slice the potatoes lengthwise, as thinly as possible. You can use a mandoline, a vegetable peeler, or a very sharp knife.
4. Combine the potato slices in a medium bowl and drizzle with the olive oil; toss to coat. Transfer to the air fryer basket.
5. Place the air fryer basket onto the baking pan and slide into Rack Position 2, select Air Fry and set time to 12 minutes. Use tongs to gently rearrange the chips halfway during cooking time.
6. Sprinkle the chips with the rosemary, cayenne pepper, and sea salt. Serve with the chipotle sauce for dipping.

Indian Masala Omelet

Prep time: 10 minutes | Cook time: 12 minutes | Serves 2

4 large eggs
½ cup diced onion
½ cup diced tomato
¼ cup chopped fresh cilantro
1 jalapeño, deseeded and finely chopped
½ teaspoon ground

turmeric
½ teaspoon kosher salt
½ teaspoon cayenne pepper
Olive oil, for greasing the pan

1. Preheat the air fryer oven to 250°F (121°C). Generously grease a baking pan.
2. In a large bowl, beat the eggs. Stir in the onion, tomato, cilantro, jalapeño, turmeric, salt, and cayenne.
3. Pour the egg mixture into the prepared pan.
4. Slide the baking pan into Rack Position 1, select Convection Bake and set time to 12 minutes, or until the eggs are cooked through. Carefully unmold and cut the omelet into four pieces.
5. Serve immediately.

Traditional Queso Fundido

Prep time: 10 minutes | Cook time: 25 minutes | Serves 4

4 ounces (113 g) fresh Mexican chorizo, casings removed
1 medium onion, chopped
3 cloves garlic, minced
1 cup chopped tomato
2 jalapeños,

deseeded and diced
2 teaspoons ground cumin
2 cups shredded Oaxaca or Mozzarella cheese
½ cup half-and-half
Celery sticks or tortilla chips, for serving

1. Preheat the air fryer oven to 400°F (204°C).
2. In a baking pan, combine the chorizo, onion, garlic, tomato, jalapeños, and cumin. Stir to combine.

3. Slide the baking pan into Rack Position 1, select Convection Bake and set time to 15 minutes, or until the sausage is cooked, stirring halfway through the cooking time to break up the sausage.
4. Add the cheese and half-and-half; stir to combine. Bake for an additional 10 minutes, or until the cheese has melted.
5. Serve with celery sticks or tortilla chips.

Sweet Corn and Carrot Fritters

Prep time: 10 minutes | Cook time: 10 minutes | Serves 4

1 medium-sized carrot, grated
1 yellow onion, finely chopped
4 ounces (113 g) canned sweet corn kernels, drained
1 teaspoon sea salt flakes
1 tablespoon chopped fresh cilantro

1 medium-sized egg, whisked
2 tablespoons plain milk
1 cup grated Parmesan cheese
¼ cup flour
$1/3$ teaspoon baking powder
$1/3$ teaspoon sugar
Cooking spray

1. Preheat the air fryer oven to 350°F (177°C).
2. Place the grated carrot in a colander and press down to squeeze out any excess moisture. Dry it with a paper towel.
3. Combine the carrots with the remaining ingredients.
4. Mold 1 tablespoon of the mixture into a ball and press it down with your hand or a spoon to flatten it. Repeat until the rest of the mixture is used up.
5. Spritz the balls with cooking spray. Arrange them in a baking pan, taking care not to overlap any balls.
6. Slide the baking pan into Rack Position 1, select Convection Bake and set time to 10 minutes, or until they're firm.
7. Serve warm.

Peppery Brown Rice Fritters

Prep time: 10 minutes | Cook time: 10 minutes | Serves 4

1 (10-ounce / 284-g) bag frozen cooked brown rice, thawed
1 egg
3 tablespoons brown rice flour
1/3 cup finely grated carrots
1/3 cup minced red bell pepper
2 tablespoons minced fresh basil
3 tablespoons grated Parmesan cheese
2 teaspoons olive oil

1. Preheat the air fryer oven to 380°F (193°C).
2. In a small bowl, combine the thawed rice, egg, and flour and mix to blend.
3. Stir in the carrots, bell pepper, basil, and Parmesan cheese.
4. Form the mixture into 8 fritters and drizzle with the olive oil. Put the fritters carefully into the air fryer basket.
5. Place the air fryer basket onto the baking pan and slide into Rack Position 2, select Air Fry and set time to 10 minutes, or until the fritters are golden brown and cooked through.
6. Serve immediately.

Spinach and Carrot Balls

Prep time: 10 minutes | Cook time: 10 minutes | Serves 4

2 slices toasted bread
1 carrot, peeled and grated
1 package fresh spinach, blanched and chopped
1/2 onion, chopped
1 egg, beaten
1/2 teaspoon garlic
powder
1 teaspoon minced garlic
1 teaspoon salt
1/2 teaspoon black pepper
1 tablespoon nutritional yeast
1 tablespoon flour

1. Preheat the air fryer oven to 390°F (199°C).
2. In a food processor, pulse the toasted bread to form bread crumbs. Transfer into a shallow dish or bowl.

3. In a bowl, mix together all the other ingredients.
4. Use your hands to shape the mixture into small-sized balls. Roll the balls in the bread crumbs, ensuring to cover them well.
5. Put them in the air fryer basket. Place the air fryer basket onto the baking pan and slide into Rack Position 2, select Air Fry and set time to 10 minutes.
6. Serve immediately.

Sweet Potato Soufflé

Prep time: 10 minutes | Cook time: 30 minutes | Serves 4

1 sweet potato, baked and mashed
2 tablespoons unsalted butter, divided
1 large egg, separated
1/4 cup whole milk
1/2 teaspoon kosher salt

1. Preheat the air fryer oven to 330°F (166°C).
2. In a medium bowl, combine the sweet potato, 1 tablespoon of melted butter, egg yolk, milk, and salt. Set aside.
3. In a separate medium bowl, whisk the egg white until stiff peaks form.
4. Using a spatula, gently fold the egg white into the sweet potato mixture.
5. Coat the inside of four ramekins with the remaining 1 tablespoon of butter, then fill each ramekin halfway full.
6. Place the ramekins into Rack Position 1, select Convection Bake and set time to 15 minutes.
7. Remove the ramekins from the oven and allow to cool on a wire rack for 10 minutes before serving

Chapter 11 Holiday Specials

Classic Churros

Prep time: 35 minutes | Cook time: 10 minutes | Makes 12 churros

4 tablespoons butter
¼ teaspoon salt
½ cup water
½ cup all-purpose flour
2 large eggs

2 teaspoons ground cinnamon
¼ cup granulated white sugar
Cooking spray

1. Put the butter, salt, and water in a saucepan. Bring to a boil until the butter is melted on high heat. Keep stirring.
2. Reduce the heat to medium and fold in the flour to form a dough. Keep cooking and stirring until the dough is dried out and coat the pan with a crust.
3. Turn off the heat and scrape the dough in a large bowl. Allow to cool for 15 minutes.
4. Break and whisk the eggs into the dough with a hand mixer until the dough is sanity and firm enough to shape.
5. Scoop up 1 tablespoon of the dough and roll it into a ½-inch-diameter and 2-inch-long cylinder. Repeat with remaining dough to make 12 cylinders in total.
6. Combine the cinnamon and sugar in a large bowl and dunk the cylinders into the cinnamon mix to coat.
7. Arrange the cylinders on a plate and refrigerate for 20 minutes.
8. Spritz the air fryer basket with cooking spray. Place the cylinders in the basket and spritz with cooking spray.
9. Put the air fryer basket on the baking pan and slide into Rack Position 2, select Air Fry, set temperature to 375ºF (190ºC) and set time to 10 minutes.
10. Flip the cylinders halfway through the cooking time.
11. When cooked, the cylinders should be golden brown and fluffy.
12. Serve immediately.

Garlicky Olive Stromboli

Prep time: 25 minutes | Cook time: 25 minutes | Serves 8

4 large cloves garlic, unpeeled
3 tablespoons grated Parmesan cheese
½ cup packed fresh basil leaves
½ cup marinated, pitted green and black olives
¼ teaspoon crushed

red pepper
½ pound (227 g) pizza dough, at room temperature
4 ounces (113 g) sliced provolone cheese (about 8 slices)
Cooking spray

1. Spritz the air fryer basket with cooking spray. Put the unpeeled garlic in the basket.
2. Put the air fryer basket on the baking pan and slide into Rack Position 2, select Air Fry, set temperature to 370ºF (188ºC) and set time to 10 minutes.
3. When cooked, the garlic will be softened completely. Remove from the oven and allow to cool until you can handle.
4. Peel the garlic and place into a food processor with 2 tablespoons of Parmesan, basil, olives, and crushed red pepper. Pulse to mix well. Set aside.
5. Arrange the pizza dough on a clean work surface, then roll it out with a rolling pin into a rectangle. Cut the rectangle in half.
6. Sprinkle half of the garlic mixture over each rectangle half, and leave ½-inch edges uncover. Top them with the provolone cheese.
7. Brush one long side of each rectangle half with water, then roll them up. Spritz the basket with cooking spray. Transfer the rolls to the basket. Spritz with cooking spray and scatter with remaining Parmesan.
8. Select Air Fry and set time to 15 minutes.
9. Flip the rolls halfway through the cooking time. When done, the rolls should be golden brown.
10. Remove the rolls from the oven and allow to cool for a few minutes before serving.

Kale Salad Sushi Rolls with Sriracha Mayo

Prep time: 10 minutes | Cook time: 10 minutes | Serves 12

Kale Salad:

1½ cups chopped kale
1 tablespoon sesame seeds
¾ teaspoon soy sauce
¾ teaspoon toasted

sesame oil
½ teaspoon rice vinegar
¼ teaspoon ginger
⅛ teaspoon garlic powder

Sushi Rolls:

3 sheets sushi nori
1 batch cauliflower rice
½ avocado, sliced
Sriracha

Mayonnaise:
¼ cup Sriracha sauce
¼ cup vegan mayonnaise

Coating:

½ cup panko bread crumbs

1. In a medium bowl, toss all the ingredients for the salad together until well coated and set aside.
2. Place a sheet of nori on a clean work surface and spread the cauliflower rice in an even layer on the nori. Scoop 2 to 3 tablespoon of kale salad on the rice and spread over. Place 1 or 2 avocado slices on top. Roll up the sushi, pressing gently to get a nice, tight roll. Repeat to make the remaining 2 rolls.
3. In a bowl, stir together the Sriracha sauce and mayonnaise until smooth. Add bread crumbs to a separate bowl.
4. Dredge the sushi rolls in Sriracha Mayonnaise, then roll in bread crumbs till well coated.
5. Place the coated sushi rolls in the air fryer basket.
6. Put the air fryer basket on the baking pan and slide into Rack Position 2, select Air Fry, set temperature to 390ºF (199ºC) and set time to 10 minutes.
7. Flip the sushi rolls halfway through the cooking time.
8. When cooking is complete, the sushi rolls will be golden brown and crispy. .
9. Transfer to a platter and rest for 5 minutes before slicing each roll into 8 pieces. Serve warm.

Milky Pecan Tart

Prep time: 2 hours 25 minutes | Cook time: 26 minutes | Serves 8

Tart Crust:

¼ cup firmly packed brown sugar
⅓ cup butter, softened

1 cup all-purpose flour
¼ teaspoon kosher salt

Filling:

¼ cup whole milk
4 tablespoons butter, diced
½ cup packed brown sugar
¼ cup pure maple

syrup
1½ cups finely chopped pecans
¼ teaspoon pure vanilla extract
¼ teaspoon sea salt

1. Line the baking pan with aluminum foil, then spritz the pan with cooking spray.
2. Stir the brown sugar and butter in a bowl with a hand mixer until puffed, then add the flour and salt and stir until crumbled.
3. Pour the mixture in the prepared baking pan and tilt the pan to coat the bottom evenly.
4. Slide the baking pan into Rack Position 1, select Convection Bake, set temperature to 350ºF (180ºC) and set time to 13 minutes.
5. When done, the crust will be golden brown.
6. Meanwhile, pour the milk, butter, sugar, and maple syrup in a saucepan. Stir to mix well. Bring to a simmer, then cook for 1 more minute. Stir constantly.
7. Turn off the heat and mix the pecans and vanilla into the filling mixture.
8. Pour the filling mixture over the golden crust and spread with a spatula to coat the crust evenly.
9. Select Bake and set time to 12 minutes. When cooked, the filling mixture should be set and frothy.
10. Remove the baking pan from the oven and sprinkle with salt. Allow to sit for 10 minutes or until cooled.
11. Transfer the pan to the refrigerator to chill for at least 2 hours, then remove the aluminum foil and slice to serve.

Teriyaki Shrimp Skewers

Prep time: 10 minutes | Cook time: 6 minutes | Makes 12 skewered shrimp

1½ tablespoons mirin
1½ teaspoons ginger juice
1½ tablespoons soy sauce
12 large shrimp
(about 20 shrimps per pound), peeled and deveined
1 large egg
¾ cup panko bread crumbs
Cooking spray

1. Combine the mirin, ginger juice, and soy sauce in a large bowl. Stir to mix well.
2. Dunk the shrimp in the bowl of mirin mixture, then wrap the bowl in plastic and refrigerate for 1 hour to marinate.
3. Spritz the air fryer basket with cooking spray.
4. Run twelve 4-inch skewers through each shrimp.
5. Whisk the egg in the bowl of marinade to combine well. Pour the bread crumbs on a plate.
6. Dredge the shrimp skewers in the egg mixture, then shake the excess off and roll over the bread crumbs to coat well.
7. Arrange the shrimp skewers in the basket and spritz with cooking spray.
8. Put the air fryer basket on the baking pan and slide into Rack Position 2, select Air Fry, set temperature to 400ºF (205ºC) and set time to 6 minutes.
9. Flip the shrimp skewers halfway through the cooking time.
10. When done, the shrimp will be opaque and firm.
11. Serve immediately.

Jewish Blintzes

Prep time: 5 minutes | Cook time: 10 minutes | Makes 8 blintzes

2 (7½-ounce / 213-g) packages farmer cheese, mashed
¼ cup cream cheese
¼ teaspoon vanilla extract
¼ cup granulated white sugar
8 egg roll wrappers
4 tablespoons butter, melted

1. Combine the farmer cheese, cream cheese, vanilla extract, and sugar in a bowl. Stir to mix well.

2. Unfold the egg roll wrappers on a clean work surface, spread ¼ cup of the filling at the edge of each wrapper and leave a ½-inch edge uncovering.
3. Wet the edges of the wrappers with water and fold the uncovered edge over the filling. Fold the left and right sides in the center, then tuck the edge under the filling and fold to wrap the filling.
4. Brush the wrappers with melted butter, then arrange the wrappers in a single layer in the air fryer basket, seam side down. Leave a little space between each two wrappers.
5. Put the air fryer basket on the baking pan and slide into Rack Position 2, select Air Fry, set temperature to 375ºF (190ºC) and set time to 10 minutes.
6. When cooking is complete, the wrappers will be golden brown.
7. Serve immediately.

Pigs in a Blanket

Prep time: 10 minutes | Cook time: 8 minutes | Makes 16 rolls

1 can refrigerated crescent roll dough
1 small package mini smoked sausages, patted dry
2 tablespoons melted
butter
2 teaspoons sesame seeds
1 teaspoon onion powder

1. Place the crescent roll dough on a clean work surface and separate into 8 pieces. Cut each piece in half and you will have 16 triangles.
2. Make the pigs in the blanket: Arrange each sausage on each dough triangle, then roll the sausages up.
3. Brush the pigs with melted butter and place of the pigs in the blanket in the baking pan. Sprinkle with sesame seeds and onion powder.
4. Slide the baking pan into Rack Position 1, select Convection Bake, set temperature to 330ºF (166ºC) and set time to 8 minutes.
5. Flip the pigs halfway through the cooking time.
6. When cooking is complete, the pigs should be fluffy and golden brown.
7. Serve immediately.

Bourbon Monkey Bread

Prep time: 15 minutes | Cook time: 25 minutes | Serves 6 to 8

1 (16.3-ounce / 462-g) can store-bought refrigerated biscuit dough
¼ cup packed light brown sugar
1 teaspoon ground cinnamon
½ teaspoon freshly grated nutmeg
½ teaspoon ground ginger
½ teaspoon kosher salt
¼ teaspoon ground allspice
⅛ teaspoon ground cloves
4 tablespoons (½ stick) unsalted butter, melted
½ cup powdered sugar
2 teaspoons bourbon
2 tablespoons chopped candied cherries
2 tablespoons chopped pecans

1. Preheat the air fryer oven to 310ºF (154ºC).
2. Open the can and separate the biscuits, then cut each into quarters. Toss the biscuit quarters in a large bowl with the brown sugar, cinnamon, nutmeg, ginger, salt, allspice, and cloves until evenly coated. Transfer the dough pieces and any sugar left in the bowl to a round cake pan, metal cake pan, or foil pan and drizzle evenly with the melted butter.
3. Slide the pan into Rack Position 1, select Convection and set time to 25 minutes, or until the monkey bread is golden brown and cooked through in the center.
4. Transfer the pan to a wire rack and let cool completely. Unmold from the pan.
5. In a small bowl, whisk the powdered sugar and the bourbon into a smooth glaze. Drizzle the glaze over the cooled monkey bread and, while the glaze is still wet, sprinkle with the cherries and pecans to serve.

Golden Nuggets

Prep time: 15 minutes | Cook time: 4 minutes | Makes 20 nuggets

1 cup all-purpose flour, plus more for dusting
1 teaspoon baking powder
½ teaspoon butter, at room temperature, plus more for brushing
¼ teaspoon salt
¼ cup water
⅛ teaspoon onion powder
¼ teaspoon garlic powder
⅛ teaspoon seasoning salt
Cooking spray

1. Line the air fryer basket with parchment paper.
2. Mix the flour, baking powder, butter, and salt in a large bowl. Stir to mix well. Gradually whisk in the water until a sanity dough forms.
3. Put the dough on a lightly floured work surface, then roll it out into a ½-inch thick rectangle with a rolling pin.
4. Cut the dough into about twenty 1- or 2-inch squares, then arrange the squares in a single layer in the basket. Spritz with cooking spray.
5. Combine onion powder, garlic powder, and seasoning salt in a small bowl. Stir to mix well, then sprinkle the squares with the powder mixture.
6. Put the air fryer basket on the baking pan and slide into Rack Position 2, select Air Fry, set temperature to 370ºF (188ºC) and set time to 4 minutes.
7. Flip the squares halfway through the cooking time.
8. When cooked, the dough squares should be golden brown.
9. Remove the golden nuggets from the oven and brush with more butter immediately. Serve warm.

Air Fried Spicy Olives

Prep time: 10 minutes | Cook time: 5 minutes | Serves 4

12 ounces (340 g) pitted black extra-large olives
¼ cup all-purpose flour
1 cup panko bread crumbs
2 teaspoons dried thyme

1 teaspoon red pepper flakes
1 teaspoon smoked paprika
1 egg beaten with 1 tablespoon water
Vegetable oil for spraying

1. Preheat the air fryer oven to 400ºF (204ºC).
2. Drain the olives and place them on a paper towel–lined plate to dry.
3. Put the flour on a plate. Combine the panko, thyme, red pepper flakes, and paprika on a separate plate. Dip an olive in the flour, shaking off any excess, then coat with egg mixture. Dredge the olive in the panko mixture, pressing to make the crumbs adhere, and place the breaded olive on a platter. Repeat with the remaining olives.
4. Spray the olives with oil and place them in a single layer in the air fryer basket.
5. Place the air fryer basket onto the baking pan and slide into Rack Position 2, select Air Fry and set time to 5 minutes, or until the breading is browned and crispy. Serve warm

Lush Snack Mix

Prep time: 10 minutes | Cook time: 12 minutes | Serves 10

½ cup honey
3 tablespoons butter, melted
1 teaspoon salt
2 cups sesame sticks
2 cup pumpkin seeds

2 cups granola
1 cup cashews
2 cups crispy corn puff cereal
2 cup mini pretzel crisps

1. In a bowl, combine the honey, butter, and salt.
2. In another bowl, mix the sesame sticks, pumpkin seeds, granola, cashews, corn puff cereal, and pretzel crisps.
3. Combine the contents of the two bowls.

4. Preheat the air fryer oven to 370ºF (188ºC).
5. Put the mixture in the air fryer basket. Place the air fryer basket onto the baking pan and slide into Rack Position 2, select Air Fry and set time to 12 minutes. Shake the basket frequently during cooking.
6. Put the snack mix on a cookie sheet and allow it to cool completely. Serve immediately.

Pão de Queijo

Prep time: 37 minutes | Cook time: 12 minutes | Makes 12 balls

2 tablespoons butter, plus more for greasing
½ cup milk
1½ cups tapioca

flour
½ teaspoon salt
1 large egg
⅔ cup finely grated aged Asiago cheese

1. Put the butter in a saucepan and pour in the milk, heat over medium heat until the liquid boils. Keep stirring.
2. Turn off the heat and mix in the tapioca flour and salt to form a soft dough. Transfer the dough in a large bowl, then wrap the bowl in plastic and let sit for 15 minutes.
3. Break the egg in the bowl of dough and whisk with a hand mixer for 2 minutes or until a sanity dough forms. Fold the cheese in the dough. Cover the bowl in plastic again and let sit for 10 more minutes.
4. Grease the baking pan with butter.
5. Scoop 2 tablespoons of the dough into the baking pan. Repeat with the remaining dough to make dough 12 balls. Keep a little distance between each two balls.
6. Slide the baking pan into Rack Position 1, select Convection Bake, set temperature to 375ºF (190ºC) and set time to 12 minutes.
7. Flip the balls halfway through the cooking time.
8. When cooking is complete, the balls should be golden brown and fluffy.
9. Remove the balls from the oven and allow to cool for 5 minutes before serving.

Supplì al Telefono (Risotto Croquettes)

Prep time: 1 hour 40 minutes | Cook time: 54 minutes | Serves 6

Risotto Croquettes:
4 tablespoons unsalted butter
1 small yellow onion, minced
1 cup Arborio rice
3½ cups chicken stock
½ cup dry white wine
3 eggs
Zest of 1 lemon
½ cup grated Parmesan cheese

2 ounces (57 g) fresh Mozzarella cheese
¼ cup peas
2 tablespoons water
½ cup all-purpose flour
1½ cups panko bread crumbs
Kosher salt and ground black pepper, to taste
Cooking spray

Tomato Sauce:
2 tablespoons extra-virgin olive oil
4 cloves garlic, minced
¼ teaspoon red pepper flakes
1 (28-ounce / 794-g) can crushed tomatoes

2 teaspoons granulated sugar
Kosher salt and ground black pepper, to taste

1. Melt the butter in a pot over medium heat, then add the onion and salt to taste. Sauté for 5 minutes or until the onion in translucent.
2. Add the rice and stir to coat well. Cook for 3 minutes or until the rice is lightly browned. Pour in the chicken stock and wine.
3. Bring to a boil. Then cook for 20 minutes or until the rice is tender and liquid is almost absorbed.
4. Make the risotto: When the rice is cooked, break the egg into the pot. Add the lemon zest and Parmesan cheese. Sprinkle with salt and ground black pepper. Stir to mix well.
5. Pour the risotto in a baking sheet, then level with a spatula to spread the risotto evenly. Wrap the baking sheet in plastic and refrigerate for1 hour.
6. Meanwhile, heat the olive oil in a saucepan over medium heat until shimmering.
7. Add the garlic and sprinkle with red pepper flakes. Sauté for a minute or until fragrant.
8. Add the crushed tomatoes and sprinkle with sugar. Stir to mix well. Bring to a boil. Reduce the heat to low and simmer for 15 minutes or until lightly thickened. Sprinkle with salt and pepper to taste. Set aside until ready to serve.
9. Remove the risotto from the refrigerator. Scoop the risotto into twelve 2-inch balls, then flatten the balls with your hands.
10. Arrange a about ½-inch piece of Mozzarella and 5 peas in the center of each flattened ball, then wrap them back into balls.
11. Transfer the balls to a baking sheet lined with parchment paper, then refrigerate for 15 minutes or until firm.
12. Whisk the remaining 2 eggs with 2 tablespoons of water in a bowl. Pour the flour in a second bowl and pour the panko in a third bowl.
13. Dredge the risotto balls in the bowl of flour first, then into the eggs, and then into the panko. Shake the excess off.
14. Transfer the balls to the baking pan and spritz with cooking spray.
15. Slide the baking pan into Rack Position 1, select Convection Bake, set temperature to 400ºF (205ºC) and set time to 10 minutes.
16. Flip the balls halfway through the cooking time.
17. When cooking is complete, the balls should be until golden brown.
18. Serve the risotto balls with the tomato sauce.

Honey Yeast Rolls

Prep time: 10 minutes | Cook time: 12 minutes | Makes 8 rolls

¼ cup whole milk, heated to 115°F (46°C) in the microwave
½ teaspoon active dry yeast
1 tablespoon honey
⅔ cup all-purpose flour, plus more for

dusting
½ teaspoon kosher salt
2 tablespoons unsalted butter, at room temperature, plus more for greasing
Flaky sea salt, to taste

1. In a large bowl, whisk together the milk, yeast, and honey and let stand until foamy, about 10 minutes.
2. Stir in the flour and salt until just combined. Stir in the butter until absorbed. Scrape the dough onto a lightly floured work surface and knead until smooth, about 6 minutes. Transfer the dough to a lightly greased bowl, cover loosely with a sheet of plastic wrap or a kitchen towel, and let sit until nearly doubled in size, about 1 hour.
3. Uncover the dough, lightly press it down to expel the bubbles, then portion it into 8 equal pieces. Prep the work surface by wiping it clean with a damp paper towel (if there is flour on the work surface, it will prevent the dough from sticking lightly to the surface, which helps it form a ball). Roll each piece into a ball by cupping the palm of the hand around the dough against the work surface and moving the heel of the hand in a circular motion while using the thumb to contain the dough and tighten it into a perfectly round ball. Once all the balls are formed, nestle them side by side in the air fryer basket.
4. Cover the rolls loosely with a kitchen towel or a sheet of plastic wrap and let sit until lightly risen and puffed, 20 to 30 minutes.
5. Preheat the air fryer oven to 270°F (132°C).
6. Uncover the rolls and gently brush with more butter, being careful not to press the rolls too hard.
7. Place the air fryer basket onto the baking pan and slide into Rack Position 2, select Air Fry and set time to 12 minutes, until the rolls are light golden brown and fluffy.
8. Remove the rolls from the oven and brush liberally with more butter, if you like, and sprinkle each roll with a pinch of sea salt. Serve warm.

Chapter 12 Sauces, Dips, and Dressings

Lemony Tahini

Prep time: 5 minutes | Cook time: 0 minutes | Serves 4

¾ cup water
½ cup tahini
3 garlic cloves, minced
Juice of 3 lemons
½ teaspoon pink Himalayan salt

1. In a bowl, whisk together all the ingredients until mixed well.

Hummus

Prep time: 5 minutes | Cook time: 0 minutes | Serves 2

1 (19-ounce / 539-g) can chickpeas, drained and rinsed
¼ cup tahini
3 tablespoons cold water
2 tablespoons freshly squeezed lemon juice
1 garlic clove
½ teaspoon turmeric powder
⅛ teaspoon black pepper
Pinch pink Himalayan salt, to taste

1. Combine all the ingredients in a food processor and blend until smooth.

Cashew Mayo

Prep time: 5 minutes | Cook time: 0 minutes | Makes 18 tablespoons

1 cup cashews, soaked in hot water for at least 1 hour
¼ cup plus 3 tablespoons milk
1 tablespoon apple cider vinegar
1 tablespoon freshly
squeezed lemon juice
1 tablespoon Dijon mustard
1 tablespoon aquafaba
⅛ teaspoon pink Himalayan salt

1. In a food processor, combine all the ingredients and blend until creamy and smooth.

Avocado Dressing

Prep time: 5 minutes | Cook time: 0 minutes | Makes 12 tablespoons

1 large avocado, pitted and peeled
½ cup water
2 tablespoons tahini
2 tablespoons freshly squeezed lemon juice
1 teaspoon dried
basil
1 teaspoon white wine vinegar
1 garlic clove
¼ teaspoon pink Himalayan salt
¼ teaspoon freshly ground black pepper

1. Combine all the ingredients in a food processor and blend until smooth.

Classic Marinara Sauce

Prep time: 15 minutes | Cook time: 30 minutes | Makes about 3 cups

¼ cup extra-virgin olive oil
3 garlic cloves, minced
1 small onion, chopped (about ½ cup)
2 tablespoons minced or puréed sun-dried tomatoes (optional)
1 (28-ounce / 794-
g) can crushed tomatoes
½ teaspoon dried basil
½ teaspoon dried oregano
¼ teaspoon red pepper flakes
1 teaspoon kosher salt or ½ teaspoon fine salt, plus more as needed

1. Heat the oil in a medium saucepan over medium heat.
2. Add the garlic and onion and sauté for 2 to 3 minutes, or until the onion is softened. Add the sun-dried tomatoes (if desired) and cook for 1 minute until fragrant. Stir in the crushed tomatoes, scraping any brown bits from the bottom of the pot. Fold in the basil, oregano, red pepper flakes, and salt. Stir well.
3. Bring to a simmer. Cook covered for about 30 minutes, stirring occasionally.
4. Turn off the heat and allow the sauce to cool for about 10 minutes.
5. Taste and adjust the seasoning, adding more salt if needed.
6. Use immediately.

Dijon and Balsamic Vinaigrette

Prep time: 5 minutes | Cook time: 0 minutes | Makes 12 tablespoons

6 tablespoons water
4 tablespoons Dijon mustard
4 tablespoons balsamic vinegar
1 teaspoon maple

syrup
½ teaspoon pink Himalayan salt
¼ teaspoon freshly ground black pepper

1. In a bowl, whisk together all the ingredients.

Balsamic Dressing

Prep time: 5 minutes | Cook time: 0 minutes | Makes 1 cup

2 tablespoons Dijon mustard
¼ cup balsamic

vinegar
¾ cup olive oil

1. Put all ingredients in a jar with a tight-fitting lid. Put on the lid and shake vigorously until thoroughly combined. Refrigerate until ready to use and shake well before serving.

Enchilada Sauce

Prep time: 15 minutes | Cook time: 0 minutes | Makes 2 cups

3 large ancho chiles, stems and seeds removed, torn into pieces
1½ cups very hot water
2 garlic cloves, peeled and lightly smashed
2 tablespoons wine

vinegar
1½ teaspoons sugar
½ teaspoon dried oregano
½ teaspoon ground cumin
2 teaspoons kosher salt or 1 teaspoon fine salt

1. Mix together the chile pieces and hot water in a bowl and let stand for 10 to 15 minutes.
2. Pour the chiles and water into a blender jar. Fold in the garlic, vinegar, sugar, oregano, cumin, and salt and blend until smooth.
3. Use immediately.

Teriyaki Sauce

Prep time: 5 minutes | Cook time: 0 minutes | Makes ¾ cup

½ cup soy sauce
3 tablespoons honey
1 tablespoon rice wine or dry sherry
1 tablespoon rice

vinegar
2 teaspoons minced fresh ginger
2 garlic cloves, smashed

1. Beat together all the ingredients in a small bowl.
2. Use immediately.

Mushroom Apple Gravy

Prep time: 5 minutes | Cook time: 10 minutes | Serves 4

2 cups vegetable broth
½ cup finely chopped mushrooms
2 tablespoons whole wheat flour
1 tablespoon unsweetened applesauce
1 teaspoon onion

powder
½ teaspoon dried thyme
¼ teaspoon dried rosemary
⅛ teaspoon pink Himalayan salt
Freshly ground black pepper, to taste

1. In a nonstick saucepan over medium-high heat, combine all the ingredients and mix well. Bring to a boil, stirring frequently, reduce the heat to low, and simmer, stirring constantly, until it thickens.

Southwest Seasoning

Prep time: 5 minutes | Cook time: 0 minutes | Makes about ¾ cups

3 tablespoons ancho chile powder
3 tablespoons paprika
2 tablespoons dried oregano
2 tablespoons freshly

ground black pepper
2 teaspoons cayenne
2 teaspoons cumin
1 tablespoon granulated onion
1 tablespoon granulated garlic

1. Stir together all the ingredients in a small bowl.
2. Use immediately or place in an airtight container in the pantry.

Cashew Pesto

Prep time: 10 minutes | Cook time: 0 minutes | Makes 1 cup

¼ cup raw cashews
Juice of 1 lemon
2 garlic cloves
¹/₃ red onion (about 2 ounces / 56 g in total)
1 tablespoon olive oil

4 cups basil leaves, packed
1 cup wheatgrass
¼ cup water
¼ teaspoon salt

1. Put the cashews in a heatproof bowl and add boiling water to cover. Soak for 5 minutes and then drain.
2. Put all ingredients in a blender and blend for 2 to 3 minutes or until fully combined.

Pico de Gallo

Prep time: 5 minutes | Cook time: 0 minutes | Serves 2

3 large tomatoes, chopped
½ small red onion, diced
⅛ cup chopped fresh cilantro
3 garlic cloves, chopped

2 tablespoons chopped pickled jalapeño pepper
1 tablespoon lime juice
¼ teaspoon pink Himalayan salt (optional)

1. In a medium bowl, combine all the ingredients and mix with a wooden spoon.

Cashew Ranch Dressing

Prep time: 15 minutes | Cook time: 0 minutes | Serves 12

1 cup cashews, soaked in warm water for at least 1 hour
½ cup water
2 tablespoons freshly squeezed lemon juice

1 tablespoon vinegar
1 teaspoon garlic powder
1 teaspoon onion powder
2 teaspoons dried dill

1. In a food processor, combine the cashews, water, lemon juice, vinegar, garlic powder, and onion powder. Blend until creamy and smooth. Add the dill and pulse a few times until combined.

Hemp Dressing

Prep time: 5 minutes | Cook time: 0 minutes | Makes 12 tablespoons

½ cup white wine vinegar
¼ cup tahini
¼ cup water
1 tablespoon hemp seeds
½ tablespoon freshly squeezed lemon juice
1 teaspoon garlic powder
1 teaspoon dried

oregano
1 teaspoon dried basil
1 teaspoon red pepper flakes
½ teaspoon onion powder
½ teaspoon pink Himalayan salt
½ teaspoon freshly ground black pepper

1. In a bowl, combine all the ingredients and whisk until mixed well.

Asian Dipping Sauce

Prep time: 15 minutes | Cook time: 0 minutes | Makes about 1 cup

¼ cup rice vinegar
¼ cup hoisin sauce
¼ cup low-sodium chicken or vegetable stock
3 tablespoons soy sauce

1 tablespoon minced or grated ginger
1 tablespoon minced or pressed garlic
1 teaspoon chili-garlic sauce or sriracha (or more to taste)

1. Stir together all the ingredients in a small bowl, or place in a jar with a tight-fitting lid and shake until well mixed.
2. Use immediately.

Caesar Salad Dressing

Prep time: 5 minutes | Cook time: 0 minutes | Makes about ²/₃ cup

½ cup extra-virgin olive oil
2 tablespoons freshly squeezed lemon juice
1 teaspoon anchovy paste

¼ teaspoon kosher salt or ⅛ teaspoon fine salt
¼ teaspoon minced or pressed garlic
1 egg, beaten

1. Add all the ingredients to a tall, narrow container.
2. Purée the mixture with an immersion blender until smooth.
3. Use immediately.

Appendix 1 Measurement Conversion Chart

VOLUME EQUIVALENTS(DRY)

US STANDARD	METRIC (APPROXIMATE)
1/8 teaspoon	0.5 mL
1/4 teaspoon	1 mL
1/2 teaspoon	2 mL
3/4 teaspoon	4 mL
1 teaspoon	5 mL
1 tablespoon	15 mL
1/4 cup	59 mL
1/2 cup	118 mL
3/4 cup	177 mL
1 cup	235 mL
2 cups	475 mL
3 cups	700 mL
4 cups	1 L

VOLUME EQUIVALENTS(LIQUID)

US STANDARD	US STANDARD (OUNCES)	METRIC (APPROXIMATE)
2 tablespoons	1 fl.oz.	30 mL
1/4 cup	2 fl.oz.	60 mL
1/2 cup	4 fl.oz.	120 mL
1 cup	8 fl.oz.	240 mL
1 1/2 cup	12 fl.oz.	355 mL
2 cups or 1 pint	16 fl.oz.	475 mL
4 cups or 1 quart	32 fl.oz.	1 L
1 gallon	128 fl.oz.	4 L

TEMPERATURES EQUIVALENTS

FAHRENHEIT(F)	CELSIUS(C) (APPROXIMATE)
225 °F	107 °C
250 °F	120 °C
275 °F	135 °C
300 °F	150 °C
325 °F	160 °C
350 °F	180 °C
375 °F	190 °C
400 °F	205 °C
425 °F	220 °C
450 °F	235 °C
475 °F	245 °C
500 °F	260 °C

WEIGHT EQUIVALENTS

US STANDARD	METRIC (APPROXIMATE)
1 ounce	28 g
2 ounces	57 g
5 ounces	142 g
10 ounces	284 g
15 ounces	425 g
16 ounces (1 pound)	455 g
1.5 pounds	680 g
2 pounds	907 g

Appendix 2 Air Fryer Cooking Chart

Beef

Item	Temp (°F)	Time (mins)	Item	Temp (°F)	Time (mins)
Beef Eye Round Roast (4 lbs.)	400 °F	45 to 55	Meatballs (1-inch)	370 °F	7
Burger Patty (4 oz.)	370 °F	16 to 20	Meatballs (3-inch)	380 °F	10
Filet Mignon (8 oz.)	400 °F	18	Ribeye, bone-in (1-inch, 8 oz)	400 °F	10 to 15
Flank Steak (1.5 lbs.)	400 °F	12	Sirloin steaks (1-inch, 12 oz)	400 °F	9 to 14
Flank Steak (2 lbs.)	400 °F	20 to 28			

Chicken

Item	Temp (°F)	Time (mins)	Item	Temp (°F)	Time (mins)
Breasts, bone in (1 ¼ lb.)	370 °F	25	Legs, bone-in (1 ¾ lb.)	380 °F	30
Breasts, boneless (4 oz)	380 °F	12	Thighs, boneless (1 ½ lb.)	380 °F	18 to 20
Drumsticks (2 ½ lb.)	370 °F	20	Wings (2 lb.)	400 °F	12
Game Hen (halved 2 lb.)	390 °F	20	Whole Chicken	360 °F	75
Thighs, bone-in (2 lb.)	380 °F	22	Tenders	360 °F	8 to 10

Pork & Lamb

Item	Temp (°F)	Time (mins)	Item	Temp (°F)	Time (mins)
Bacon (regular)	400 °F	5 to 7	Pork Tenderloin	370 °F	15
Bacon (thick cut)	400 °F	6 to 10	Sausages	380 °F	15
Pork Loin (2 lb.)	360 °F	55	Lamb Loin Chops (1-inch thick)	400 °F	8 to 12
Pork Chops, bone in (1-inch, 6.5 oz)	400 °F	12	Rack of Lamb (1.5 – 2 lb.)	380 °F	22

Fish & Seafood

Item	Temp (°F)	Time (mins)	Item	Temp (°F)	Time (mins)
Calamari (8 oz)	400 °F	4	Tuna Steak	400 °F	7 to 10
Fish Fillet (1-inch, 8 oz)	400 °F	10	Scallops	400 °F	5 to 7
Salmon, fillet (6 oz)	380 °F	12	Shrimp	400 °F	5
Swordfish steak	400 °F	10			

Vegetables					
INGREDIENT	**AMOUNT**	**PREPARATION**	**OIL**	**TEMP**	**COOK TIME**
Asparagus	2 bunches	Cut in half, trim stems	2 Tbsp	420°F	12-15 mins
Beets	1½ lbs	Peel, cut in ½-inch cubes	1Tbsp	390°F	28-30 mins
Bell peppers (for roasting)	4 peppers	Cut in quarters, remove seeds	1Tbsp	400°F	15-20 mins
Broccoli	1 large head	Cut in 1-2-inch florets	1Tbsp	400°F	15-20 mins
Brussels sprouts	1lb	Cut in half, remove stems	1Tbsp	425°F	15-20 mins
Carrots	1lb	Peel, cut in ¼-inch rounds	1 Tbsp	425°F	10-15 mins
Cauliflower	1 head	Cut in 1-2-inch florets	2 Tbsp	400°F	20-22 mins
Corn on the cob	7 ears	Whole ears, remove husks	1 Tbps	400°F	14-17 mins
Green beans	1 bag (12 oz)	Trim	1 Tbps	420°F	18-20 mins
Kale (for chips)	4 oz	Tear into pieces,remove stems	None	325°F	5-8 mins
Mushrooms	16 oz	Rinse, slice thinly	1 Tbps	390°F	25-30 mins
Potatoes, russet	1½ lbs	Cut in 1-inch wedges	1 Tbps	390°F	25-30 mins
Potatoes, russet	1lb	Hand-cut fries, soak 30 mins in cold water, then pat dry	½ -3 Tbps	400°F	25-28 mins
Potatoes, sweet	1lb	Hand-cut fries, soak 30 mins in cold water, then pat dry	1 Tbps	400°F	25-28 mins
Zucchini	1lb	Cut in eighths lengthwise, then cut in half	1 Tbps	400°F	15-20 mins

Appendix 3 Recipe Index

Made in the USA
Columbia, SC
16 February 2021